BRITAIN AND AMERICA

BRITAIN AND AMERICA

A Comparative Economic History, 1850–1939

Graeme M. Holmes

DAVID & CHARLES

NEWTON ABBOT   LONDON   VANCOUVER

BARNES & NOBLE BOOKS   NEW YORK
(a division of Harper & Row Publishers, Inc)

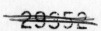

© Graeme M. Holmes 1976

ISBN 0 7153 7256 4 (Great Britain)
ISBN 0-06-492941-8 (United States)

This edition first published in 1976
in Great Britain by
David & Charles (Publishers) Limited
Newton Abbot   Devon

Published in Canada by
Douglas David & Charles Limited
1875 Welch Street   North Vancouver   BC

First published in the USA by
Harper & Row Publishers Inc
Barnes & Noble Import Division

Printed in Great Britain by
Latimer Trend & Company Ltd   Plymouth

CONTENTS

Introduction   7

One   **The Mid-Century Economies**   9
Britain and America in Mid-Century   9
Expansion and Reorientation, 1850–73   13
The American Civil War, 1861–5   20

Two   **Economic Change Before World War I**   25
The Difference in Economic Growth   25
The Fluctuations of Economic Life, 1873–1914   33

Three   **Human Aspects of Economic Change,**
1850–1914   40
The Moving Frontier Thesis   40
Immigration   44
Entrepreneurship   48
Trade Unions and the Labour Force   54

Four   **The Changing Balance of Economic**
Structure, 1850–1914   64
Agriculture   64
The Development of Industry   71
Railways and the Economy   80

Five   **Markets and Finance, 1850–1914**   88
Overseas Trade   88
Capital Export and Commercial Policy   92
The Banking Structure   100

Six   **From War to Depression, 1914–33**   106
The War and Its Immediate Consequences   106
Contrasts in Prosperity, 1922–9   112
The Great Crash, 1929–33   120

Seven   **Contrasts in Economic Recovery, 1933–40**   132

Eight Agriculture, Industry and the Labour
       Force, 1914–39   146
       Agriculture   146
       Industry   155
       The Industrial Labour Force   164

Nine Finance and Markets, 1914–39   173
       International Trade and Tariffs   173
       International Finance   179
       Banking   185

Ten The Changing Role of the State   191

References   205

Books Used and Further Reading   208

Index   221

INTRODUCTION

This book, within a severely limited length, compares the economic experience of Britain and America between 1850 and 1939. Although not the first book to deal with the topic, it aims more than its predecessors did to draw the attention of first-year university students to issues debated by economic historians and to significant features of comparison and contrast between the two countries. Hence the emphasis is not so much on a digest of facts as on topics for discussion. References have been kept to a minimum but it is hoped that the text taken in conjunction with the book list for each chapter makes clear where information has been obtained.

Wherever the word billion is used in this book to refer to any American statistics, it is used in the American sense. That is to say, it means a thousand million, or milliard.

CHAPTER ONE

THE MID-CENTURY ECONOMIES

Britain and America in Mid-Century

To many historians industrialisation is a magic process and it may be that a belief in the superiority of industrial over agricultural societies springs from the political influence arising from industrial power. Such an outlook has tended to breed notions of an international economic league football table where Britain was once champion to be subsequently supplanted by America and some other nations. In the year 1850 it seemed that Britain had done particularly well in the recent past in applying labour and capital to her own and other people's resources. It might be flattering to British arrogance to say that Britain was the foremost industrial nation by 1850 and that arrogance was expressed by the Great Exhibition in the Palace of Industry and Trade in 1851 which was a declaration of British industrial supremacy to the world.

Modern opinion would be rather less dogmatic. In the course of evolution to becoming complex industrial economies, Britain and America in 1850 were in an interesting transitional phase. Both of them were by no means wholly dependent on agriculture yet by later standards neither country was overwhelmingly industrial. If, in 1851, agriculture accounted for only 20.9 per cent of the occupied labour force in Britain, that proportion was still the largest for any occupational group, female domestic servants being in second place. America had a much higher proportion of agricultural workers – 64 per cent in 1850 – but the essential point was that both countries had achieved a framework of institutions where further industrialisation and diversification was possible. Present-day economists would no doubt point to figures of net national product and one recent estimate gives the United States in 1840 a net national product per capita from 71 to 83 per cent of that of Britain.[1] Contemporaries pointed rather to apparent British supremacy in heavy industry and engineering, and American backwardness seemed to be shown by the degree to which America was still dependent on manufactured imports, especially those from Britain. In 1850 out of a total of $173,509,000 of imports into America no less than $121,475,000 were semi-manufactures or manufactures compared with only $30,568,000 for crude foods plus raw materials and $21,466,000 for manufactured foodstuffs. This pattern was quite different from that in Britain where wheat was imported to the extent that in 1851 one estimate reckoned a quarter of all bread consumed to be foreign. Conversely, British exports of many manufactures and mineral products were significant, in the export for example of cotton and wool, copper, lead, tin and tinplate, coal, iron, salt and even soda and heavy chemicals. Perhaps nine-tenths of Britain's merchandise exports in 1850 consisted of manufactures. Different proportions of imports and exports reflected different balances in the two economies dictated by the nature of their industrial development. American manufacturing consisted of elementary processing of raw materials on or near their location or where transportation obstacles occurred. The three major resource oriented industries were lumber, meat packing and flour milling, located in the West with centres at Cincinnati and Chicago. Most other manufacturing occurred in the North East where in 1850 three-quarters of America's manufacturing employment involved cotton goods, boots and shoes, men's clothing, iron, leather, woollen goods and machinery. Both in America and in Britain the cotton textile industry was enormously important yet its relative functioning involved important differences in demand. In America the growing size of the domestic market was emphasised by two English commissions which investigated United States manufacturing in the 1850s, whereas in Britain a major factor for the cotton textile industry had been demand from overseas. The localisation of the British cotton industry was partly a reflection of overseas demand since, with some 312,000 workers in Lancashire, 58,000 in Lanarkshire and 55,000 in Cheshire and the West Riding out of a total of 527,000 cotton workers, there was a concentration occurring particularly in the region of ports. Similarly, Britain's iron industry, foremost in quantity and even in quality in world iron production, depended significantly on overseas sales. By 1840 Britain produced 52 per cent of the world's pig iron. Between

1840 and 1870 Britain kept pace with the increase of world production of between 50 and 75 per cent per decade and went on producing about half of the world's pig iron. In 1856 total British pig iron production was 3,586,377 tons and exports of iron (wrought, pig or bar iron) amounted to 1,275,000 tons.

The important difference, therefore, was Britain's greater involvement with overseas trade. Ashworth comments on the expansion deriving from favourable circumstances for overseas trade and believes that from 1850 to 1875 Britain had consistently more than a fifth and sometimes more than a quarter of all international trade. Britain's apparent industrial supremacy, an impression derived largely from the iron industry, depended to some extent on her ability to maintain such a large share of world markets. Yet the situation was not altogether favourable since Britain had nearly always had an adverse balance of trade with physical imports exceeding physical exports. The deficit was counter-balanced by 'invisible' exports from freight shipping earnings, banking and insurance services and returns on overseas investments. A. H. Imlah has estimated that between 1851 and 1855 there was an annual average deficit of £27.5 million on physical trade which was offset by invisible earnings of £42.3 million. Shipping earnings were the chief item at £18.7 million but interest on foreign investment was already as high as £11.7 million which showed an appreciation by British investors of the importance of the development of the international economy.

America, by contrast, could regard the international economy as a useful outlet for certain exports but not as a fundamental condition of her economic existence. Yet for certain sectors exports were vital. In 1850 raw cotton exports amounted to $71,984,616 or nearly half of the total value of American exports for that year of $144,376,000. Foreign demand for cotton was increasing significantly. Other significant exports were tobacco, rice, lumber products, wheat and flour, even if their trends were erratic. From 1830 manufactures had shown a modest gain. The importance of cotton had been that it had provided a major expansive force in the American economy. Since Britain took almost one-half of American exports including considerable cotton exports and since America took about one-third of her imports from Britain there was an important reciprocal element in the Anglo-American economies. In the Anglo-American relationship invisible items were important. Despite a favourable trend in the American balance of trade in the 1840s there was usually an adverse balance of payments and in 1850 American aggregate indebtedness amounted to $222.1 million. During the expansion of the fifties that figure rose to $379 million. That indebtedness largely represented British willingness to invest in future American development.

The foresight of British investors was soundly based. Already in 1835 Cobden had said on a visit to America that 'here will one day centre the civilisation, wealth, the power of the entire world' and in March 1851 an article appeared in *The Economist* commenting favourably on the quality of the American people: 'From the relative progress of the two countries within the last sixty years, it may be inferred that the superiority of the United States to England is ultimately as certain as the next eclipse.' It was, indeed, the accessions of capital and population to America which promised so much since it had already become apparent that America possessed potentially fertile but as yet undeveloped land in abundance. In 1850 the number of immigrants to the United States from the United Kingdom alone amounted to 215,089, a figure to be substantially exceeded in the year following. Although immigration figures fluctuated considerably from year to year their continually high average incidence meant that America had a fruitful addition of willing hands. If their only outlet had been agricultural work there would no doubt have been a fairly slow rate of economic growth. Yet already there were signs that America was becoming, even if it had not yet become, a highly sophisticated economy. Even if Europe and especially Britain received the bulk of American exports there had been in the last two decades or so a significant expansion of trade in eastern Asia. The signing of the treaty in 1844 with China involving extra-territorial privileges and the visit of Commodore Perry to Tokyo Bay in 1853 were two episodes revealing America's increasing Pacific interests. Quite apart from the widening market, however, was the high rate of capital accumulation. If there is enough capital invested some of that investment will possibly spill over into fruitful technical development, a possibility which will be much further enhanced if there is an awareness of the advantages of technical change. It had become clear by 1851 that some Americans had keen awareness of productive advantages to be gained from machines. In his visit in 1835 Cobden had noted labour-saving machinery in a woollen mill as well as labour-saving agricultural machinery. E. W. Watkin, a leading British railway engineer, reported on a visit to the USA in 1851 that the American railway workshops had 'tools equal or superior to ours in all respects'. Goulding's condenser was widely used in the New England wool spinning industries by 1850. At the Great Exhibition in Britain in 1851 McCormick's reaping machine and Singer's sewing machine both aroused comment. Yet for the moment there was no threat to Britain in such a situation. 'Inventive as the Americans were, their typical inventions were hardly competitive with British manufacturing industry. They supplemented it; went beyond it; or met needs which it had not yet been called upon to meet.'[2] The fact was that the economies of Britain and America involved a significant measure of complementarity, a situation which was to continue for two or more decades. It was only when the potential development of America brought competition and when the impact of American tariffs helped to change the balance of trade between the two countries that Britain's vulnerability in the international situation was to be more noticeable. That situation was in the future. In 1850 there were in both countries grounds for economic optimism and satisfaction.

Expansion and Reorientation, 1850–73

With some reservations of detail, historians are generally agreed that the period between 1850 and 1873 witnessed great prosperity in the international economy. The expansion of the fifties was associated with rapidly improving transport, with increased use of machinery and with additional sources of currency appearing in circulation as a result of discoveries of gold in California and Australia and of silver in Nebraska. Until 1860 there were significant complementary or reciprocal elements in Anglo-American trade to which the heavy volume of shipping on the North Atlantic route bore witness. During the sixties the importance of the 'Atlantic economy' as a distinct trading area tended to decline partly as a result of the American Civil War, of America's imposition of tariffs and of a relative shift by Britain away from the United States to other markets. The buoyancy of the fifties and sixties was a prelude to new difficulties since it was a time of increasing complexity for international trade, but while conditions remained buoyant the problems inherent in that complexity were easily borne. This section endeavours to analyse the reasons for prosperity and the difficulties to which it gave rise.

The first and perhaps most traditional explanation for mid-century dynamism lies in the money supply. The world's supply of precious metals rose by an estimated 30 per cent in the period 1848–56 at a time, especially in the early fifties, when interest rates were low. Hence there was little constraint on investment and Britain was able to invest in enterprise on a world-wide scale. This investment was made in railways in Europe, North America and India, and in textile factories, iron and locomotive works and ships in many countries. Britain's large merchant fleet and advantageous trading position with the gold-producing nations of America and Australia enabled her to trade her industrial products for the new gold. The gold came to Britain as payment but, since expanding British manufactures required increased supplies of raw materials, much of the new gold went out again in payments to foreign countries. Since Britain acted as an entrepôt for the new gold, production especially in California supplied an expanding monetary base to world economic activity.

Economic expansion connoted a flow of labour and capital across national boundaries which was new in scale. This sense of movement was summed up for contemporaries by railway development. Even if historians are now rather more cautious than they once were in casting railways as the key growth factor, the statistics of new railway mileage were impressive. In 1847 the amount of British railway mileage was 3,945 and in 1860 it was 10,443, an increase of about two and a half times in thirteen years. American mileage increased more spectacularly from some 9,000 miles in 1850 to over 30,000 miles in 1860. From an international viewpoint, however, it was important that so many countries experienced railway expansion simultaneously. While the amount of additional track in each country might be modest the cumulative international effect was considerable. Yet even internally railways might have repercussions in knitting economies, and particularly the British economy, into a more closely integrated market. Crude statistics of railway mileage may be important only as an index of demand for one kind of construction activity; their real importance may not be quantifiable since for the fifties they symbolised the elusive entity known as business confidence.

For both Britain and America business confidence seems to

have arisen from uniquely favourable circumstances. If not all new investment was wisely undertaken, as shown in the economic crisis of 1857, it seems to have been the combination of money supply, improvement in transport and wider application of machinery which resulted in a greater awareness of opportunity than hitherto. The favourable features for Britain and America were that they were able to achieve a widening internal market and participate simultaneously in expanding world trade. Nevertheless, the degree of involvement in world trade was of different proportions. It can be argued, therefore, that during the fifties and sixties trends occurred which set the pattern for later contrasts in economic performance. Britain's share of world trade was phenomenal for so small a country. In 1850 British exports were £71.4 million and by 1860 they nearly doubled to £135.8 million. American exports more than doubled from some $144 million (£30 million) in 1850 to $333.5 million in 1860 when cotton exports amounted to $191.8 million or nearly three-fifths of the whole. The high increase in American raw cotton exports was in large degree a function of sales of British manufactured cotton exports to Indian and Far Eastern markets. Conversely, American imports rose in nearly the same proportions from $180 million in 1850 to $367 million in 1860. Even so, the British share in American imports was declining yet one must notice that America did not take the lion's share of British exports even in 1850 when out of total British exports of £71.4 million America took £14.9 million compared with £16.7 million to northern Europe and £12.3 million to the Near and Far East. By 1860, however, exports to America had risen to £22.9 million compared with £31.4 million to northern Europe and £30.1 million to the Near and Far East. In other words, the North American share of British exports fell during the decade from just over 20 per cent to just under 16 per cent.

This declining share was an indication that the reciprocal elements of Anglo-American trade were declining relative to the total international trade in which the two countries were involved. The sixties saw a slow continuation of the same trend. Although the view has been held that the year 1860 marked a dividing line for the Atlantic economy before the imposition of the Morrill tariff in 1861–4, change did not occur in a single year. Before 1860 reciprocal elements in trade were raw materials (especially raw cotton) from America in return for cheap manufactures from Britain. The majority of immigrants to America were British or Irish just as the major portion of capital flowing into America was also British. There were some particularly strong linkages such as the export of American cotton to Lancashire on one side and the export of south Wales tinplate, Staffordshire pottery and British iron rails to America on the other. As Potter has shown, America was an important customer for a number of British manufactures between 1815 and 1860 yet the balance of the Anglo-American relationship changed. By the late 1850s America had become Britain's main supplier of foodstuffs. From the mid-forties Britain had a deficit on visible trade with America, a deficit becoming much larger by the late fifties. In 1860 the computed real value of imports from America (including carriage) was slightly more than twice the declared value of exports (including carriage), the figures being £44.7 million against £21.7 million. Even if the Morrill tariff of 1861–4 marked a change it represented for Britain an accentuation of existing tendencies rather than a drastic re-orientation. There was a relative diminution of exports to America offset by increased exports to other parts of the world and there was possibly an undue reliance on America for some cheap foodstuffs. The real impact of the Morrill tariff on British trade came in the seventies rather than in the sixties. Whatever dislocations might be caused by the American Civil War – the cotton famine in south Lancashire and Britain's search for alternative sources of raw cotton supply such as Egypt being among them – world trade continued to be buoyant in the sixties. There was as yet no marked decline in the supply of new currency and the impact of the 'transport revolution' continued apace. The railways and the iron steamship seemed to serve as the key symbols of mid-Victorian prosperity.

The most spectacular American transport developments were associated with Chicago, which became the centre of a whole western network transforming the balance of regional economic development. A city of 30,000 inhabitants in 1850, Chicago became a focal point for railway building. The Illinois Central was the most interesting of eleven railroads serving Chicago in 1860, being the beneficiary of the first land-grant act aiding the building of a railroad and, with 700 miles of track on its main-line completion in 1856, being the longest railroad in the world. Furthermore, canals became increasingly used, with

shipments from the West through the Erie Canal growing substantially between 1845 and 1848; these shipments were the
beginning of a relatively new trade flow and the railway
accentuated the East-West linkage in the fifties. There was a
strong shift to a market-dominated agriculture with grain exports out of Chicago rising from approximately 2 million
bushels in 1850 to 50 million bushels in 1861 as well as increases
in livestock and other produce. Rising productivity of agriculture in Illinois was shown by relative percentage of farmers
increasing by 39 per cent but improved acreage increasing by
163 per cent and gross farm value by 350 per cent. Finally,
there was a marked relative shift away from the old flow between West and South via the Mississippi.

American expansion in the West connoted not merely a
great increase in agricultural activity but the development of a
complex infrastructure. This infrastructure was in sharp contrast to the South which relied on a few staple commodities,
especially cotton. A problem for cotton was the tendency for
over-production to occur relative to demand, although in the
late forties and fifties cotton prices tended to move upwards in
some years with sharp falls occurring in the trough years of 1849
and 1852. Overall, the high level of cotton exports did not
bring major accruing benefits to the South. There was a notable
lack of urbanisation in the South apart from ports serving the
cotton trade. Investment in education was conspicuously lower
in the South than in the West and North East and local industries and services were conspicuously fewer than elsewhere.
By contrast, the West's agricultural expansion was supplemented by lead, copper, iron and timber production. These
'basic' industries brought advantages for associated industries
such as flour processing, corn meal, ham, bacon, salt pork and
whisky. Soap and candles at Cincinnati, McCormick reaper
plant at Chicago and the agricultural machinery and implement industry in Canton and Dayton, Ohio, were additional manufactures. Because of the virtual non-existence of
slavery, income was more evenly distributed in the West than
in the South. Hence rising income from the export sector
affected consumer demand from Western inhabitants for the
services provided in a growing number of small towns and for
the goods of small industries such as machine and tool shops,
printing and publishing, leather goods, glass and stone products
and so on. Finally, the attitude of Westerners towards invest-

ment in skills, training and education led to an early willingness to raise taxation for education and training.

Likewise in Britain regional development coupled with investment in skills, knowledge and technology was a feature of expansion. Some development reflected reciprocal Anglo-American trade. For example, the expansion of the south Wales tinplate industry reflected the rise of the American canning industry with exports of tinplate and backplate rising nearly four-fold between 1850 and 1870. Nevertheless, regional development in Britain was widespread over all the existing industrial regions. That development was expressed essentially in an extension and continuation of the trends traditionally associated with the so-called Industrial Revolution: steam power, the use of coal, manufacture of cotton and woollen textiles and the production of iron (with the new emergence of steel in quantity) together with the application of heavy engineering. The continuity of earlier trends is shown by the extent of mechanical improvement in the 1850s in cotton and wool production. In the cotton industry steam horsepower rose from 71,005 in 1850 to 281,663 in 1861 and in Lancashire the larger factories integrated spinning and weaving within the same plant. Technical improvement was also noticeable in shipbuilding, in iron and steel, in coal and in engineering. In the 1850s psychological resistance on the part of buyers and builders to steamships was being overcome and by 1860 the proportion of new steam to sailing vessels was 25.4 per cent. The greater use of steam vessels was shown in the carriage of coastwise coal by iron-screw colliers, the tonnage of coal carried from Newcastle to London increasing a hundred-fold between 1852 and 1862. Conversely, by 1858 the great clipper sailing ships had few buyers. One aspect of British technical advance was the increasing use of British iron ships on the North Atlantic and the carriage of American goods was increasingly done in British ships.

Similarly in some other industries Britain remained in the forefront of technical advance. Perhaps the most spectacular development was the appearance of the new Bessemer process which made possible the speedy mass production of steel. By 1870 Britain was world leader in steel production at $\frac{1}{2}$ million tons per annum whereas the United States produced one-quarter of that figure. Between 1847 and 1865 British production of pig iron nearly trebled and the production per blast furnace rose from a weekly make in tons of iron of 120 in 1845 to between 450 and 550 in 1865 with increasingly less coal being needed per ton of iron.

Up to 1873 Britain's technological leadership, supremacy in quantity and quality of production in those activities which had brought her industrial greatness seemed to be undisputed. The phrase 'workshop of the world' still had some meaning. Nevertheless, once the interruption of normal activity occasioned by the Civil War was over, the American economy between 1867 and 1873 seemed to achieve a new upsurge. Once again, new railroad mileage seemed to be an infallible index of business confidence and in those six years 30,000 new miles of track were built. In 1869 the first trans-continental line was completed. The aftermath of the war seemed to produce a wave of business confidence which may itself have been an important result of Northern victory. Both nations were experiencing a widening of economic horizons and the creation of a national market. In 1873 the publication of Bagehot's *Lombard Street* acknowledged that the Bank of England was performing the functions of a central bank and by implication that Britain had achieved a degree of economic and monetary unity not known a generation before. While America might yet be in the process of creating a national market, the widening prospects of sales for agriculture brought increasing specialisation by regions and the prospect of an adequate living for farmers. Even if the pattern of landownership in the two countries was very different the relative prosperity of rural life did much to give a wide basis to the upsurge of the fifties and sixties. Indeed, it is doubtful if periods of prosperity experienced subsequently – the 'climacteric' in Britain of the 1890s or the American consumer boom in the 1920s – brought anything approaching the diffusion of expansion in virtually all branches of economic activity. It was the apparently general pervasiveness of prosperity which made the fifties and sixties an age of business confidence. This confidence persisted in spite of the economic downturns of 1857 and of 1866, in spite of the problems occasioned by the Civil War and in spite of the existence of large pockets of poverty unacceptable to later generations. Those decades experienced a degree of Anglo-American complementarity and involvement with an expanding international economy which would never recur again with quite the same degree of mutual benefit. The full impact of the Morrill tariff and the realisation that a steady drift of emphasis from complementarity to competition was occurring did not come until the economic downturn of the seventies. That is the justification for ending this section in 1873.

The American Civil War, 1861–5

The episode of the Civil War requires separate treatment because of the controversy over whether the war constituted a profound turning-point in American industrial, financial and commercial history. Whereas older interpretations commencing with Beard and Hacker suggested that it was difficult to overemphasise the war's significance, more recent writing has minimised the importance of the conflict. Perhaps one of the most forthright critics of traditional views has been D. C. North who has pointed to the high economic growth occurring between 1830 and 1860. Quoting Gallman's work on commodities he has stressed decade rates of growth in commodity output (at constant prices) which were in excess of 60 per cent for the 1850s and 1870s whereas for the 1850s the rate was only 23 per cent. Hence he believes that the United States 'took time out' for a costly and fratricidal blood-bath.

North's approach may imply that the war was somehow irrelevant to economic development. Yet development takes place within a given social and political context and is often far from being a smooth continuum. Expansion often brings its own social difficulties and institutional bottlenecks which have to be resolved if further expansion is to follow. From this viewpoint the Northern states may have succeeded in imposing their own interpretation on events. If the Civil War overcame the barriers that threatened development it was easy to assume that the war speeded an industrial revolution since within two decades of the end of the conflict America emerged as the leading manufacturing nation in the world.

From this point of view the real economic importance of the war may have been to resolve a situation in which economic power was imperfectly represented in the prevailing system of political power. The small oligarchy which ruled the South also dominated the federal government. Between 1828 and 1860 that southern oligarchy controlled the Presidency, the Senate, the Supreme Court and the House of Representatives for substantial periods of time. Yet the balance of political power was clearly changing in the 1850s with the developments of the old North West. A key state was Illinois where railroads and slavery became interconnected issues: they became so because economic and railroad development resulted in proposals to create new states whose attitudes to slavery were as yet undefined. A proposal that Congress should leave the inhabitants of the two new territories of Kansas and Nebraska free to settle the issue of slavery for themselves was virtually a contradiction of the Missouri Compromise of 1820 which prohibited slavery from all western territory north of 36° 30'. That proposal of 1854 revived old passions in a heightened form and what began as a discussion about a railroad ended by being a national debate about slavery. If the slavery question aroused strong emotions the essential economic change was that the increasingly important agricultural regions of the North West became linked with North-Eastern ports. The North West became more sympathetic than hitherto towards a tariff system which would promote industrial cities and enlarge the eastern market. By favouring donation of public lands and a trans-continental railroad the new Republican party won the adherence of prospective western settlers. With a split in the Democratic party in 1860, the Republicans gained an election victory. The slave-holding South interpreted the results of the 1860 election as heralding the doom of her national control.

Hence it was the very economic development of the North and North West which provided a reason for the shifting balance of power. It was industrialisation in the North East and the opening up of the West and Far West which were primarily responsible for the growth of the American economy in the 1840s and 1850s. The role of cotton in the economy declined in relative importance after 1839. Yet in absolute terms income from cotton continued to grow especially during the prosperous era of the 1850s. It is certainly wrong to suggest that the cotton plantation economy of the South was nearing exhaustion in 1860. Its defect was that it did not encourage additional kinds of economic activity, industry or commerce and the unequal distribution of income with most of the labour force enslaved tended to prevent more diversified activities. Nevertheless, the South was not a stagnating economy. The researches of Conrad, Meyer, Fogel and Engerman among others have shown that slavery was a viable undertaking since the price of slaves was rising and slavery for cotton production was a profitable undertaking.

The reassessment of the economic importance of slavery should be a reminder that traditional Northern interpretations of the effects of the war should be received with caution. Clearly, once the war had began in 1861, there was short-term expansion in some sectors, decline in others and a considerable amount of dislocation. The historian's task, however, is to distinguish short-term from long-term disequilibrium effects. No one has yet done so entirely satisfactorily which is one reason for continuing controversy. In a recent work J. G. Williamson points to four important factors. The first was a rise in the share of gross net capital formation in GNP, a rise of 7 percentage points in the 1860s, and the fact that the new plateau of the savings rate in the 1870s was maintained for the rest of the century. Secondly, there was a considerable decline in capital goods' prices between the 1850s and the 1870s. Hence the greater volume of savings could increasingly command a better price on producer durables. Thirdly, the tariffs of 1861 and 1864 meant a shift to a policy of very stiff protection. Finally, the composition of capital formation expenditures changed significantly following the Civil War, with railroads accounting for an enormous share of capital formation activity throughout much of the early and mid-1870s.[3] Apart from these factors some other possible long-term effects could be related to currency and banking. Measures adopted included the issue of $150 million in treasury notes after February 1862, the so-called 'Greenbacks' because of the ink with which they were printed. Within a year two additional issues were authorised and, by June 1865, there were $462,687,966 in greenbacks outstanding. This inflationary trend could support the contention that a shift to profits occurred during wartime inflation or that borrowing could occur at an effective rate of interest lower than the nominal rate at the time of borrowing, thus encouraging investment. Furthermore, an enormous loan policy resulted in the national debt incurred during the war amounting by June 1865 to $2,616,446,199. So far were government financial operations mingled with the banking system that the Treasury used the bankers to sell its obligations and placed its funds in private banks as depositories. Congress established a national banking system, giving banks the precious privilege of issuing notes based upon government bonds.

There is little way of knowing whether some of these trends such as a rise in savings or a decline in capital goods' prices or railroad construction in the 1870s would have occurred in any event without the war. The debate about tariffs, currency and banking may be more open to argument in the sense that one can pinpoint particular events like the tariff measures of 1861 and 1864 or the greenback issues or the National Banking Acts of 1863–4 as events clearly associated with the war. Nevertheless, it is possible that higher tariffs would have come in any event since the United States was already depending less on British imports. Even if tariff measures appealed to the nationalist economic sentiments of Northern industrialists, recent opinion is sceptical about the overall effect of tariffs on industrial development and questions whether they made any great difference. In discussing the inflation issue Engerman is sceptical about a substantial increase in profits during wartime, and points to the possibility that businessmen were reluctant to borrow during the war in anticipation of a postwar fall in prices. Further, the National Banking Acts by no means solved all future financial difficulties as the growth of small country banks after 1875 testified.

In spite of the doubts raised over any definitive answers concerning the above aspects there are two features of the war about which it is possible to be rather more certain. The first is the effect on the Southern economy. There is little doubt that the abolition of slavery and the policy of Northern-dominated governments towards the South after 1865 led to severe dislocation and the retardation of development in Southern industry. In that sense the war constituted a decisive political and economic turning-point but not in any positive contribution to economic growth since the South failed to participate fully in the significant changes of the American economy between 1870 and 1900. If those changes can be summed up as the process of industrialisation the question has been raised by T. C. Cochran whether the war retarded industrialisation. His approach is certainly different from those traditional writers who have urged that the war speeded an industrial revolution, yet it is worth noting that as long ago as 1928 Victor Clark in his massive book on United States manufactures was sceptical about the degree of impetus which the Civil War provided for industry. Clark, writing a fairly straightforward narrative account, employed a somewhat different methodology from that of Cochran who attempted to compile an industrial balance sheet by using statistical series of the output of different industries. Cochran believes that lavish expenditure and speculation by a small group of contractors and speculators gambling on inflation created a legend of wartime prosperity but concludes that collectively the statistical estimates support a conclusion that the Civil War retarded industrial growth. Past interpretations reflected a desire of teachers for neat periodisation so that up to 1860 America was agricultural and after 1865 it was industrial. Isolated facts were seized upon and no comparison was made with other decades. While Cochran's approach has not been universally accepted it has epitomised the cautious and critical view of the war by recent writers. Perhaps the cautions to be made can be typified by two industries, the oil industry and the iron industry. Both of these industries experienced some wartime expansion. Yet the essential point about them is that in 1860 they were industries with considerable potential in which demand and supply patterns were changing rapidly. Oil had been discovered only in 1859, a date which made expansion between 1861 and 1865 to some extent coincidental. New technologies in iron and steel were again a feature of the 1850s and 1860s ensuring that ferrous metal would be more widely used. With many industries it is difficult to show that the war in itself generated whole new patterns of demand largely because it was a non-mechanised war. Overall, in the present state of the debate one can do worse than follow Engerman's conclusion that 'much work still remains on the analysis of the economic effects of the war but, at present, reservations regarding the traditional interpretation seem justified'.

CHAPTER TWO

ECONOMIC CHANGE BEFORE WORLD WAR I

The Difference in Economic Growth

After the previous background description of the two economies in mid-century, attention can now turn to discussion of the problem why America achieved a faster rate of growth than Britain between 1850 and 1914. The different scale and prospects of the two economies was becoming apparent to contemporaries by the 1880s, and before 1914 British industrialists were admiring some of the features of American industry and organisation. While general impressions provide background evidence economic historians have been concerned for some time to give more precision to the differences in growth. There is a considerable and growing literature about the reliability of different statistical methods but here there is only space to indicate particular findings. In view of the great difference in land area or in population between countries economists now usually prefer to judge performance by the increase in gross or net national product per head of the population. Deane and Cole show that British national income per head (at 1913 prices) rose from £26.8 per head in 1870 to £48.2 per head in 1910 or less than a doubling, while American historical statistics show that gross national product (at 1929 prices) per head grew from $223 as an average of 1869–73 to $608 in 1907–11 or some two and three-quarter times. Maddison gives a rise in net output per capita between 1870 and 1913 of 1.3 per annum for Britain and of 2.2 per cent for America.[1] Elsewhere we point out that between 1920 and 1939 the overall performance of the two countries was not dissimilar. The statistics for the period between 1850 and 1873 are less reliable. For the period from 1870 to 1914 (or perhaps to 1920), on the other hand, there is general agreement that the American economy performed much better than that of Britain. Contemporary impressions have been confirmed by economists' computations.

At a simple level we can no doubt say that higher growth was achieved by a superior mixture of land, labour and capital. Yet when one analyses each factor in turn or attempts to judge the way in which various factors combined it is not easy to say precisely why America should have achieved superior performance. The difficulty of analysis can be shown in respect of the one factor which has often been thought a fairly obvious cause of growth, namely land. Since land in the economists' sense connotes natural resources it might be thought that here was the key explanation particularly since time was to show how America possessed considerable resources in coal, oil, timber, iron ore, gold and silver, copper and lead. By 1850 the land area of the United States was 1.9 thousand million acres. In square miles the United States in our period could be reckoned as containing 2,977 million square miles compared with an area for Great Britain and Northern Ireland of 94,000 square miles. We are not including the later Republic of Ireland with a land area of 26,000 square miles whose economic benefits to Britain until 1922 were questionable. Hence as a very approximate measure the United States could exploit a land area some thirty times greater than that of Britain. On general grounds a country with a very large land area need not enjoy higher economic growth than a much smaller country. Estimates of growth of national income per capita agree that between 1850 and 1950 Sweden and Japan achieved higher growth than America and these were countries – Japan with some 145,000 square miles and Sweden with some 179,000 square miles – with far less land than America. Sometimes a very large land area may be thought a disadvantage – as in India and China until fairly recently – since it may connote a very large traditional agricultural sector in which rapid change is difficult to effect. In terms of people employed on the land the proportion of the labour force in American agriculture was still as large as 64 per cent in 1850. Nevertheless, most discussions give land a prominent place as a factor in American growth for several reasons.

The first approach is psychological and stresses the attraction to the newcomer (usually a regional migrant but sometimes an immigrant) of opening up and improving fertile land. This approach began perhaps with the 'frontier thesis' in the 1890s but was a derivative of contemporary expressions of optimism, for example railroad advertisements about land potential or reports from farmers who had themselves prospered. By contrast, there was the problem of farmer discontent which is difficult to quantify. Nevertheless, the optimism has been sufficiently enduring for historians to be influenced by the undoubted fact that considerably more land was brought under cultivation. A second approach is technical and stresses the lack of labour relative to the large amount of land available. Hence if the land were to be fully exploited there needed to be a considerable injection of capital and it was the high capital/labour ratio symbolised by mechanical reapers, harvesters and the like which distinguished American agriculture from that of more peasant economies. The backward and forward linkages between agriculture and industry – making equipment for exploiting the land and processing of agricultural products – was a special feature of the American scene. Finally, a third approach would point to the market situation. The growth of agricultural production depended upon the growth of markets. A dynamic internal market associated with growing towns with expanding industries and services may have provided an important initial stimulus to agricultural development say to 1875, but even if the domestic market continued to expand the emphasis in the last quarter of the century lay in the export sector. Even as late as 1900 some four-fifths of American physical exports consisted of agricultural products either crude or processed. Some of those exports, especially raw cotton, had been important items for a long time. The repercussions of expanding markets for the service sector – distribution and transportation – are obvious. It may well be that insufficient attention has been paid to the reasons why American exports could achieve such considerable growth, those reasons lying to some extent in demand conditions in the importing countries as well as in American supply conditions. Hence markets illustrate the general point about American land and agricultural development that complex linkages with other sectors of the economy were, on the whole, operating in favour of general expansion.

The land situation in Britain was somewhat different. There were, of course, some natural resources (besides agricultural land) which brought undoubted benefits, of which the outstanding example was coal. It is a simple if often neglected point to make that the approximately five-fold rise in coal production from 57 million tons in 1851 to 287 million tons in 1913 was impossible without the existence of abundant reserves. More problematic, however, is whether the existence of so much coal in a relatively small land area did not have a fundamental influence on popular conceptions about the correct balance of the economy. Apart from London all the major industrial regions had substantial coal production. Of course, America came to have a higher absolute production of coal by 1913 at 509 million tons, but the production rise was steep in the twenty years before 1913 and was linked with the rapid rise of industry. The essential point was that the American coal regions were small in relation to the country's total land mass whereas the fictional 'Coketown' of Charles Dickens's *Hard Times* could stand as a symbol of British industrialism. Already by 1850 the importance of the British coal-bearing regions was indisputable and was linked to some extent with the existence of iron ore in the same locations. Although by the 1870s some regions had exhausted their iron ore deposits – south Wales being a good example – the rapid growth in manpower terms of the coal industry could be adduced as evidence of a popular belief in the desirability of industrial as distinct from agricultural activity as a rewarding occupation. The American appeal to go west was primarily to the land whereas the movement of British agricultural workers away from the land was a prominent feature of the 1870s and beyond. Hence the proportion of British workers employed on the land fell from 14.1% in 1871 to 8% in 1911. This low proportion of less than 10 per cent was quite remarkable even among industrial countries and prompts the question whether the British economy was unbalanced.

It was certainly true that compared with France and Germany Britain allowed her agriculture to decline even if the decline was highly uneven as between different agricultural products with falls in production being noticeable in wheat, barley and oats. The difference in commercial policy between the two continental countries and Britain – the contrast between tariffs and free trade – involved the preservation of a larger agricultural labour force in those countries. No doubt the arguments at the time had a certain simple logic. Manufacturers believed that Britain's relative inability to produce cheap food and the availability of cheap imported food meant that wage costs and hence manufacturing costs could be reduced by allowing food imports into the country. Resultant cheaper manufactured exports would be more competitive abroad and export earnings would offset the food import bill. Even if the argument gained widespread assent and the cry of cheap food had a seductive appeal to workers it failed to recognise elements of choice in the situation. Firstly, it was not necessarily true that tariffs on some items of imported food would necessarily meet with retaliation against all British exports. For example, since coal exports went mainly to Europe and to South America, tariffs aimed to reduce the import of American and Russian wheat need not have caused coal exports to decline since the coal purchasers would be little affected. There was no attempt at a careful statistical evaluation of proportionate alternatives and the slogan of Free Trade or Tariffs obscured the possibility of a multitude of choices about the possible amount of custom duties to be levied. Secondly, there was little thought of opportunity costs. The choice of allowing farming to decline might mean a reduction of some farm income which could have downward multiplier effects on the rural economy and linked crafts. Thirdly, there seems to have been little consideration of substitution of factors: even if dearer home-produced food had resulted in higher wages those wages might have acted as a spur to substitute labour by capital with the installation of machinery. These hypothetical arguments draw attention to contemporary thinking, which assumed a somewhat different attitude to the land in each country. The small land area of Britain relative to a growing population may have encouraged the belief that agriculture overall provided little prospects for growth. Yet the sociology of landownership might also be important in colouring contemporary attitudes. With the fall in land values in Britain some of the larger landowners tended to spread their risk and either sold some of their estates to effect improvement on the rest or took a greater interest in industrial or commercial ventures. Their relative pessimism may itself have affected the situation just as relative optimism influenced expansion and development in America.

Nevertheless there were objective factors influencing the course of events especially in the application of technology. Agriculture was relevant to technology in two ways. Firstly, as David has suggested in relation to the introduction of the mechanical reaper, 'the landscape of Britain's principal grain-producing districts ... was on balance inimical to the immediate successful introduction of the mechanical innovation ...' Secondly, there is the general question of a different capital/labour ratio in the two countries. If land were abundant and labour relatively scarce then the land could be exploited to its full potential only by the introduction of labour-saving tools and machinery. Was the labour supply crucial or the nature of the land or a mixture of both in bringing about American mechanisation? Yet in Britain also the capital/labour ratio was changing and it can be claimed that the cold blast of foreign competition made British agriculture more efficient and productive per man employed than hitherto, perhaps rather more by improvements in drainage or in crop rotation or in breeding or in changing balances within mixed farming than by mechanisation.

Mechanisation was relevant not only to agriculture but also to industry as an explanation of American progress. Abramovitz has concluded that between the 1870s and 1944–53 productivity accounted for the greater part of the growth in output per head. Productivity, however, is really a statistical measure of the relationship between inputs and outputs and hence 'may be taken to be some sort of measure of our ignorance about the causes of economic growth in the United States.[2] Higher productivity linked with technical superiority has often been put forward for the faster growth of American industrial production, perhaps the best known exponent being Habakkuk, who tended to assume American technical superiority and then proceeded to explain it on the basis of the relative scarcity of labour. With a higher capital/labour ratio becoming both a necessity and a habit for American entrepreneurs they consistently invested more in machinery than their British counterparts and the cumulative result of continuous technological investment was higher output per man-hour.

Nevertheless recent discussion has urged caution on the question McCloskey has raised as to whether labour productivity in coal and steel was so much higher in America (as compared with Britain) as has been thought.[3] Equally, Floud has pointed out the difficulties of measuring British productivity even if 'there is now general agreement that (the period 1870–1913) saw a slackening in the rate of growth of labour productivity in the economy as a whole, (but) there is much less agreement on the causes of this slackening or on its implications for the position of the United Kingdom vis-á-vis the other industrial economics'.[4] We need to know a great deal more about particular industries and individual firms before being too certain about the extent of superiority of American productivity

and about its causes. Nevertheless, productivity can be connoted with that hoary old phenomenon of social psychology
– the will to work. This feature is not in itself directly measur-
able, since it is interlinked with other factors. The open nature
of American society with few rigid class barriers was claimed to
allow greater opportunities for personal advancement than in
Britain and Europe. Hence personal incentives were greater
and there was less reluctance to resist giving full personal effort
in work. Obviously these generalisations need considerable detailed study since not everyone in America was successful in improving his standard of living substantially. The gap between
rich and poor was wide. Nevertheless, the generally less militant
nature of American trade unions and the enthusiastic reports of
immigrants' letters to their relatives in their native land provide
impressionistic evidence. Yet incentives did not only apply to
wage rates and to employers' attitudes towards the labour which
they employed. It could also be argued that educational opportunity was also greater in America in the sense that a greater
proportion of the population learned to read and to write and
to develop the general skills necessary as a background to learning more specialised tasks in industry and commerce. It is
noticeable how champions of the 'comprehensive' principle in
Britain in the 1960s referred back to the different educational
traditions of the two countries, contrasting the class-ridden traditions of Britain with the more open and accessible nature of
education in America with the community school providing a
good basic education for most children in the community. In
retrospect there is almost certainly an element of exaggeration
in any appraisal of education which contrasts a higher investment per head in human capital in America than in Britain.
The difficulties of measuring investment as distinct from consumption in education are notorious. From an economic point
of view expenditure on formal education in schools or colleges
is not necessarily an indication of the possible rate of return
from that expenditure. For industry, commerce and agriculture
a good deal of fruitful education might be informal in the sense
that acquired expertise – learning by doing – might be in-
corporated into current practice and passed on to all members
of an organisation including the most junior members. The
educational influence on the economy of newspapers and trade
journals must not be discounted. In this sense there is still a
great deal more that we need to know about nineteenth-century

educational development and it is noticeable that some recent contributions on the subject, like those of West or Sanderson, have been more optimistic about the efficacy of British changes whether in schools or in universities than opinion twenty years ago.

Whatever the difficulties involved in estimating precisely the inputs and outputs involved in aspects of labour, there is now reasonable agreement among economists that a large part of the explanation for American growth consisted of residual factors associated with labour rather than with land and capital. The same approach is now fashionable in Britain with its implicit rejection of the Harrod-Domar model which emphasises the place of capital investment in the growth process. It is not so much the quantity of capital invested which is important but rather the nature of its utilisation. Utilisation depends partly on capacity to absorb capital and there is little doubt that America's capacity of absorption was greater than Britain's. America imported capital right until 1914 even if in the early twentieth century with her widening overseas commitments she was beginning to export capital as well. A considerable amount of capital imported into America was British capital which possibly amounted in 1914 to between £750 and £800 million or about one-fifth of Britain's total capital export of £4,100 million. Hence one sees the essential difference between the two countries in the international economy with Britain providing in 1914 over 40 per cent of world exports of capital and France a long way behind at just under 20 per cent with the United States furnishing not even 10 per cent. Apart from the complex question whether the high proportion of overseas investment diverted potentially fruitful investment away from the internal British economy it is not difficult to point to misplaced internal British investment such as the later railways, like the Great Central Railway, which were not really viable and largely duplicated existing facilities. Nevertheless, there is misplaced investment in every economy and examples of waste or over-commitment were common enough in the United States, as the crises of 1873, 1897 and 1907 showed clearly enough. Yet the readiness to invest capital which was characteristic of American entrepreneurs was possibly a function both of size of the country and of population expansion simultaneously which created potential fruitful projects and widening markets.

The railroads are an often quoted example of how the major

opportunities for new construction were exhausted in Britain after 1870 whereas new American lines were constructed well into the 1890s and even beyond. The railroads may have been overstressed as an unfailing yardstick of nineteenth-century economic progress but their respective differences in the two countries do draw attention to the fact that Britain may have entered a period of diminishing marginal returns on well-established activities like cotton spinning or iron and steel manufacture. The 'early start thesis' which suggests that Britain was entering a phase where her excessive specialisation in and commitment to her staple industries was now proving a handicap is by no means disproved. Yet the fact was that even in 1913 Britain still had a remarkable share of some items of world trade, some 35 per cent of world trade in iron and steel and perhaps three-quarters of all world sea-borne coal exports. Capital was still being invested in new coal mines or in new shipbuilding facilities in the expectation of reasonable profits. Recent writing is not disposed to criticise British entrepreneurship and foresight overmuch. If American entrepreneurship and investment appeared to be more dynamic and profitable than in Britain then the explanation seems to lie more in objective circumstances and greater investment opportunities in America than in the relative virtues or defects of the entrepreneurs themselves. Entrepreneurship, itself described as a 'slippery concept', underlines the slippery nature of debate over the reasons for growth. All that has been done in this section has been to draw attention to some of the problem areas. Further discussion on them occurs in the next two chapters.

The Fluctuations of Economic Life, 1873–1914

Although there may be general agreement about America's relatively high growth rate after 1870 there is a residue of debate over the degree of optimism or pessimism which should properly be ascribed to late nineteenth-century economies. This debate is shown by Williamson's book published in 1974 which can refer in one chapter heading to 'the Great Depression: 1873–96' and in another heading to 'the Gilded Age: 1870–90'. In traditional text-books turning points have been placed at 1873 and 1896. Between those dates both the British and American economies are said to have experienced a phase of business depression and pessimism whereas after 1896 there was a renewal of confidence and activity. The explanation provided has been in terms of the quantity of money and of the price level. After 1873 the production of new gold and silver was less great than previously, whereas after 1896 new gold from South Africa caused the international economy to be more buoyant.

This neat formulation in terms of money and prices is now seriously questioned. Ever since a classic article by H. L. Beales some forty years ago there has been an acknowledgement that the period 1873–96 was not as bleak as some writers would suggest. It is now generally accepted that in spite of the defects of the British economy after 1870 the really marked deceleration in British growth came after 1900 and that the truly disquieting period was between 1900 and 1914. More recently S. B. Saul has argued against the existence of a Great Depression in Britain in any unified sense between 1873 and 1896 in spite of unusual and worrying economic difficulties in the last quarter of the century. In a sense the debate has been over the accuracy of the impressions of observers at the time in the light of the more refined enquiries of later statistical and quantitative investigators. Confusion has been generated between general economic progress over two or more decades (as measured by the usual indicators of GNP, industrial production and so on) and the incidence of particular cyclical movements of boom and slump generating a mood of uncertainty and gloom among investors and businessmen. E. C. Kirkland, for example, discusses the new era of depression between 1873 and 1897 commencing with the Jay Cooke panic of the former year and points to three long phases of American business prostration: 1873–8, 1882–5 and 1893–7. 'Two [years of depression], 1873 and 1897, join 1837 and 1929 as the worst in American history.' *The Commercial and Financial Chronicle* of 1877 compared monetary circulation to that of the blood, with movement of economic confidence resembling those of the nerves. Buoyancy and vigour could not be restored until trouble in the nervous centres had been relieved. A measure of uncertainty was the contemporary belief that 95 per cent of American capitalists had failed. Similarly in Britain the title of the Royal Commission on the Depression in Trade and Industry in 1885 gave later historians the cue for labelling the quarter century after 1873 as 'the Great Depression'.

The article by Beales mentioned above pointed out that a rise in real wages and a significant increase in industrial production, not to mention a substantial if erratic increase in national income, were not normally features associated with a depression. Saul points out that the great peaks and slumps in prices and employment produce a semblance of unified long periods which turn out to be a fiction on closer investigation. He emphasises the complexity of the circumstances affecting Britain and rejects any unicausal explanation. The same point can be made of America. Indeed, it is probable that the money supply in America, including gold, silver, bank notes and drafts, cheques, and bills of exchange rose somewhat in the seventies and by 1897 the money supply was rather over twice what it had been in 1873. Yet despite such elements of expansion the period has been presented as one of economic difficulty. Perhaps an explanation can be found in the remarkable presidential speech to the Iron and Steel Institute in 1871 made by William Menelaus, general manager of the Dowlais Iron Company, in which he expressed his foreboding about the industry's new difficulties in view of the price differentials operating against it in a period of increasing uncertainty. The theme of uncertainty is the common element in the forebodings of the late nineteenth century and was of a different order from that of a previous generation in that it was induced by rapid change due to opportunities engendered by improved technology (especially in transport), by the resultant widening of markets and by intensification of competition. The iron steamship became the normal rather than the exceptional means of ocean transport and made possible movements of goods and people on an unprecedented scale. It was one aspect of a technologically more sophisticated, more closely linked yet unregulated international economy. Along with technological innovation, the arbitrary decisions of governments and the faulty state of economic intelligence might all be relevant to uncertainty. It was an age which found economic progress difficult to digest. Two detailed examples of a tendency to supply excess goods or services because of undue optimism partly generated by improved techniques could be seen in over-production of American agriculture and in over-supply of shipping services influenced considerably by Britain. Ashworth points out that the world's shipping supply increased over four and a half times between 1870 and 1910 which must have been considerably more than the increase in the amount of cargo available. Intense competition could arise and since shipping involves high overheads as a proportion of total costs, rates were liable to be driven down for long periods as it would have been even more unprofitable to lay-up a vessel than to run it for an income which just covered the prime cost of operation. Subsidies from some governments were a further complication. In such circumstances British shipping companies could not expect to maintain steadily rising profits. Even in an apparently buoyant industry like coal there were considerable cyclical problems. In 1896 D. A. Thomas pointed out that new coal investment occurred on the upswing of the cycle but since the consequent new production took time to achieve it tended to appear when a new downswing was on the way. Hence prices were down more rapidly than might otherwise be the case. Rapid expansion of the industry after 1870 was a highly uneven process in which individual bankruptcies for the smaller or more chancy enterprises were legion and in which the fluctuating rewards for workers reflected the nature of an industry where 'hire and fire' tended to be the order of the day. Cyclical fluctuations could be seen equally in the steel industry, one example being the great strike at Carnegie steelworks in 1894 which was related to a new downturn in America.

Yet in spite of the uncertainty of the later nineteenth century it is clear that the performance of the American economy was remarkably good. Conrad has claimed that there were two periods of accelerated growth; one occurring between 1869–70 and 1881–3 when the average annual growth rate was 9 per cent, and the other between 1894 and 1903 when the rate was almost 6 per cent. He emphasises the importance of railroad promotion in the 1870s when railroad expenditure accounted for over 20 per cent of total gross capital formation. This expansion involved credit creation by state governments, by English banks and by stock market issue with consequent multiplier effects. Another great impetus to capital formation came in the 1890s with public utilities and street railways. Capital intensity in telephones, in electric light and power and in electric street railways was considerable. At the same time, the appearance of the holding-company in raising the parameters dependent upon the availability of credit was important since it facilitated borrowing and the absorption of funds available for investment.

While Conrad's diagnosis may not be universally accepted it does provide a comment on differences between the British and American economies. Railway construction slackened in the

1870s and 1880s and only exceptional lines built for a highly specific purpose after 1870 made much profit, the Barry railway in south Wales being an obvious example. Electricity, by contrast, did have potential for development in Britain since the electrical industry was small; but it has been pointed out that a highly efficient British gas industry gave little incentive for substantial investment in electricity. Because of the widespread use of relatively cheap coal and steam power for energy purposes the advantages of electric power at prevailing prices did not immediately reveal themselves to British investors. Electricity constituted an economic substitute for coal to a greater extent in America than in Britain.

The importance of coal raises in turn the question of the export balance of the two economies. The development of the British coal industry was a reflection both of internal demand and of the stimulus of the export trade. By 1913 approximately one-third of production was accounted for by exports whether direct or by sales from bunkering stations overseas. Although coal was a fast-growing export industry between 1870 and 1914 the other staple export industries – cotton and woollen textiles, iron and steel, and shipbuilding – continued to be important. The figures given by S. B. Saul for 1913 – Britain's 29.9 per cent of world exports of manufactured goods compared with America's 12.6 per cent – provide some comparison of the relative export involvement of industry. Clearly, the rapid rise of America as the world's greatest manufacturing nation between 1870 and 1900 took place largely because of the growth of America's domestic market. In turn, this different relationship of the two countries towards foreign markets may have accounted for their somewhat different performance. At least one line of approach is to suggest that many of the problems in the British economy before 1914 – a dangerously narrowing surplus in the balance of payments, possibly an undue reliance on invisible exports and a measure of complacency both in government and among private entrepreneurs – all these were a measure of British assumptions that exports should continue to enjoy high priority. Unfortunately, any neat correlation between export performance and growth performance comes up against the difficulty that no one is quite sure when the important problems of the British economy really started to appear. Coppock and Musson believe that deceleration in British growth became more marked after 1873 even if it was a long-term process lasting until 1914. Another interpretation has seen the British economy reaching a 'climacteric' in the 1890s after which progressive sluggishness occurred and Matthews has argued that between 1899 and 1913 Britain achieved only 1.1 per cent growth per annum in national income compared with 2 per cent between 1856 and 1899. Even if there is general agreement that Edwardian Britain saw relative stagnation there is no consensus of opinion over the reasons for sluggishness. As Pollard has pointed out 'it is not difficult to point to weaknesses in the British industrial structure before 1914 but they would not have been easy to prove to contemporaries'. Partly the difficulty was that British industry was still making substantial profits and was achieving a marked increase in absolute production. If contemporaries were not overwhelmingly alarmed by the greater dynamism of Germany and America it was presumably because there was a general mood of satisfaction with activities as they were.

The question is whether this mood of satisfaction was justified. No doubt there was an impression of greater business dynamism in America where business confidence in spite of the crashes of 1893 or of 1907 remained high. Two symbols of that confidence were R. W. Sears and William C. Durant, both of whom tried to lead their respective firms – Sears Roebuck and General Motors – into substantial over-commitment. The ultimate example of American business confidence in the period would be Henry Ford with his relentless pursuit of solving the problem of mass-producing a cheap, reliable passenger car; a problem solved by putting his Model T into production on a moving assembly line in 1914. Yet the considerable advances in Britain by firms such as Brunner Mond or Courtaulds in relatively new industries, and the production increases in British coal and shipbuilding, also gave grounds for optimism. The problem is whether one should take the quantitative evidence of a low growth rate in the Edwardian period at its face value or whether one argues that the period was one of inevitable pause, a phase when the structure of the economy was commencing to change partly in response to world trends. It is a problem bedevilled by hindsight with the knowledge that major distortions with consequent unemployment occurred in the 1920s. If historians now concede that undue reliance was placed by Britain upon a number of specialised lines of activity, it can be argued that the major difficulties arose from World War I. Without the war the highly disadvantageous position of coal, iron and steel and shipbuilding might have been avoided in its catastrophic proportions and a change in emphasis towards newer industries could have occurred in more orderly fashion.

World War I had the effect of placing the economic problems of 1914 in a new context producing strange and rather sudden effects. Between 1896 and 1914 there was a considerable degree of structural change in both countries even if it occurred rather more slowly in Britain. One aspect of that change was the degree of disquiet in both countries over certain aspects of the social and economic system. In America immigration policy, the banking system, tariffs and the provision of social welfare were all under review. In Britain the pressure on real earnings after 1900 for workers in Britain's traditional export industries caused industrial discontent. The growing assertion of trade union influence coupled with uneasiness about measures for social welfare illustrated a background of social flux. Yet after the war there was a tendency to look back to the days before 1914 as years of solid and orderly progress. If America had emerged as the world's leading industrial nation and had continued to expand and to achieve increasing productivity in agriculture, Britain had still performed remarkably well up to 1914 in view of the considerable changes and vicissitudes associated with her high degree of involvement in the international economy. The extent of her influence over the international monetary system and of her importance in the complex network of world trade was a reflection of the economic strength which she achieved between 1850 and 1914. Complacency may not have been altogether justified but it was understandable.

CHAPTER THREE

HUMAN ASPECTS OF ECONOMIC CHANGE, 1850–1914

A perennial theme to explain America's economic progress is the nature of American society. A highly mobile society in which personal advancement was accepted and rewarded encouraged men and women to work hard and to be confident about the future. This simple correlation conceals the problem that it is often difficult to know whether social factors are cause or effect of economic change. In any event, the question is highly complex because both Britain and America were not simple homogeneous societies as befitted the degree of industrialisation which they attained after 1850. Hence generalisations about one section or aspect of society may not be valid for others. These difficulties are relevant to the problems treated in this chapter of which the first is the moving frontier.

The Moving Frontier Thesis

It was perhaps inevitable that towards the end of a period of rapid development obvious enough to contemporaries there should come an interpretation explaining economic growth in terms of developing new land. This interpretation was Frederick Jackson Turner's famous essay in 1893 on 'The Significance of the Frontier in American History'. Although Turner was writing about three previous centuries his thesis is specially applicable to the 1850–90 period since the pace of change was then so great in absolute terms. Billington has summarised the Turner thesis as the lure of adventure in search for wealth. In an abundant land area old laws were inapplicable and there was scope for innovation and experiment. Materialism, mobility and hard work came to be a habit. Traditional class distinctions were meaningless and a democratic social system was natural.

Individualism and political democracy became ideals. These characteristics were revitalised as the frontier moved westward so that they evolved into a distinct American way of life and thought.

This thesis raises problems. The frontier itself is difficult to define but if it was an area where extremely sparse settlement involved pioneering then it is difficult to see how it could induce very advanced innovation because of the risks involved. If, however, the frontier concept is taken to mean a large area of the trans-Mississippi West which may have been pioneering country in 1850 but which was subject to increasing economic development throughout this period, then the concept is largely an exercise in regional development theory. In terms of population the trans-Mississippi West was the fastest growing area in the United States: whereas in 1850 it was an area containing 14 per cent of the American people, in 1910 it contained over 26 per cent. Billington admits the difficulty in the frontier thesis when he writes that: 'The area lying immediately behind the spatial frontier contributed far more substantially to the growth of the country's economy. There production could be stimulated only by technological improvement and expansion of markets, as abundant resources scarcely scratched by the pioneering generation were gradually brought into full use.'[1] Hence the concept invites semantic confusion and one must think in terms of the relatively unexploited land of the trans-Mississippi West.

In terms of population the West's proportionate increase was more rapid than any other area of the United States, yet by 1910 the population of the North East was still much greater than that of the West. In the work of Harvey S. Perloff and his collaborators eight regional divisions are adopted of which four (New England, Middle Atlantic, Great Lakes and South East) accounted between them for 73.8 per cent of population in 1910 as compared with 26.2 per cent in the Western regions (Plains, South West, Mountain and Far West).[2] These proportions urge cautions against exaggerated claims of the importance of 'the frontier'. Yet population is not a decisive economic indicator. The relative distribution of purchasing power together with the contribution by value of certain economic activities to total economic life may be equally significant. The most important feature of the West lay in its contribution to the major 'natural resource' industries of which agriculture was clearly the most important. Between 1870 and 1910 there was a striking change. In 1870 agriculture accounted for 89 per cent of the value of all resource industries and within that percentage the North East accounted for 49 per cent as opposed to 14 per cent by the West. By 1910 agriculture still accounted for 80 per cent of the value of 'natural resource industries' but within that percentage the West now accounted for 35 per cent as opposed to the North East's 27 per cent.[3] Similarly in mineral extraction the West achieved a striking relative advance, from 1.20 per cent in 1870 to 4.35 per cent in 1910 compared with the North East's increase from 4.18 per cent to 6.01 per cent. In such developments the year 1910 was of greater significance than 1890 when the 'frontier' was reputedly closed. Until 1910 there was still a great deal of territory capable of more intensive exploitation because of its low population density.

Low population density is not in itself a guarantee of development. The development of agriculture and mining in the West was to a large extent a reflection of demand for agricultural and mineral products. For demand to be satisfied, communication and distribution systems were of immense importance. In view of its size both in population and in manufacturing the North East generated much of the demand and the development of the West could be written in terms of regional interplay between East and West. For interplay to occur, the links provided by urban centres were necessary. Perhaps the most important urban centre of all was Chicago which for purposes of regional classification came in the Great Lakes area of the westernmost part of the North East. As regional centres St Louis and Denver grew while Minneapolis, Oklahoma and Kansas became flour-milling centres of great size.

For Western economic development to proceed capital had to be imported from the East. New York financiers played a part in the growth of railroads and of flour-milling even if the necessity to raise Eastern loans was resented by the millers with every effort being made to rely less on Eastern finance as time went on. With increasing agricultural exports to Europe the Eastern ports, especially New York and Boston, became natural centres for the financing of international transactions. Hence the economic development of the West was a function of total American development in which the growth of internal manufacturing and of exports were two important features. A good example of these changing relationships would be meat packing. Although Chicago and Cincinnati were early centres of the industry, meat packing moved westward and with the emphasis on the range-cattle industry between 1865 and 1885 St Louis and Kansas City and Omaha became important centres. The export importance of meat packing is shown by the fact that in 1900 manufactured foodstuffs were rather over 23 per cent by value of American exports. Nevertheless, home demand in the industrial North East also increased considerably.

Hence the economic development of the West involved several elements which would be a normal feature of regional economic development. The features of technical innovation and experiment, hard work, love of material possessions, greater opportunity and upward social mobility alleged to belong to the frontier were features associated with a society in the course of rapid change, and rapid change applied to most of America and not just to one part of it. Habakkuk, for example, has written about American technology with scarcely a mention of the frontier. Cochran and Miller have described the rise of a business society by emphasising the growth of finance capitalism and the cities of the East. The greatest personal opportunities lay in the cities and the farmers remained a relatively impoverished group. The young T. A. Edison travelled east to Boston and New York and not west to the Dakotas. Moreover, upward social mobility existed over a wide section of American society and was a feature to which more than one English visitor drew attention. The best evidence of social equality for those who compared British and American institutions was the common school system. The educational system provided a basis for upward social mobility, and fairly rapid economic development over a wide area ensured widespread opportunities.

In short, the moving frontier thesis is an over-statement for our period, yet there is no need to disparage development occurring in the West since that development was important both for agricultural exports and for a more highly specialised system of agriculture. Regional interdependence arising from a large new area provided new outlets for consumer goods and manufactures. Interdependence was a continuing feature, and to write of the closing of the frontier in 1890 is to obscure the very real increase in production and productivity occurring in the trans-Mississippi West between 1890 and 1910. To emphasise the 'frontier' is to overlook the complexities of the situation in the manufacturing North East where society was far from static and where opportunity existed with increasing frequency for men of ability and ambition. America was indeed a land of opportunity but its attraction lay in the diffusion of opportunity in more than one region.

Immigration

Another possible contribution to the dynamism of American society lay in immigration. All historians agree that the volume of immigration to America after 1850 was phenomenal. According to Conway, about 5 million immigrants came before the Civil War, most of them between 1847 and 1857. Over 30 million arrived between 1860 and 1930 with peak periods from 1880 to 1890 and from 1900 to 1920.[4] In any single decade between 1860 and 1910 the percentage of immigrants in American population varied between 13.1 and 14.7 per cent. The immigrants, moreover, belonged almost entirely to the productive age group between 15 and 64 years of age. It is usually assumed that economic development was furthered by immigration but the precise contribution is often difficult to measure because of the disparate character of the immigrants. Furthermore, immigration may have been rather more beneficial at some points in time than at other points. It is not easy to be certain on the matter partly because the concept of human capital is one which economists are still in the stage of refining.

Nevertheless, there is reasonable agreement that the absorptive capacity of the American economy was high because most branches of economic activity were capable of expansion given extra labour, not least agriculture and activities such as mining which consisted of natural resource exploitation. Furthermore, the fact that immigrants were speedily able to enter work resulted in increased earnings and consumption and an expansion of the American domestic market. The variety of occupations open to immigrants was matched by a variety of tasks which they were capable of performing since they were relatively mobile and non-specialised. Nevertheless, a significant minority were skilled. In 1910, for example, the proportion of total male skilled workers was 14.2 per cent of the occupied male population whereas foreign male workers provided 18 per cent skilled workers from their number and an exceptional group – the Scots – provided 32.5 per cent. Even the Irish, often reputed to be unskilled, provided 19.6 per cent. Of course these figures from the United States Population Census of 1910 did not necessarily reflect the most recent immigration and some of the men included may have entered the country years before. Definitions of 'skill' may also be questionable. Nevertheless, they provide a warning that in spite of defects alleged against the 'new' immigrants from south-eastern Europe, by 1910 the immigrant proportions were larger than those of the indigenous population in most socio-economic groups except for farmers and farm labourers. Only 9.9 per cent of the foreign male workers were farmers compared with 19.5 per cent of the total male working population and 5 per cent were farm labourers as against 15.6 per cent. On the other hand, 15 per cent of the foreigners were factory and building construction labourers as compared with 8.5 per cent of total workers. Hence the immigrants provided labour of the kind required by an increasingly industrial society.

Nevertheless, the outcry around 1910 against so-called new immigrants from south-eastern Europe might be significant. It was said that the immigrants were unskilled and provided a social problem in town ghettos where they constituted a pool of cheap unemployed or underemployed labour. It was possible that the absorptive capacity of the American economy was less great than in earlier decades or less in particular occupations or activities because of the financial panic and downturn of 1907. Hence the appointment of the Dillingham Commission to investigate the problem might indicate a turning point around 1910. The situation was complex in that the attraction of the United States to newcomers was relative to the attractions of moving to other developing lands or of simply not moving at all. It does seem clear that contemporaries were correct in assuming that a marked shift in the geographical origins of immigrants had taken place. Of the 788,000 immigrants who arrived in 1882, 87 per cent came from northern and western Europe and only 13 per cent from southern and eastern Europe. In 1907 the positions were reversed when out of 1,285,000 immigrants the proportions were 19.3 per cent and 80.7 per cent respectively. The shift came relatively late; not until 1896 did the volume of 'new' immigration exceed the 'old' and the disparity between the two groups became really marked only after the turn of the century. As Maldwyn Jones points out, the strictures of the commission against the 'new' immigrants were by no means justified. Accusations about illiteracy or about a low proportion of unskilled workers were exaggerated.

The Dillingham Commission episode, however, does prompt enquiry about the relationship between the receiving country – the United States – and the supplying countries and about the reasons for the uneven incidence of immigration as between particular years. Brinley Thomas has analysed the problem in terms of the interdependence of the Atlantic community of nations; the expansion of the whole entailed the transfer of labour and capital from east to west. There was a mutual relation between the minor secular fluctuations in the British and American economies. When the United States experienced a strong upsurge in activity she absorbed large quantities of labour and capital from Britain and the rate of growth in Britain slackened. When the American system was digesting what it had swallowed, Britain's appetite for home investment would increase and her real income would grow faster than usual. Conditions in the supplying countries were important and each crisis of over-population was a milestone in the building of America's industrial strength; the periodic flows of redundant labour had a powerful influence on the rate of growth, the technique of production and the social structure of America. The inverse relationship ceased when the United States practically stopped importing labour from Europe and began to export capital on a considerable scale and this coincided with the emergence of the United States as the predominant industrial power. Accordingly, international migration and especially immigration into the United States was one key flow of resources which, along with the flow of capital, helped the smooth working of the pre-1914 gold standard as a mechanism for ensuring adjustments or equilibrium between debtor and creditor countries.

Even if the views of Thomas are not universally accepted, they have influenced discussion considerably, especially about capital movements rather than labour. Some would give rather more emphasis to America than Britain as the source of inverse movements, and no doubt the precise nature of the inverse relationship will continue to be debated. It does not seem controversial that movement of labour before 1914 was beneficial both for the international economy and for the United States. One beneficial aspect was the effect on the age composition of the American labour force. With declining fertility after about 1825, by the 1850s the excess of births over deaths accounted for only a little more than 2 per cent annual population growth while immigration supplied almost another 1 per cent. As long as population growth was desirable for the fuller exploitation of resources and for a more complex division of labour, then immigration was an advantage. Between 1820 and 1920 the median age of immigrants was 24 and well over half the immigrants were from 14 to 44 years old, the most productive age. From 1899 to 1914, 80 per cent or more were in this age group. Over the whole period 1820–1920, 60 per cent or more were males. In purely quantitative terms unskilled labourers predominated, forming 42 to 50 per cent of immigrants up to 1900 and 35 per cent in the decade 1901–10. Hence there was a reserve of unskilled labour which both facilitated industrial expansion and formed a cushion for agriculture especially in periods of depression. However, immigrant labour tended to concentrate in certain industries throughout the country, for the most part in heavy industry requiring large numbers of unskilled. In 1910 foreign-born whites comprised 20.5 per cent of male workers in all industries and in twenty-three selected industries including mining, clothing, railroad shops, steel, textiles, rubber and construction, the proportion of foreign-born varied between 40 and 76 per cent. It was argued by native workers that unskilled immigrants lowered wage rates but the indirect effect may have been to push native workers out of the unskilled class into more skilled and higher paid occupations. There were short-run periods where immigration was too large for immediate absorption, causing consequent dislocation in the labour market and adverse repercussions on wages; the classic example of such a period would be around 1907 which influenced the Dillingham Commission. Moreover, the flow of poor prolific peoples to a prosperous and growing economy could not have continued indefinitely without a radical transformation of American society. National self-preservation was bound to come into play. Because of the many variables interacting with it, few economists would probably see immigration as the key element in American growth but the evidence does suggest that without it the rate of economic growth would have been lower than that achieved between 1860 and 1910. Perhaps the campaigns to restrict immigration which occurred in the twentieth century were a sign that the American economy was entering a new phase when immigration was no longer so important for economic development as in the past.

Entrepreneurship

In so-called 'capitalist' societies it is not surprising if apparent American social dynamism has been symbolised by the superiority of the American entrepreneur. In the last ten years or so an explanation of growth in terms of entrepreneurship has been put forward and then largely abandoned. This brief section attempts to show the problems concerned with such an explanation.

The first problem is to define the entrepreneur's role and function. According to Schumpeter producers can manipulate consumer's tastes by advertising and by control of the market; in his system the entrepreneur is essentially an innovator in technology or in business methods. Hence successful entrepreneurship depends largely on successful innovation. Such an approach is at variance with that of classical economic theory which assumes a state of perfect competition in production and in consumption: since the consumer is king, the art of entrepreneur is to respond to if not to foresee the way in which consumers' tastes evolve. There is an element of chance in such an exercise and hence the essential element in entrepreneurship – as for Edith T. Penrose – may lie in risk taking. '[It is] a psychological predisposition on the part of individuals to take a chance in the hope of gain and, in particular, to commit effort and resources to speculative activity.'[5] Yet a third approach stresses the many-sided aspects of entrepreneurship which involves both setting business aims and co-ordinating the activities of management, marketing, finance, technology and public relations. It is not difficult to see that for some writers the entrepreneur plays a causative or determining role in the economic system whereas for others he is largely an associated feature of the system and may be moulded by it.

Hence it is not surprising if historians have wavered between different approaches. The American entrepreneur has usually been considered something of a folk-hero even if in recent years the study of his performance has become more subtle in terms of distinguishing the merits and demerits of different approaches to management problems. Cochran and Miller point out that the ideals of business leaders became the ideals of the great majority of Americans in the nineteenth century, and Habakkuk has drawn attention to a strongly entrenched social system in Britain limiting social mobility so that there was 'a haemorrhage of capital and ability from industry and trade into landowner-ship and politics'. The implication of such remarks is that the entrepreneur was largely a creature of his environment with the implication that a more dynamic American environment pro-duced more dynamic American entrepreneurs.

A different approach was adopted by Aldcroft in 1964 when he cast the entrepreneur in a causative role by asserting that after 1870 'Britain's relatively poor economic performance can be attributed largely to the failure of the British entrepreneur to respond to the challenge of changed conditions'. He quoted examples from the coal, iron and steel and tinplate industries and pointed out that it was foreign enterprises and not British which contributed most to the development of chemicals, ma-chine tools, scientific instruments, motor vehicles and electrical manufacture. There was a lack of appreciation by British in-dustrialists of the importance of science and technology and its application to industry. The 'inescapable' conclusion was that the British economy could have been more viable if there had been a concerted effort of adaptation on the part of British industry. Only a year later Charles Wilson replied by pointing out that the new industries were all the product of vigorous and ingenious entrepreneurs as dynamic as any of their predecessors. A list of enterprising businessmen either in promoting new industries or developing new territories could contain such names as Lever, Beecham, Cecil Rhodes, Alfred Beit, Barney Barnato, George Taubman Goldie, Ludwig Mond, George Newnes, Alfred Harmsworth, the Iliffes, Lipton, Cadbury, Rowntree, Guinness, Boot, Courtauld, Charles Parsons and W. D. Pearson.

The defect of the approach of both Aldcroft and Wilson was that it was highly selective. The greater complexity of the situa-tion was shown by S. B. Saul who studied the problem by way of one industry. The title of his article 'The Market and the Development of the Mechanical Engineering Industries' showed an awareness that engineering was not homogeneous, a point which could be applied to almost any industry one cared to name. Engineering consisted of such diverse branches as textile machinery, railway locomotives, steam engines, boilers, ma-chine tools, agricultural machinery, agricultural steam engines, cycles, motor cycles and motor vehicles. The performance of different sectors varied greatly. Perhaps the most dynamic sec-tor was textile machinery, a subject strangely neglected by historians even though in 1907 it was the largest branch of British engineering and an overwhelmingly dominant force in world trade. One firm, Platts of Oldham, had an output in 1914 equal to that of the whole American industry put together. In some parts of the world Platt's machinery was standard for all cotton mills. Unlike the American industry, which had grown so customer-conscious in its fight for American southern mill orders that it was prepared to grant all kinds of design concessions to individual millmen, the British were in a position to insist on standardised products. There were other engineering sectors such as stationary and marine steam-engines or sewing machinery which were very advanced commercially and technologically. Where success varied as with agricultural machinery, locomotives and machine tools, it was in part at least conditioned by the nature of the market. With railway locomotives the institutional framework resulted not only in the market being created in an entirely different manner in Britain and America but in the building of entirely different technical products. The British engine was a high quality product with a long life, relatively expensive and difficult to service, closely tailored to the needs of the line for which it had been specifically designed. Clearly the market was not the complete answer to all the questions about engineering and to understand more fully its lags and successes there would be a need for more detailed study of training and institutional patterns. Nevertheless, in engineering Saul would argue that the slowing down of growth after 1870 was due more to objective economic factors than had been previously recognised. It might be that in explanations of relative response to technological change, the firm and individuals within it remained the residual factor. Unfortunately, such a belief did not help one in determining how important the residual factor was.

Saul's article probably constitutes a landmark since after it there has been much less disposition to make generalisations about national qualities of entrepreneurs. In 1968 Aldcroft was prepared to admit that condemnation was begun by the Victorians themselves and that the situation was highly complex in varying from industry to industry. A key problem is to know what criteria of judgement should be employed. Much historiography may be beside the point because it views British performance from the standpoint of the 1920s and 1930s when export demand had turned down. It is interesting that recent

American writings are not disposed to support the more extreme condemnations of Britain. Temin, for example, has argued that British steelmasters might have been somewhat more dynamic than they were, but their inherent difficulties meant that the scope for improvement over actual performance was not enormous: he has estimated that, had certain hypothetical changes taken place after 1890, the average annual growth rate of the British steel industry would have increased from the actual figure of 3.4 per cent to one of 4.6 per cent per year. The merit of Temin's approach is that he puts forward a target, however hypothetical, against which actual performance can be judged. Even so, his work has been criticised on the grounds that he over-estimates productivity growth in the American steel industry and that he assumes mistakenly that productivity change fell in proportion to the fall in the growth of output in Britain.

More fundamental considerations, however, are raised by McCloskey and Sandberg. They point out that entrepreneurship is a residual factor and that it is not a satisfactory line of argument to discuss a variety of hypotheses, discarding them one by one on qualitative grounds, to arrive at a final conclusion about one factor. Qualitative argument by isolation brings the critical difficulty that the size of the isolated residual variable is left a matter of faith rather than fact. Scattered cases of entrepreneurial success or failure do not add up to a general proof of entrepreneurial failure. Following their approach one may argue that some apparently brilliant American success stories show that elements of chance and of external circumstance were operative. No one doubts that Thomas Alva Edison was a superb innovator, yet his success shows that an American environment was essential. He spent some ½ million dollars between 1878 and 1884 in research and development before he was able to make incandescent electric lighting a practicable proposition, and the necessary financial backing obtained from Pierpoint Morgan and others would almost certainly not have been available in Britain, not merely because of the size of the investment but because Britain's efficient gas-lighting industry made the rapid supersession of gas by electricity a much less feasible proposition in Britain than in America. Similarly, the career of John D. Rockefeller was uniquely American. The biography by Nevins shows that however formidable Rockefeller's personal qualities may have been it was of crucial importance that his early business career lay in Cleveland, Ohio, which was a strategic point for oil on the Atlantic & Great Western Railway and, secondly, that through his business contacts and aquaintances Rockefeller was able to borrow the necessary funds for expansion in the vital first decade of the rise of the industry. America had oil under its surface and Britain did not.

The value of individual case-studies is simply that they show the particular elements of choice and environment making a framework within which the entrepreneur has to operate. A major problem is the extent to which the framework can be altered by the entrepreneur. To what extent is it true that the 'businessman gets the demand he deserves'? In the absence of clear objective yardsticks by which to judge entrepreneurial potential, historians have fallen back on criteria seemingly objective such as size of firm, social mobility and willingness to innovate. On examination these criteria reveal little. Size of firm has been treated by P. L. Payne who has no difficulty in showing that in 1905 American firms were larger than British firms. In analysing the fifty largest firms in each country he found that if one omitted the two largest firms (US Steel and American Tobacco on the one hand and Imperial Tobacco and Watney, Combe & Reid on the other), the average capital of American firms came out at rather more than two and a quarter times that employed in Britain. If one included the two largest firms the average capital would be more like three and a half times in favour of America because of the enormous size of US Steel and American Tobacco. Payne explains the relatively smaller size of British firms in a number of ways. British manufacturers pursued a policy of specialisation and product differentiation, exploiting the imperfections of the market created by the ingrained preference of British consumers for articles exhibiting craftmanship and individual character. Yet specialisation tends to become irreversible since special merchant relationships, skilled labour and particular managerial skills develop which makes the entrepreneur's position inflexible. Hence too many British entrepreneurs failed to diversify. Another factor limiting size of firm was that oft-quoted failing of family control. Even when mergers took place, vendors attempted to retain their hold over the business. Leadership by inheritance applied in a great range of industrial activities in Britain, thus inhibiting the ascent of the brilliant salaried official, whereas in America the widespread acceptance of the democratic principle meant that capable persons were prepared initially to accept a fairly low status because they were aware of the possibility of promotion. Payne concludes that sociological factors explained the differences in the growth of big business in the two countries before World War I.

The danger may be in confounding cause and effect. One has to show that new markets were available on a wide scale so as to make larger firms and subsequent economies of scale worthwhile. In America the growth of Sears Roebuck and of General Motors before 1914 shows that the founders of those firms – Richard Warren Sears and William C. Durant – came to regard continuing expansion as an almost inevitable state of existence; in each case their over-commitment eventually caused difficulties leading to changes in management and organisation, but the crucial point was that both men could exercise heady enthusiasm for a number of years during which their firms grew considerably because the market could bear such expansion. In Britain the situation induced understandable caution because the benefits of large-scale operation were not overwhelmingly apparent. A good example of such caution would be in the south Wales tinplate industry. Considerable expansion was achieved before 1891 when the McKinley tariff came into operation, making the American market difficult to penetrate. Expansion had been achieved by relatively small firms but subsequent difficulties did not suggest that a large organisation could surmount marketing problems better than a number of small ones. One firm – Richard Thomas & Co Ltd – did come by 1916 to acquire about a quarter of the mills operating in the industry but there was little evidence that its size suggested great improvement in efficiency.

The tinplate industry also provides a warning that social mobility in industry may be largely irrelevant to entrepreneurial performance. It is not difficult to show that there were a number of men of humble origins in south Wales who rose to directorship. The vital point was that in an age when no formal promotion arrangements existed a firm would turn to any candidate who seemed a feasible successor. In both countries candidates with a good education stood a better chance of appointment than those of meagre learning, and even in America educational arrangements were not so democratic that boys with poor parents easily obtained entry to high school or college. Mabel

Newcomer's sample of big business executives in 1900 and T. C. Cochran's sample of sixty-one railroad leaders between 1845 and 1890 have both shown that American business leaders came from relatively high social status. Psychologists, after all, still find it a considerable point of debate how far ability is a matter of nature and nurture. The dynamic entrepreneur may well more often come from upper social groups. The more important point of difference, however, between America and Britain, lay in the more rapid expansion of firms which made possible rapid personal promotion. Thus an attitude arose in America of relatively rapid mobility within the firm which may not be the same as general social mobility. Opportunities for business ascendancy were more numerous in America but it was still the upper social groups who stood to gain from those opportunities.

If the American entrepreneur was superior to the British entrepreneur before 1914, it was largely because of the difference of the environment. Individual businessmen made wrong decisions on both sides of the Atlantic. No one yet seems to have done a study of comparative British and American nineteenth-century industrial bankruptcy, but the results of such a study might not be so unfavourable to Britain. Objective comparative measurements of entrepreneurs are hardly possible because of the different circumstances within which entrepreneurs operated, different circumstances occurring even within the same industry. What one can say is that British entrepreneurs or some of them did superbly well in those industries which played such an important part in British exports, and American entrepreneurs did superbly well over a number of industries catering specially for the needs of the domestic consumer. If the American entrepreneur gave the impression of greater drive and confidence it was because of his more favourable situation; the extreme blanket condemnation of entrepreneurs in Britain has not been proven.

Trade Unions and the Labour Force

In the process of economic growth, labour is no doubt an important contributory factor. Yet we still know far too little about the mechanisms by which higher output per man has been or is being achieved and, therefore, we find it difficult to analyse labour in all its facets. One area of discussion, however, lies in the rewards or wages provided to workers in return for their labour and in the question whether wages are improved by the actions of trade unions. This area of discussion may be highly inconclusive but it does throw some light on the differences in human terms between the British and American economies.

Part of the student's problem is that while there is a great deal of literature about trade unions from an institutional or organisational point of view there is much less on the contribution made by trade unions to improving the worker's standard of living especially by raising wages. Trade unions set some store on their influence over wages yet it is arguable from the historical record that, in spite of weaker trade union organisation, real industrial wages grew more rapidly in America than they did in Britain between 1850 and 1914. As Phelps Brown has shown, the actual factor by which the real wage has been multiplied over a hundred years (between 1860 and 1960) is between 4 and $4\frac{1}{2}$ in France, Germany and the United Kingdom, and about $6\frac{1}{2}$ in Sweden and the USA. It was an uneven process but, according to Phelps Brown, the tendency for wages to rise faster in America than in Britain appeared in the 1870s and 1880s and become manifestly clear between 1895 and 1914.[6] These wage rises occurred in spite of much lower American trade union membership and in spite of the relative lack of involvement of unions in social and political struggles compared with their British counterparts. To explain the American advantage one must consider the total situation determining wage and salary structures and not least the factors influencing notions of social status which are an important psychological element in the fixing of wage levels. As Phelps Brown says, 'do money wages rise because there is an excess of vacancies over applicants in the labour market, or because profits have gone up or because trade unions are pushing harder? One cannot appeal to everyday experience for a certain and an exclusive answer, and then use it to identify cause and effect when they make their appearance in the record. One has to start with the record, and ask whether any systematic association appears between money wage rises and the movements of some other variables . . . here difficulties multiply.'[7] In view of these difficulties all that the present section claims to do is to explain why trade unions seemed to become more influential as time went on.

According to one authority, a labour union is 'a continuous

association of wage earners for the purpose of improving their economic and social well-being'.[8] In both countries the important point to note is that many unions were not continuous, having an intermittent existence with some disappearing and others re-emerging under a different name. From the viewpoint of labour movements it might be argued that Britain achieved a common organisation with the formation of the Trades Union Congress in 1868 which soon achieved some political influence with the election of 'Lib-Lab' members to Parliament in 1874 (just two of them) and the setting up of a parliamentary committee of the TUC. In time – especially between 1900 and 1914 – there was to emerge a Labour party which around 1909–10 had no less than fifty-three members in Parliament. By contrast, the labour movements which might have some general appeal in America were much less influential. The Knights of Labor was an interesting but essentially short-lived attempt at a general approach to labour organisation which flourished in the early 1880s but lost support after the 'Haymarket episode' of 1886. The American Federation of Labor (AFL) which developed as a federation of skilled unions centred around particular crafts, increased its membership from the late 1880s to 1914 but remained largely outside the particular arena. The AFL became bitterly opposed to the aims and methods of the Industrial Workers of the World (the Wobblies) formed in 1905 to serve the interests of semi-skilled and unskilled workers. The 'dual unionism' existing in America in the early twentieth century was a contrast with the apparent unity in Britain where both 'craft' and 'general' unions co-ordinated policies under the umbrella of the TUC and the Labour party.

As Pelling has shown, British labour leaders were highly critical of the weaknesses of American unions by the early twentieth century, yet half a century earlier there was considerable admiration in Britain for American society and the position of the industrial worker. This change in attitude was partly because of the institutional and legal achievements of British unions which appeared to offer a contrast with the vulnerability of the American worker and the subservience of American unions attached to the AFL to the pressure of employers. The important question is to know whether the institutional gains achieved in Britain did result in gains for workers in their wages and standard of living. From this point of view the evidence is by no means conclusive.

In institutional terms the British trade union movement appeared to achieve marked success between 1850 and 1875. It was a period in which the unions moved from a position of legal disability and public hostility towards them to the legal protections afforded by the Acts of 1871 and 1875. After the Act of 1825 they were allowed to exist but enjoyed no legal status in the sense of being able to sue or be sued in the courts. An absconding treasurer could make off with the funds. Middle-class opinion was often hostile since unions were often regarded as conspiracies against the normal operation of a free market for labour. Hence the courts could usually be relied upon to uphold the employers' cause in any contentious issue. In older histories such as that of the Webbs a turning point is usually placed in the year 1851 with the formation of the Amalgamated Society of Engineers, labelled a 'New Model' because of its emphasis on organisation which other unions began to imitate. As a skilled craftworkers' union the ASE under its efficient secretary William Allan broke down old regional loyalties and imposed the necessary discipline for an effective national union. The problem for the historian is to know to what extent the development of the ASE or the formation of the London Trades' Council in 1860 were offensive in character – the initiative of particularly gifted men taking advantage of new circumstances such as the widening of the labour market associated with improved transport; and to what extent defensive – a response to the growing size of firms and of power among employers. It is perhaps an intractable problem to be solved by partisan prejudice. Yet it seems undeniable that the dialogue between employers and unions shifted in context when, in the 1860s, union officials were drawn into politics by a number of factors. The London builders' strike revealed potential allies of trade unions among professional men. The general debate over the extension of voting qualifications could hardly leave the unions uncommitted. It was a fluid situation in which opinion might move either way. The 'Sheffield outrages' of 1866 involving acts of violence against non-unionists in the Sheffield cutlery trades and leading to the appointment of a Royal Commission had a potentially injurious effect. In the event, trade unionists or their supporters favourably impressed the commission and its report resulted in a change of public attitude. Between 1867 and 1875 a tide of events seemed to help trade unions. Voting qualifications were extended in 1867 to include skilled craftsmen. A meeting at Manchester in 1868 was the effective historic foundation of the TUC. In 1871 legal recognition was given to trade unions and they could protect funds by registering under the Friendly Societies Act. Even if picketing was still illegal there was now a political arm of the trade unions in the guise of the Parliamentary Committee of the TUC appointed in 1871 which could campaign for alteration of the criminal law. In 1875 the Disraeli Conservative government was prepared to pass a measure expressly legalising picketing and at the same time the law of conspiracy was not to apply in trade disputes unless the actions concerned were criminal in themselves. In the election of 1874 two trade union candidates were elected to Parliament as members of the Liberal party, the forerunners of the 'Lib-Labs'.

In view of these developments it may be surprising that British observers should comment so favourably upon the situation in America. As V. L. Allen has pointed out, however, unions have to be seen not as separate institutions leading an autonomous existence but in the context of the general socio-economic environment. The American environment, as British visitors noted, was one where high wages were common and where social equality seemed to prevail to a much greater extent than in Britain. John Wilson, a British miner who spent some years in Pennsylvania during the Civil War was impressed by the freedom and social equality that he encountered in the mining villages. He wrote: 'The highest citizen was not a long way up. There was no need for a social telescope to see him.'[9] If Habakkuk's argument is correct that there was, in general, a shortage of labour which employers were obliged to recognise by granting relatively high wages, then the necessity for trade unions as a bargaining agency was not so marked as in Britain. Yet even the more highly rewarded workers were not immune from fluctuations inherent in trade union activity and there were important differences between particular trades or occupations or between regions. Hence it may be that attempts at American union organisation were primarily defensive. The printers were the first to attempt a national organisation by a convention of 1850 issuing instructions to local printers' unions nation-wide and by a second convention of 1852 forming the National Typographic Union. By 1857 ten more national unions had been established but only three survived the financial panic of that year. Five more national craft unions were established between 1857 and 1860. By 1873 the shoemakers, the Knights of St Crispin, formed the largest union with a membership of 50,000. The financial depression of 1866 caused a general membership decline but, with unemployment and the anti-labour campaign of employers, trade unionists turned to agitation for the eight-hour day. Several trades called simultaneously for national organisation to unify the movement and a congress at Baltimore formed the National Labor Union, the first permanent organisation of labour in America on a national scale. It lacked funds and was unable precisely to define its membership. Its annual congress dwindled to only seven persons by 1872. If it had any influence it was presumably that of giving its participants some pragmatic training in the task of organising and administering a central labour union.

Hence in an organisational sense British unions seemed to make greater headway. Nevertheless, little was achieved for the great mass of workers, and unions of cotton workers, miners, gasworkers, builders' labourers, agricultural labourers and railwaymen all enjoyed only limited success at best. The unskilled labourers and workers in sweated trades remained outside the interest of the Parliamentary Committee of the TUC. Divisions or sectional interests often appeared, an example being the miners' split between the Miners National Union and the Amalgamated Association of Miners with the AAM eventually being swept out of existence. Around 1875, therefore, it is not altogether clear that British trade unions were 'in advance' of their American counterparts, even if attempts in America to form national unions were not altogether fruitful. Probably the greater size of America and the more fluid nature of American society resulted in a situation where workers did not view combination as a defence against employers in quite the same way as they did in Britain. Nevertheless, movements of the trade cycle and particularly the greater economic uncertainty occurring in the 1870s and 1880s may have acted as a stimulus to new departures. These were especially the rise and fall of the Knights of Labor in America and the rise of general unions in Britain. In both countries there was a need to change custom and traditional attitudes to wages by propaganda to gain public sympathy, by political action and by increasing attention to greater solidarity to counter the threat of punitive legislation.

The hostility of the American public at large to unionism may explain the need for the rise of the Knights of Labor, an extraordinary union originally composed of district assemblies of garment-makers practising secret rituals. It had no national organisation in its early years after 1869, but the long depression of the 1870s and the railroad strike of 1877 seems to have acted as a catalyst. Rayback believes that the strike involved the largest number of persons in any labour conflict during the nineteenth century. In every locality railway workers were joined by other groups such as miners, millhands, sewer-men, stevedores and the unemployed. There was a sudden rush of interest in the Knights of Labor and by the end of 1877 eleven more district assemblies had been created. Expansion brought a need for national organisation which was achieved early in 1878. The ultimate aim of the order was the establishment of productive and distributive co-operative institutions which would enable labour and capital to live harmoniously together. A national organisation did not prevent internal conflict over issues such as secrecy, involvement with politics, strike action and wage bargaining, and organisation by industrial unions rather than by trades. Nevertheless, the Knights acquired prestige from leadership of the railroad strikes of 1884 and 1885. At the same time the rank and file became interested in the eight-hour movement which in 1885 attracted an influx of unskilled workers. Terence V. Powderly, the overall leader, warned against such a general movement with possibly irresponsible leadership. Many so-called members joined in a wave of emotion and their allegiance was virtually untested. If the eight-hour movement was a failure it was not so serious as the 'Haymarket episode' of 1886 during which ten people were killed in a demonstration meeting at Haymarket Square, Chicago. In the ensuing reaction eight probably innocent men were convicted of murder and many state legislatures passed laws curbing freedom of action by labour organisations. 'In the public mind the Haymarket affair was a climax to ten years of labour violence. It was no accident that the American Federation of Labor began its long period of dominance when public disillusionment with the Knights became widespread.'[10]

The experience of the Knights of Labor was in contrast with the experience of the 'New Unionism' emerging in Britain in the mid-eighties which secured public sympathy during the dockers' strike of 1885 and the match-girls' strike of 1889. In Britain public conscience was aroused even if only fitfully, by the plight of the lower-paid unskilled worker. Although Hobsbawm has shown that between 1885 and 1914 most unskilled or general unions existed for only a relatively short time and that there were a great number of them with loose or non-existent links between each, there is justification for the view that the thirty-year period before 1914 saw a coalescence of interest and organisation, however tenuous, between different unions, which found practical expression in the emergence of the Labour party after 1906. No doubt it is easy to exaggerate the strength of the British labour movement before 1914 but there is little doubt that the debate over social and political rights to be enjoyed by working men was of a different order from that conducted in America. The contrast is most easily shown by the way in which skilled and unskilled unions were drawn together in the Labour Representation Committee after 1900 and then in the Labour party after 1906 in Britain whereas in America the skilled unions centred around particular crafts which combined in the growing American Federation of Labor (AFL) were bitterly opposed to the aims and methods of the Industrial Workers of the World (the Wobblies) formed in 1905 to serve the interests of semi-skilled and unskilled workers.

The Wobblies continued the tradition, if it can be called a tradition, of dual unionism deriving from the Knights of Labor. The AFL represented craft organisations not disposed to pursue violent tactics nor to strike except in extreme necessity. Its policies under Samuel Gompers, who was president almost continuously from 1886 to 1924, were cautious and conservative. It was hostile towards the Knights and the Wobblies because those bodies infringed on the activities of craft unions. By contrast, Hobsbawm's conclusion for Britain is that workers 'on both sides of the gap' kept to their proper stations as 'artisan' and 'labourers' which was of considerable advantage to the general unions in their formative period and avoided the competition with the 'crafts' which wrecked the Knights of Labor. Yet the rise of general unions in Britain took place against the background of a more widespread debate not only about the distribution of wealth in society but about the law concerning trade unions and the place of trade unions in industrial arrangements. It was certainly true that there was a tendency both in Britain and America for firms to grow larger in size whether by their own self-induced expansion or by industrial combination. The rapid expansion in membership of the AFL between 1898 and 1904 took place against such a background. In Britain, the combination movement seemed in its incidence to be rather less dramatic; but it was still true that the apparent increase in employers' bargaining power during the first decade of the twentieth century at a time of legal decisions such as Taff Vale in 1901 or Osborne in 1908, apparently adverse to trade unions, aroused a sense of unity lacking in America. The shock of the Taff Vale decision of 1901 which made unions liable for damages incurred during a strike promoted increasing union membership and support for the Labour Representation Committee which aimed at distinctly separate working-class representation in Parliament. The Osborne judgement of 1908 appeared to threaten the expanding Labour party by declaring the use of trade union subscriptions illegal. Such episodes provided a rallying cry for the unity of labour. The rise of the Labour party with no less than forty-two Labour members of Parliament seemed a remarkable advance. Yet appearances were deceptive and while it might be a gain that Labour politicians could influence concessions such as the Miners' Eight Hours Act of 1909, it was still true that there was growing violence on the British labour scene.

During the decade or so before 1914 industrial wages rose rapidly in America; hence the cause of political representation might be an outlet for industrial frustration in Britain. Inasmuch as skilled craft unions became embroiled in the political movement their reasons for doing so might be in defence of legal rights or might be economic because real wages were rising less rapidly than in previous decades. In America, co-operation of the AFL with employers seemed to bring monetary reward. Just one example of the contrasting scene would be the reception given to the ideas of Frederick Winslow Taylor and the scientific management movement. 'Taylorism' was anathema to British trade union leaders whereas American workers had little resistance to offer to Henry Ford's moving assembly line especially when that method of operation connoted wages of $5 a day.

The trade union record, then, provides intriguing but inconclusive evidence. Trade union historians who provide the evidence invariably write from an institutional viewpoint which draws attention to the personalities and policies of trade union leaders, to constitutional arrangements within and between trade unions, and to the nature of the collective bargaining arrangements between employer and employed. Such influences might be a means of persuasion upon employers but the central problem is to know the extent of their influence. Even where unions do not exist because they are 'bought off', the extent to which they are bought off will presumably depend on their ability to influence conditions in the remainder of the particular industry or section of the labour market. Similar considerations may apply to the effectiveness or otherwise with which employers may enforce yellow-dog contracts. There is also the question of the influence of the community and of public opinion. The evidence seems to be reasonably clear that public opinion and the operation of the law were more favourable to unions in Britain than in America. Nevertheless, on balance employers in America were prepared to pay higher wages even if differentials there between skilled and unskilled were marked. Thus it may be a reasonable conclusion that in a faster growing economy wages to some extent take care of themselves, that a labour market is by no means a matter entirely of custom and rigidity. If it is an acceptable interpretation that the significance of trade unions was defensive rather than positive as an influence on wages, then the disillusionment of British trade unionists with the actions of American trade union leaders between 1900 and 1914 becomes clear. Apart from underprivileged groups, some of whom joined the Wobblies, the American leaders saw no great reason to be dissatisfied whereas British unions were inclined to emphasise the power of the trusts and the brutality of the struggle between capital and labour in America and were disillusioned with the apparent ineffectiveness of American trade unions. Altogether, therefore, trade union history tends to bring out the contrasts in human rewards because of the differing performance of the two economies.

CHAPTER FOUR

THE CHANGING BALANCE OF ECONOMIC STRUCTURE, 1850–1914

Agriculture

In some models of economic development like those of Arthur Lewis or of Rostow the importance of agriculture tends to be overlooked because of a preoccupation with the benefits to be derived from continuing industrialisation. Yet in terms of the labour force involved before 1914 whether in Britain or America, agriculture was the largest occupation. If such an important sector could raise production or productivity then it could contribute to growth in its own right. In fact, it constituted a considerable element of economic change but the change was uneven because agriculture was not a single homogeneous industry. Some branches were more influenced than others by the growth of international transport and by the widening of the international market. The repercussions were to be seen in a changing balance between different agricultural sectors and in alternating periods of apparent prosperity and distress which sometimes drew forth torrents of farmers' complaints. One feature is that agricultural historians seem to be reasonably satisfied with the conventional divisions of the period around 1873 and 1896. In these divisions they do not stress monetary factors so much as changing markets due to transport improvements and to changing patterns of demand brought about by general economic growth allied with changing features of expenditure.

Between 1850 and 1873 agriculture on both sides of the Atlantic experienced prosperity. Despite gloomy forebodings of Tory landowners when the act to repeal the corn laws was passed in 1846 the demand for home grain in the British market remained high because of rising living standards and population increase and because imports of wheat and corn, even if rising, did not increase enough to undermine the market advantages enjoyed by British farmers because of their lower transport costs compared with foreign competitors. Since Europe and Britain had much the same climate, grain prices in both areas tended to move the same way. Before 1873 American competition in British grain markets was small by comparison with its volume after 1879. By the 1880s with greatly improved ocean-going transport the predictions of the Tory landowners of the 1840s were at last realised. Yet if those landowners had seemed to be unjustified pessimists their predictions had shown considerable awareness that the days of Britain's agricultural exports were over and that an industrialised society was coming to import food in greater quantities. Hence it is important to note that with the upsurge in international trade in the 1850s and 1860s agricultural products were traded in greater amounts. A good example would be the increase in exports of American raw cotton to Britain before the Civil War; it illustrates the point that the products being traded internationally were not those with a high risk of perishability. Thus while wheat was traded it could not yet be carried extremely long distances because of the slowness of sailing ships and of the risk of rotting at sea. The expansion of agriculture in both countries up to 1875 constituted a mixture of demand generated by earnings from buoyant exports (though not necessarily agricultural exports) and by demand generated from home expansion.

Until 1875 the expansion of agriculture played an integral part in the economic development of both countries. Virtually every agricultural sector showed vitality. In America the spectacular changes were the opening up of the mid-and far mid-West with new settlers taking advantage of the Homestead Act of 1862 to increase production of grain on the Prairies. In addition, raw cotton production reached phenomenal levels in the 1850s only to suffer in the Civil War, but tobacco continued to benefit both from overseas and from home demand. Finally, livestock and dairy farming, fruit growing and market gardening all prospered from demand associated with growing towns. Likewise in Britain better transport facilities brought increased demand to virtually all agricultural products. As Court has observed, the acreage under the plough generally and for wheat specifically was higher in Britain in 1869–70 than at any subsequent time. Even so, a vital question to be posed for both countries is to ask how far mid-century patterns of expansion and investment were misconceived, leading in part to the difficulties and anxieties which bedevilled farmers in the 1880s and 1890s. If the conventional treatment of Britain has been to describe the period from 1850 to 1873 as a Golden Age the description is applicable in that an undoubted rise occurred in farm incomes which in turn contributed to industrial expansion through greater purchases of machinery and other producer goods. If agriculture was generally profitable the major part of the improvement in profits was being earned by the producers of meat, dairy produce and vegetables. Within patterns of mixed farming the emphasis tended to shift away from wheat and grain towards livestock rearing. The old reliance on wheat as the prime market crop was slowly diminishing. Yet the relative diminution of arable farming was prolonged because of the natural conservatism of some farmers which found expression in investment in expanding arable output at a time when a free market threatened to make intensive methods of arable farming quite uneconomic. There were undoubtedly many cases of misdirected investment which was lost when the so-called 'Great Depression' minimised the hope of satisfactory returns in the arable districts where so much of the improvement had been concentrated.

The difficulties of English arable farming as they emerged in the 1880s and 1890s were partly a reflection of the great expansion of American arable farming in the 1850s and 1860s especially in Iowa and Illinois and the Great Plains. Already by the end of the 1840s the prairie farmers had wide horizons for their markets. The expansion of those markets was due to developments in transport, in processing techniques and in marketing methods which made it possible for prairie farmers to compete with others. If at first in the 1850s and 1860s the markets to be satisfied were mainly in America itself, by the late 1870s the development of the great corn belt of the mid-West meant that American exports of wheat to Europe increased dramatically to the consternation of English corn-farmers who could not compete with the relatively low prices at which America could sell wheat in Britain after 1880. Yet to conclude that because a successful penetration of European markets had been made there were no problems would be to distort the position. On the contrary, there is a long tradition that between 1866 and 1896 the American farmer suffered from depression. Prices of agricultural commodities fell as did general prices during the period. Since primary producers always suffer during periods of falling prices it is not surprising that there were strong farmers' protests.

The historical problem for America as for Britain is to determine what value to give to contemporary outbursts of discontent and to assess the relative performance of the different sectors of agricultural activity. Increasingly in both countries success lay with those farmers who were prepared either to specialise or to undertake a judicious combination of the relatively profitable activities. For Britain, Fletcher has reassessed the so-called Great Depression to show that depression was far from being a generalised overall condition of British agriculture before 1900. On the contrary, there was increasing production of meat and vegetables, dairy produce and fruit not only because diet was becoming more varied but because nearness to markets brought an inherent advantage for those products. The items which declined were wheat especially and, to a lesser extent, barley and wool. Similarly in America the more extreme complaints made at the time by the Grangers, Populists and others need cautious interpretation since there was a variety of experience among different farmers. In the 1880s the more progressive farmers of the prairie triangle appreciated that the best policy was to increase the size of farm unit to be able to utilise new technology. Profit lay in the right combinations of corn, hogs and cattle with oats, grasses and clovers becoming necessary as grass commons disappeared. Perhaps the real problem was one of over-production with expansion proceeding at a faster pace than demand. There were too many would-be farmers, partly because of an over-reckless attitude. As Bogue says, 'Some owners failed miserably. Land was often a lucrative speculation no less than a factor of production.'[1]

The difficulty of estimating the problem partly reflects the diversified nature of land-holding. Yet in Britain the nobility with their great estates still constituted a powerful section of the land-owning community. The experience of the great British landowners reflected the different fortunes of arable and livestock farmers. Lord Derby was an exceptional owner who managed to increase rents on his Fylde estate between 1870 and 1896 but the general British experience was that rents fell from a peak reached in 1874–8 until the middle of the 1890s and that thereafter they were stabilised at a new level. The amount of the fall varied markedly between different parts of the country.

The prosperity of Durham farmers depended on the price of beef, mutton and dairy produce, and on the state of local industrial activity in the coal and metal industries. On the Marquess of Bath's Longleat estate severe depression was experienced only on the part which lay in the Wiltshire corn country and was characterised by sheep and corn farming; elsewhere, in Wiltshire dairy country and in the Cheddar and Frome districts of Somerset, life was normal and rents held up. It was landowners of arable estates who were hard hit for, where gross rents were halved, the whole way of life was inevitably altered. Demand for land collapsed partly because of a decline in the political and social advantages of landownership but also because of a belief in the widespread nature of the depression and gloom over the future. Only Wales escaped the fall in capital values because the market there saw the land-hunger of a peasant society. Capital values may provide some insight, if only of one kind, to the fortunes of tenant farmers, about whom too little is known.[2]

If diversity of experience was a feature in Britain it was even more so in America. There were clearly both failures and success stories. The difficulty of generalisation about America could be found in the very large number of farmers and in the great variety of soils in a vast land area. Some had meagre capital relative to the task before them and in order to continue were obliged to incur considerable debt. Almost certainly family tenure in any one place was much shorter than in Britain. The Thirteenth Census (1910) revealed 54 per cent of the farm population living on tracts they had occupied for not more than five years. The number of farms in the United States grew from about 2,000,000 in 1860 to 5,737,000 in 1900 and the total land in farms rose from 407,312,000 to 838,592,000 acres. This increase was not due primarily to the Homestead Act of 1862 since 80 million acres of homesteads were issued between 1860 and 1900 or, in other words, even if all the homesteaders had kept their holdings and lived on them, less than a sixth of the new homes and a little over a sixth of the acreage would have been on land that came as a gift from the government. Yet such vast numbers inevitably brought varying performance and complaints about difficulties. Complaints were made about railroads and grain speculators, about moneylenders and about falling prices. Complaints about railroads and grain elevator operators were exaggerated because the fall in railroad rates was striking and because grain speculators made heavy losses down to 1896, these speculators helping to narrow the difference between the average price paid to farmers and the average price charged to the ultimate consumer. Attacks on usurious rates charged by moneylenders distorted the position because the number of mortgaged farms in the United States as a whole was surprisingly small. Approximately 29 per cent of farms were mortgaged to 35 per cent of their value. Some states such as Kansas and Nebraska showed mortgage proportions of over 50 per cent but an equally striking feature was the short life-span of mortgages, perhaps from $3\frac{1}{2}$ to 5 years. Falling prices were more complex because even if farm prices fell overall less than all prices, there were differences in falls between various products. In general, the problem was one of adjustment to changing national and especially international markets providing a growing yet uncertain demand for American agriculture.

Hence the period 1865–96 constituted a difficult and uncertain period with expansion in most products occurring in America whereas in Britain there was greater unevenness. It may be that American farm income seen as a whole did not fare too badly and probably rather better than that of Britain since the researches of Bowman into the mid-West and of Bogue into the corn belt of Iowa and Illinois suggest that there were possibly periods of rising income interrupted by a very difficult decade of falling income in the 1870s. Yet one of the essential points is that adjustments had to be made not only between nations but between regions within nations, an example being those farmers of New England who had previously placed an emphasis on grain production and who had now to adjust to livestock farming, to dairy products and to market gardening in the same way as the farmers of old England.

The probability of better farm income in America compared with Britain for the period before 1896 becomes a near-certainty for the years 1896–1914, a period which has been called the Golden Age of American Agriculture. The title, if exaggerated, draws attention to farmers' relative prosperity compared with their problems before 1896 and with their depressed condition between the wars. An important point was that between 1896 and 1914 the amount of new land put into farms increased less rapidly than in previous decades whereas the urban population and the purchasing power of the industrial worker were proceeding apace. Hence there was a relative advantage accruing to the American farmer which was denied to his British counterpart at least in comparable terms. Between 1900 and 1910 American rural population increased by 11.2 per cent whereas urban population increased by 34.8 per cent, a trend which continued. Total farm production increased over 30 per cent for the two decades 1897–1917, reflecting the tendency of farming to become more efficient even before the gigantic stimulus of the war. There was little doubt of the farmer's relative prosperity, one indication being the *Yearbook of the Department of Agriculture* for 1921 which showed that with an index base of 100 for the average of 1909–13, land values rose from 45 in 1899 to 111 in 1914. Yet optimism was not unqualified since there was some concern that rural life was losing its influence and attraction. Equally, the proportion of agricultural produce in America's foreign trade tended to decline and from 1901 to 1914 the percentage of agricultural products in total exports fell from 65.2 to 47.8. The exports of some foodstuffs such as beef or wheat tended to decline but cotton and tobacco exports continued to rise. The overall decline was due to the fact that Britain, America's principal market, showed buyer resistance to rapidly rising American food prices due to American internal demand.

The overall expansion occasioned by internal demand affected different crops unevenly. Citrus fruits, sugar, oil crops (such as cottonseed, flaxseed and peanuts), and poultry and eggs expanded more rapidly than hay, grains, wool and meat production. California and Florida were the leading producers of citrus fruits while Texas expanded her production of cotton. In the regional distribution of other crops there was some shift in balance. The great wheat belt shifted farther west on the Great Plains with crops in Kansas, Nebraska and the Dakotas more than doubling. Beef cattle declined in the north-eastern states because of the growth of dairying and expanded in the prairies and the Great Plains. Wisconsin and Iowa became major dairy producers.

If, in spite of unevenness, the picture in America was one of development and change, no one would claim a Golden Age in Britain just before 1914. The share of agriculture in the national economy, if declining in both countries, was less in Britain. It has been estimated that British agriculture contributed about one-sixth of national output in 1867–9, less than one-tenth by 1890 and less than one-fifteenth by 1911–13. The number of agricultural workers remained fairly stationary, decennial census figures in thousands amounting to 1,413 in 1881, 1,351 in 1891, 1,256 in 1901 and 1,320 in 1911. The acreage of various grain and root crops (wheat, barley, oats, potatoes, turnips etc) was remarkably stable between 1900 and 1914 with some slight tendency to decline. The general impression of British farming was of apathy and, although the best farming was very good whether measured in output or in profit, there was little corporate will to improve standards both in farming and in marketing. The prime explanation, as with industrial entrepreneurship, seems to lie in market conditions. In the era of Free Trade the prospects for the British arable farmer seemed to be near hopeless and, even in other sectors, imports of refrigerated meat helped to reduce potential profit. This general apathy spilled over into the attitude of the State. In Britain the Board of Agriculture seems to have been less concerned with the broader issues of agricultural policy than the American Department of Agriculture which had been created in 1862 and given cabinet rank in 1899. As early as 1867 Congress authorised a federal Bureau of Education to collect and distribute agricultural information. Most of the data came from information supplied by agricultural colleges. By 1900 most American agricultural colleges had departments of general agricultural chemistry, general and economic entomology, an experimental station and an extension department. In short, American agriculture achieved a better performance and was better served in the two decades before 1914 than agriculture in Britain. While the reasons for such a situation were complex the disquieting feature was that British contemporaries seem to have taken a static or declining agriculture for granted, an attitude which in view of the features of weakness elsewhere in the British economy seems to have been perilously mistaken.

The Development of Industry

Continuing industrialisation was a major feature of later nineteenth-century growth. Since America emerged as the world's largest manufacturing nation by 1900 she came to impress contemporaries both by the greater diversity of her range of industries and by superior industrial performance compared with Britain. Yet a major theme of this section is that it is a mistake to assume an all-embracing American superiority. Recent consideration has shown that Britain possibly did relatively well within the constraints of much more difficult circumstances and each country performed well in those industries in which it could achieve the most favourable expansion and market opportunity. For Britain the dynamic force in industrial change seemed to lie in the export sector: hence in 1850 her strength as 'workshop of the world' lay in textiles, iron and a range of metal products, but by 1914 coal and shipbuilding had become prominent. It is arguable that the importance of exports may have been over-emphasised. Nevertheless, industrial development in America was conditioned much more by emphasis on home production with exports providing a useful surplus as time went on. The balance between home and export production and the availability of natural resources explained why industrial development showed striking differences of emphasis in the two countries.

Already in 1850 the differences were clear. Whereas Britain's orientation lay towards textiles, iron, coal, machinery and ship-building with a significant emphasis upon exports, the importance of agriculture in the American economy meant that manufacturing was far more closely linked with agricultural activities than in Britain. This feature might be normal in the early stages of industrial growth but could be reinforced by the composition of American exports where agricultural products (either crude or processed) made up the bulk of export propor-tions. The lumber industries, agricultural machinery and food processing reflected the linkage between manufacturing and agriculture. Nevertheless, the discovery or availability of natural resources other than the soil allowed the development of mining and fuel production. Coal and iron ore were obvious resources in the age of steam power which were important in both countries. The degree to which they were utilised was virtually a function of total industrial production. Lead, copper and oil, however, were in a different category. It was advantageous for America that she possessed reasonably extensive native supplies even if some copper ore was imported from Chile or elsewhere; the expansion of the home market provided a buoyant demand situation. By contrast, the relative decline of the British copper smelting industry located round Swansea was probably a func-tion of the exhaustion of British copper ore and of the con-sequent high freight charges for imported ore and for re-export of smelted copper. The copper industry is one example of the raw material difficulties facing Britain in an industry where an attempt was made to satisfy the export market as well as the home market. Oil is an even more obvious example since oil was not available in Britain and for purposes of illumination Britain developed an efficient gas-lighting industry based on the ready availability of coal. In short, although there was no doubt a degree of imperfect competition in the late nineteenth century, especially in industries like chemicals or steel requiring fairly large capital investment for entry, the overall pattern of industrial development, as Robert Higgs has recently reminded us, is explicable in terms of market forces.[3]

Hence it is almost certainly misleading to judge relative industrial development, as most older text-books seem implicitly to do, by the performance of the iron and steel industry. While it might be true that iron and steel provided basic material for the majority of industrial activities and hence did reflect general industrial development, it gave a very one-sided picture taken by itself since it was an industry like all others influenced by the relative location of raw materials and markets; by virtue of imperfect competition it was open to the influence of governments, of financiers and of agreements among producers. To compare the relative increases of production in British iron and steel with that of America as if those production figures were a real measure of the efficiency of the industry is of little value. As Payne remarks, the extraordinary lead which Britain achieved in the world iron industry between, say, 1850 and 1875, was a temporary phenomenon dependent on a technological lead built up in the late eighteenth and early nineteenth centuries.[4] That lead gave Britain a temporary advantage during the formative years of the new mass-production steel industry made possible by the Bessemer converter and Siemens open-hearth processes. In 1870 Britain produced $\frac{1}{2}$ million tons of steel and America one-quarter of that amount but by 1914 the relative figures were approximately $7\frac{1}{2}$ million and 31 million respectively, a relative increase of some 15-fold compared with perhaps 250-fold.

Such a crude comparison does not take into account the difficulties which British producers had in exporting to America once the Morrill tariff began to bite in the seventies. In the fifties and sixties, for example, the Dowlais Iron Company in south Wales (which in 1850 was the largest iron company in the world) sold considerable quantities of rail in the American market but, during the long depression of the seventies, as Duncan Burn points out, its position became extremely difficult. Roepke has shown how south-Wales iron producers in Britain responded to the impact of the new situation and to their difficulties in the exhaustion of local iron ores by rather rapid technological change in adopting the new steel processes. Nevertheless, the extent to which the British steel industry could expand overall was limited by the potential of the market. Both America and Germany, with which Britain is so often unfavourably compared in steel, had considerable availability of ores after the Thomas-Gilchrist process of 1879 made possible the use of phosphoric ores in the Bessemer process, and they also had a larger home market coupled with the political will to impose tariffs.

The way in which tariffs might influence an industry associated with iron and steel was shown by the effect of the McKinley tariff of 1890 on tinplate imported into America. The consumption of American steel for tin and terne plate rose from less than 1,000 tons in 1891 to approximately 900,000 tons in 1914. As Clark indicates, Welsh plates had a monopoly of the American market until 1890 but in 1911 the amount of foreign tinplate consumed in the United States was negligible. The brief period of active Welsh competition in the nineties stimulated improvements in machinery, in labour-saving processes and in administrative economies. It is surely inconceivable that the situation would have changed so rapidly without the McKinley tariff.

Yet American consumption of tinplate rose in the later nineteenth century because of the expansion in food canning, especially meat packing – a reminder that the linkage between manufacturing and agriculture continued to be important. Expansion was dependent on the agricultural development of the mid-and far mid-West with associated cattle ranching. Meat packing was the leading activity in food manufacture in general, a sector obviously based on agriculture and yet an activity which became to an increasing extent organised for production in factories. By 1914 the gross value of products reported by the food industries exceeded $3,500 million. In order of importance in millions of dollars various activities were divided approximately as follows: slaughtering and meat packing ($1,454 million); flour and grist-mill products ($878 million); sugar and sugar refining ($374 million); dairy products ($364 million);

miscellaneous, i.e. cereals, starch, macaroni, glucose, syrups ($249 million) and canning (except canned meats and milk) ($243 million).

The location of meat packing at Chicago, Kansas City, New York, Indianapolis, St Louis and other smaller centres reflected the great westward expansion after 1850. The most important product was pork with an annual dressed weight slaughtered of over 5 billion lb. The annual quantity of beef varied widely around the 4 billion mark while mutton and veal, although increasing rapidly, never reached an aggregate of more than 1 billion lb. Five firms – Armour, Swift, Morris, Wilson and the Cudahy Packing Company – came to control the packing industry and they virtually excluded competition by operating purchasing and selling price agreements. Inevitably they achieved considerable influence over other industries connected with livestock production such as soap, butter, eggs and milk.

Similarly, agricultural machinery expanded. The establishment in the 1840s of the Case thresher works at Racine and the McCormick harvester works at Chicago showed the westward movement of manufacture closely linked with grain production. By the 1860s Illinois, Ohio and Wisconsin were important manufacturing states although until 1900 New England continued to make a large proportion of lighter agricultural implements such as spades, forks, hand rakes and hoes. Exports flourished and Britain imported large quantities of American mowers and harvesters, partly for redistribution to other countries. As with meat packing, concentration increased, particularly with the formation of the American Harvester Company with a capital of $35 million in 1888 and then with the formation with a capital of $120 million in 1902 of the International Harvester Company which was a combination of the five principal firms making harvesters, mowers and other agricultural machinery. Overall expansion in the industry meant that between 1899 and 1914 the total value of agricultural machinery and implements manufactured in America increased from $101 to $164 million. Along with the tendency for the number of firms to decline there was marked geographical concentration in the states of Illinois, Ohio, Wisconsin, Michigan and Indiana.

Another activity linked with natural resources was the lumber industry which was made possible by America's large forests and by the demand for timber for the construction and paper industries. Considerable exploitation in the nineteenth century resulted in a migration to new forest areas where larger and more efficient plants organised by highly capitalised firms brought a process of ever more rapid felling and utilisation. Clark states that in 1909 the lumber output of the United States reached its all-time high point of over 44,000 million feet and over-exploitation brought a subsequent decline. To conclude the list of industries with agricultural linkages one might mention leather, flour milling, bakery, sugar refining, drink, tobacco, silk, cotton and wool manufacture. While some of these industries existed in Britain their usually greater size and range in America indicated either greater natural resource avilability or a larger market or a combination of both. One interesting example lay in boot and shoe manufacture where between 1887 and 1908 the number of pairs of boots and shoes exported annually rose from 351,000 to over 6,500,000. Between 1890 and 1914 the value of boots and shoes exported from America rose from $663,000 to well over $18 million. By the 1890s it was a highly mechanised industry. Allied with this development was leather production and in 1905 the United States exported more leather for soles than all the other important leather-producing countries of the world. This expansion of leather production involved substantial import of skins and hides since America could not sustain the output of raw materials from her own resources.

This situation in which special skills were developed in a manufacturing industry so that the industry came to be dependent on imported raw materials was similar to Britain's position in textile manufacture, especially cotton textiles. Raw cotton imports in Britain were made up into yarns or cloths. Yet whereas no one contends that America had too large a leather industry it has been argued often that Britain was too dependent on the textile industry before 1914 for her volume of physical exports. The charge is made that greater diversification away from cotton would have brought higher returns and that even in the cotton industry, as in coal and iron and steel, complacency was a characteristic of the industry's decision makers. In fact, as R. E. Tyson's analysis shows, the situation was complex.[5] Any rapid expansion of the British cotton industry involved overseas markets since it exported three-quarters of what it produced. From the 1870s the industry showed a marked deceleration in its rate of expansion; whereas from 1800 to 1850 growth measured by raw cotton consumption averaged over 5 per cent a year it was only 1.1 per cent from 1875 to 1900 and 1.6 per cent from 1900 to 1913. As with iron and steel, it may be suggested that Britain's dominant position in the world's cotton trade before 1870 was a matter of historical accident and could be expected to decline, not so much because of foreign competition but rather as a result of a lower proportion of cotton goods entering world trade as many countries supplied more of their own requirements. The problem became more severe after 1870 with the adoption of high tariffs in Europe, the USA and Brazil. Changes in the prices of primary products hit Britain's markets during the 1880s and 1890s but once purchasing power increased after 1900 the loss of trade through foreign competition or increasing self-sufficiency was more than compensated by a rising world demand. The reaction of manufacturers and merchants to their general problems was vigorous and new markets were developed. Tyson claims that nowhere else did the cotton industry make such a wide range of products or export such a high percentage of output so widely overseas. Its position was achieved partly by concentration within a relatively small geographical area and by a high degree of specialisation. It is a mistake to judge the industry from the perspective of the 1920s and 1930s since no one foresaw that after 1919 the volume of cotton textiles entering world trade would decline absolutely for the first time.

The same warning about hindsight applies to the British coal industry, so often castigated for labour troubles, for lack of mechanisation and for lack of development of by-products. Many later criticisms hardly seem justified from the standpoint of 1914. After 1850 the industry achieved considerable expansion and between 1875 and 1913 the output of coal from British mines rose from 133 to 287 million tons. Marked growth was achieved in exports since as late as 1860 coal exports represented as little as one-fortieth of the total value of Britain's exports, but by 1913 they were one-tenth or more in value of the export trade. In that year exports amounting to 98.3 million tons accounted for more than one-third of the total output of coal. As with cotton, it was an industry in which Britain established world supremacy in the export trade. If Germany and America achieved a more rapid rate of rise in production it was because they had the benefit of demand from rapidly expanding and industrialising home economies. In 1913, for example, America exported 24 million tons only out of a total production of 509 million tons. In per capita production and consumption Britain was scarcely behind. And if the coal industry revealed Britain's preponderance in exports so did shipbuilding, an industry in which, in the twenty years before the war, Britain built two-thirds of the new ships which were launched.

The so-called older industries showed an export emphasis in Britain and a different balance between home and export demand in America. If America developed larger iron and steel and coal industries than Britain the greater proportion of production was for the home market. The textile industries were also large industries in America. The cotton textile industry is difficult to compare in the two countries because market influences differed. Saul shows the great variety of experiences to be explained with each country having its successes and failures. If Lancashire cotton spinners have been criticised for being slow to adopt the technique of ring spinning it can be argued in their defence that differences in factor prices, in types of cotton used and of yarn spun and in the organisational structure of the two industries justified the retention of mule spinning in Britain. Conversely, Saul points out that 'some of the conservation of American textile manufacturers derived from the difficulty of modifying their large integrated and inflexible mills. They came into their own with innovations such as the Northrop loom which required simultaneous changes in vertically related stages of production – something which, like ring spinning – fitted uneasily into the disintegrated British industry.'[6]

The search for yardsticks of comparison can throw up partial and possibly misleading data. In no respect is this more true than in size of firm. P. L. Payne's article in which he lists the top fifty firms in each country by capital employed reveals two points: firstly, that Britain was not merely a land of traditional export industries but already had large firms in consumer industries, witness the tobacco firm Imperial Tobacco Company and the brewery firm Watney, Combe & Reid; and secondly, that America's much greater links with agriculture in the form of food processing or agricultural machinery were shown by firms number four to eight in the list which read: American Sugar Refining, Distilling Company of America, International Harvester, American Can, and Corn Products Refining. The National Biscuit Company was fourteenth in the American list whereas the largest British biscuit company – Huntley & Palmers – was thirty-eighth in the list of firms in Britain. Hence comparison on grounds of size raises the difficulty that different economic activities do not necessarily have the same optimum size of unit for their functioning. Another consideration is that 1905 is not necessarily the most satisfactory date for completion. R. L. Nelson – on whose evidence Payne relies – shows that the merger movement in America between 1895 and 1904 was exceptionally rapid by previous standards. There was a correlation between merger activity and stock prices, suggesting that much of the merger activity of the period had its origin in, or was influenced by the stock market. Capital market factors were more important than the level of industrial activity in influencing merger activity. Hence cost price relationships in business firms were a less important influence than many students believed.

Ten years later, in 1915, America could show gains in the much-vaunted new industries of motor vehicles and electricity. They are often quoted to show the alertness of American businessman to new ideas and his readiness to adopt new technology. A study of those industries in detail does not suggest that the situation was quite so simple as confident generalisations might suggest. As Richard Duboff points out, the spread of electrification in America between 1890 and 1900 was held back by a number of technical and economic factors, the most serious being the general lack of availability of cheap electricity. The electrical utility industry expanded rapidly only between 1905 and 1914. Steam horsepower accounted for over three-fourths of total power capacity in manufacturing from 1885 to 1904. The long-term effects of electric power – fractionalisation of power requirements, greater diffusion of power equipment, and decentralisation and intensification of individual operations – began to become appreciated in industry after 1905. The decrease in electric motor size indicated a tendency for mobile, fractionalised power to be employed in a wide range of individual processes. In average horsepower capacities, primary electric motors were more varied in size, provided a much more diverse array of possible horsepower sizes than was available during the steam era, and so played a decisive role in bringing subdivision of power loads.[7] It might thus be argued that the greater variety of size of industrial unit in America over wide distances, coupled with the superior performance of the American economy by comparison with the British economy between 1895 and 1914, created a situation where electricity had advantages over steam power in a way which was not so readily apparent in Britain with her abundant supplies of cheap coal and her engineering skills based traditionally on steam power over a long period of time.

The motor vehicle industry might appear an even more exceptional example since annual production of motor vehicles was 65,000 in 1908, 130,000 in 1909, 970,000 in 1915 and 1.9 million in 1917. The extraordinarily rapid rise of the American motor industry between 1905 and 1920 was due to special factors which could not be reproduced in the same way in any other country. Among those factors were the rapid fall in relative costs of the motor vehicle because of improved technology and the rapid rise in living standards which, as Phelps Brown has shown, became more marked in America by comparison with Britain between 1895 and 1914. A mass market for ordinary motor cars could be created because of the relative wealth of wage-earners and of some farmers compared with their European counterparts. The early motor car in Britain to 1914 was extremely expensive and had a narrow appeal to the relatively wealthy. As for commercial vehicles, they superseded horses and carts fairly rapidly but the different infrastructure and size of the two countries meant that in the USA commercial vehicles had much more scope for both supplementing and supplanting existing forms of transport than in Britain.

Hence the theme of this section has been that the peculiar circumstances in each industry must be considered separately. It is a mistake to generalise in comparative terms about British and American industry as a whole because of the different markets for products and the different factor proportions within which each industry operated. Altogether industrial performance may be seen as a response to demand pressures which themselves mirrored a host of cultural and geographical circumstances which varied between the two countries. The rapid industrialisation which America experienced between 1870 and 1914 within the framework of a largely free market was a somewhat special situation the like of which it is not easy to reproduce.

Railways and the Economy

A generation ago historians generally assumed that railways were of fundamental importance for economic development. In doing so they echoed the sentiments of contemporary witnesses bedazzled by spectacular railway speeds. It was easy to assume that such a striking innovation must be a key factor in economic growth. Since the publication of Robert W. Fogel's work in 1964 easy assumptions have been challenged and railways are more critically examined. This brief section can hardly do justice to all the complex debate which has taken place around Fogel's work. Yet the debate seems in the end rather to have rehabilitated railways even if there is now a readiness to admit that contemporary observers rather overstated the railways' importance. In tempering previous enthusiasm one would concede that the later railways, those built in Britain after about 1870 and in America after about 1890, were for the most part less likely to produce a high rate of return on investment than their forerunners.

Fogel's approach involved constructing an imaginary world in which railways were not built. He assumed that water transport was a practical alternative to the railroad for transport between regions. Taking wheat as an important commodity he calculated the least cost of carriage from primary to secondary markets firstly by allowing any form of transport and secondly by not allowing railways and finding the cost by water transport. The difference between the two least-cost figures was the estimate of social saving due to the use of the railway in wheat transport between regions. For the year 1890 it seemed that the social saving gained by railways in transport of agricultural goods between regions was about six-tenths of 1 per cent, hardly a very high figure. Within each region, however, the picture might be different. No railways would have involved both more use of water and more use of waggons. In 1890 the usual distance from a farm to a rail point might be 10 miles whereas to a water shipping point it might be 30 miles or more. Thus the local interior railroads might bring greater social saving than the more famous trunk lines. Yet to calculate social saving for transport within regions would involve allowing for less agricultural production since long waggon hauls to navigable waterways would have increased costs and caused distant land to be uneconomic. After allowing for land reduction and calculating social saving on direct and indirect costs, Fogel found social savings to lie between $111 million or slightly less than 1 per cent of GNP and $141 million or just 1.2 per cent of GNP. Thus railways were more important in short-haul than in long-haul movements, but the difference was not enormous. Fogel's conclusion was that even without railways the North Central States would have emerged as the chief grain producers since cheap transport and not necessarily rail transport was the essential condition. Railways were the most efficient means of transport but waggon and water could have provided a reasonably good substitute.

Another area of discussion lay in the multiplier effects engendered by railways on the development of the coal, iron and engineering industries in the alleged 'take-off' period in America between 1843 and 1860. Fogel pointed out that the production level of iron during 1845–9 did not depend on railways, and one could argue that nails rather than rails triggered the leap in iron production. Between 1840 and 1860 some 60 per cent of American rails came from the English market. The demand for rails did not dominate the development of the American iron industry before the Civil War. Overall, Fogel pleaded for quantitative study since many qualitative analyses contained implicit quantitative assumptions.

Yet one prominent feature of the debate has been that even those wholly sympathetic to quantitative methods have been among Fogel's strongest critics. Fishlow and David are examples. Fishlow enquired how much of a stimulus the railroad afforded and by what means, and he suggested that in 1859 true direct benefits lay between $150 million and $175 million. The higher figure would be about 4 per cent of GNP in 1859, an impressive contribution for an innovation still in its early stages. Over the thirty-year period between 1830 and 1860 the railroad yielded an internal rate of return of 15 per cent. If the last few years were more important the key point was that railroad direct benefits were making some difference by 1860 and the early period laid the foundation for substantial later resource saving. The conjecture of substantial later gains seemed to be at odds with Fogel's research relating to direct benefits in 1890. If one extrapolates Fishlow's findings for 1859 to 1890 there is a great difference between the two writers, that between a contribution of less than 5 per cent of gross national product in 1890 and of at least 15 per cent. Fishlow was sceptical of the inherent difficulties of measuring what never occurred. Elsewhere it has been pointed out that Fogel really assumes a situation where the railways were built and then abandoned, a nonsensical state of affairs.

Nevertheless, David generously praises Fogel for raising new and interesting questions. He believes that Fogel has convincingly demolished the hypothesis that American industrialisation before the Civil War rested largely on the creation of additional capacity to provide railroads. Yet David objects to Fogel's reliance on the ratio of social savings to GNP as an index of railway importance. Without railways there would have been bottlenecks which would have necessitated costs of building additional canals. Additional warehouses, grain elevators, coal bunkers and stockyards to hold greater stocks would have been needed when normal movement was interrupted by snow on roads and ice in lakes and rivers. Another objection is the idea that marginal costs remained strictly constant. By ignoring the possibility that there were enhanced opportunities for realising economies of scale and specialisation, and by implicitly assuming constant returns everywhere, one may avoid difficult index-number problems that impede unambiguous measurement. Simplification in quantification is purchased at a high price. Lastly, there is no *a priori* basis for Fogel's implication that annual social savings below one-twentieth of GNP represent a trivial magnitude on the scale of economic consequences. It may be that by 1890 the margin of railroad capital formation in the United States had already been pushed close to the point of exhausting any differential social returns from exploiting innovation, but at earlier dates the situation may have been rather different. 'It is not reckless to disregard the facts that, when the available quantitative information is put into an analytically appropriate form, it simply will not justify the disparaging tenor of Fogel's implied assessment of the social profitability of nineteenth-century railroad investment in the United States.'[8]

It is not surprising if such a controversial issue has roused an echo in Britain. Hawke in particular has studied the relationship between railways and economic growth in Britain between 1840 and 1870. His main conclusion is that 'dispensing with the railways in 1865 would have required compensation for between 7 and 11 per cent of the national income'. Other findings are that most of the direct saving of resources made possible by railways was on the transport of coal and minerals although transport charges on other merchandise were also reduced, while about 40 per cent of the social saving on railways was represented by increased comfort of personal travel. Hawke's work suggests that there was a higher social saving for Britain than for America if one relies on the work of Fogel and Fishlow. The reason was the relative difference in water costs; because America was well supplied with cheap water transport the impact of the railway was less. Such a conclusion may be true for the 1860s when railway development was still occurring in Britain at a reasonably rapid pace. Yet one would like to know the impact of the railways at other points of the nineteenth century. After 1870 the rate of new construction was much lower than in the 1850s and 1860s. As Ashworth has pointed out, post-1870 railways might yield much less than those built before: lines connecting seaside towns with existing routes might be utilised at peak capacity for only a limited period of the year. The British situation after 1870 could well contrast with America where Fishlow believes that continued rapid railway expansion from 1870 to 1890 represented a significant contribution to the economy. Because of the great size of the United States and the relatively undeveloped condition of much of the country in the 1840s railways could not be constructed adequately to cover the major regions so quickly as in Britain and the effect of economic linkages took longer to work out.

This is another way of saying that railways acted upon different economies. Although Fogel and others have adopted stimulating new approaches they do not invalidate the point made by G. C. Allen and others that the pattern of British railways was in a sense determined by previous industrial development. For the carriage of freight, railways were supplementary to existing canals and the major source of revenue until 1852 came from passenger revenue. If one makes the distinction between exploitative transport services (those carrying existing traffic more efficiently) and developmental services constructed in anticipation of new traffic then perhaps most British lines were exploitative in nature except for special coal lines such as the Stockton & Darlington or the Taff Vale, whereas American lines were mostly developmental. However, one must avoid absolute contrasts since in the American West some areas were already settled and producing a surplus of corn before railroads arrived and similarly expansion in the coalfield of east Glamorgan was occurring before the Taff Vale railway was built.

Nevertheless, a broad difference in economic function may explain the difference in social attitudes and public policy over railways in the two countries. In Britain it has been estimated that up to 1914 the average cost of construction per mile was £54,152 whereas in America it was £13,000. These figures may exaggerate the position since they overlook costs in America not borne by companies themselves – cost of bribing state legislatures by local communities desiring a railroad or costs involved granting land for railroads rather than for other purposes. Nevertheless, comparative figures provide some measure of different attitudes. In Britain the public was rather suspicious and demanding in what the railway companies should provide whereas in America, in spite of some people's misgivings, public interest resulted in land being made available relatively cheaply and not too many complaints were made about inadequacies of construction or about financial manipulation until those evils seemed to multiply and become intolerable.

The public, in fact, had ambivalent attitudes towards railways in both countries, reflecting perhaps a general confusion about the desirability of economic growth. Railways were not the only activity to reflect the confusion, coal mines being a good example. In fact, American railroads were in a difficult position because profits depended on a good reputation for service and for fair dealing yet big shippers were in a position to force reductions. Railroad officials could scarcely avoid signing secret contracts which gained traffic large enough for efficient operation yet suspicion about such contracts undermined public good will. The ambiguity in railroad presidents' conduct, maintaining rates in public and cutting them in secret, was counterbalanced by ambiguity in public attitudes. Railroads were seen as essential to development yet their receiving public aid supported a belief that they should be subject to regulation. Criticism found expression in the Inter-State Commerce Act of 1887 with its appointment of an Inter-State Commerce Commission of five members who would administer the law applying to railroads. The new act prohibited discrimination between persons, commodities or localities, and forbade pooling as well as including a clause against charging more for a short than a long haul. Subsequent laws like the Mann-Elkins Act tried to close loopholes yet it is worth noting that railroad presidents usually favoured observing the 1887 act and pressure to evade it came from shippers continuing to demand rate cuts. Hence no one could quite decide whether the railroad was a public or private enterprise and what economic criteria should apply to regulate its activity.

Ambiguity occurred equally in Britain. As Kellett points out, British railway companies were granted from the outset two unusual privileges: corporate identity and power to buy property by compulsory purchase.[9] Perhaps these privileges were a sneaking admission that railways were an essential feature of economic development with railway entrepreneurs needing encouragement, yet actual capital raising and public financial support for railways seems to have involved public authorities far less than in America. The expense of promoting railway bills in Parliament and of purchasing land was high. Nevertheless, entrepreneurs could rouse public interest in subscriptions to flotations for new companies as during the 'railway mania' of 1844–7. Yet quite early, as Parris has shown, there was a clear need for government regulation of railways which was recognised by the setting up of the Board of Trade Railway Department in 1840.[10] In that same year Peel could say 'that it was impossible to deny that railways were a practical monopoly and that they had been established by the legislature'. If government power was exercised cautiously for two decades the tendency to greater state intervention was resumed after 1868 in matters of safety, of passenger and freight rates, and of railwaymen's hours of work. The government was expected to intervene in the public interest and railways naturally were an area of activity about which public pressure could increase as more people gained the vote. Significant measures were the Regulation of Railways Act (1871), the Railway and Canal Traffic Act (1888) and the Railway and Canal Traffic Act (1894) with wide implications for safety or rate regulation. Consequently the structure of railway rates and charges became too rigid and the tendency for pooling agreements or amalgamations to occur became widespread. The declining belief in the possibility of competition between railway companies was shown when a departmental committee was appointed in 1909 to consider what further safeguards were needed to protect the public against possible abuses of railway monopoly. In its report in 1911 the committee accepted monopoly as inevitable and, if properly safeguarded, as beneficial. By 1914 one may argue that most of the vital circumstances existed to make possible the Railway Act of 1921 with its important recognition of railway monopoly and its equally important insistence on public regulation of that monopoly.

Railways, then, constitute an intriguing case study. They aroused enormous interest among contemporaries and the debate among historians is a continuing one. As usual, the size and complexity carries its own warning that not every line was as profitable as the most fully utilised ones. Econometric historians have concentrated their attention perhaps rather too much on decades when substantial claims could be made for the importance of railways and rather less on decades when railway construction or activity appeared to add little to economic development. Historians have not altogether succeeded in clarifying the confusion of contemporaries. New techniques of econometrics or of cost-benefit analysis raise important issues, but whether they resolve all the problems involved in nineteenth-century railway history is open to question.

CHAPTER FIVE

MARKETS AND FINANCE, 1850–1914

Overseas Trade

The part played by overseas trade in a nation's economic development is a matter for debate. If goods surplus to requirements can be produced at little extra cost then the returns from producing for export may be high. The income received from exports may be available for further investment and a multiplier effect of increasing investment may be generated. Without exports the level of activity would be lower. Britain's increased exports in the early nineteenth century – especially textile exports – can be quoted as an example of such a desirable multiplier effect although even there it is debatable whether the surplus arose from a conscious desire to exploit an export demand situation or whether it came from a natural surplus, generated in an expanding home market, which could then be sold abroad. There are no *a priori* grounds for determining the correct proportion of a nation's economic activity devoted to overseas trade. Particular tendencies may develop a momentum of their own which are difficult to reverse.

Hence the argument can be used that by mid-century Britain was committed to the export of certain 'staple products' because she had built up markets for those products and in so doing earned a reputation for their production which made it difficult for her to achieve greater diversification in the future. The staple products can be represented as an economic albatross. Yet in relative terms Britain was strikingly successful in exporting. In the 1850s Britain's share of world trade was something approaching a quarter of world trade and the ratio of British foreign trade to the national income was 17.1 per cent. In later decades that ratio in real terms was 22.35 per cent in 1870–2, 22 per cent in 1890–2, 21.45 per cent in 1900 and 26.5 per cent in 1911–13.

Ratio of British Foreign Trade to National Income
(not adjusted for price changes)

	%		%		%
1805–19	8.4	1860–69	26.9	1890–99	27.9
1830–39	10.4	1870–79	29.9	1900–13	27.9
1850–59	17.1	1880–89	29.5		

By contrast, the ratio of foreign trade to American national income varied around 5 per cent, exceeding that figure in the exceptional years between 1915 and 1917. Yet even a ratio as low as one-twentieth of national income may not be unimportant if the trade involved does generate strategic multiplier effects. Much may depend on the nature and composition of exports and imports including invisible exports and imports. It has been estimated that American foreign trade doubled every twenty years from 1830 to 1910. Partly because of America's faster growth in national income than Britain's her share of world trade rose steadily over the period while Britain's share declined. American trade increase can be shown by export and import figures.

American Exports and Imports ($ million)

	Exports	*Imports*
1860	316,242	353,616
1900	1,394,483	849,941
1913	2,465,884	1,813,008

Yet these striking increases should not lead to easy conclusions about American superiority in export performance. In view of the differences in resources between the two countries it can be claimed that America had an easier task. It is also difficult to decide whether the contrasts in the overseas involvement of Britain and America represented optimum proportions for the respective nations. An important point that emerges from figures of imports and exports is that America ran a deficit on the balance of trade until the 1860s. Since she was also a net importer of invisibles, particularly because of interest payments on capital borrowed from Britain, she had a marked deficit on the balance of payments. The situation began to change in the 1870s when in particular years a balance of payments surplus was achieved, in spite of America remaining a debtor in deficit on invisible account. Between 1880 and 1914, especially after 1900, substantial surpluses on the balance of trade were recorded and the balance of payments showed increasing surpluses in spite of the continuing deficit on invisibles. This relative position of visibles and invisibles was quite the opposite for Britain where a surplus on the balance of trade was never recorded in any year after 1822. The deficit on the balance of trade was made good by the surplus which Britain succeeded in gaining on invisible account by her shipping services, by banking and insurance and by interest payments received on loans made abroad.

Another development linked with America's increasing trade surplus was her growing diversity of exports. In the 1850s raw cotton constituted the greater proportion of exports and it has been argued that cotton and agricultural exports provided a powerful stimulus to the economy. This pattern changed considerably. J. G. Williamson has pointed out that the United States underwent a profound change probably in the 1860s and 1870s. The export sector and agriculture in general lost their positions of predominance and in the process the American economy gained a measure of stability in its balance of payments. Diversification and a shift towards manufactures made overall exports more stable. There was a period of transition for exports and the creation of a new stability accompanied by a decline in the relative importance of foreign trade. Even if agricultural products continued to be a much greater element in American exports than manufactures until 1910, the important point emerging from Williamson's approach is the diversification in activity after the 1860s. No longer were cotton and grain so dominant and a range of processed agricultural products – meat packing being an obvious example – became of greater significance. On the basis of production in a gigantic home market American manufactures also increased their proportions among American exports.

Yet America's increase in manufactured exports was surely not remarkable if the size of American industrial production was considered. As Saul shows, Britain accounted for 29.9 per cent of world exports of manufactured goods in 1913 and the United States for only 12.6 per cent.[1] It was true that the British percentage had declined from 41.4 per cent in 1880 whereas the American percentage had increased rather more than fourfold from 2.8 per cent in 1880. In a totally expanding international economy with her enormous natural and human resources America was in a distinctly advantageous position in having such a small initial base. In this context one may reasonably ask whether much of the literature about overseas trade has not been unfair to Britain. As Clapham has long since pointed out, a small island could not retain dominance in manufactures for ever. Between 1899 and 1913, unlike France and Germany, Britain actually increased the proportion of her manufactures exported from 42 to 45 per cent. Even if Britain did lose some of her share of world trade in manufactures to America and Germany during the later nineteenth century, she really did rather well whereas America might have been expected to increase her share of world trade in manufactures somewhat more than she did.

Yet clearly all was not well with British overseas trade. The two sources of disquiet were the range of British products and their market destinations, a feature to which Arthur Lewis has drawn attention. Lewis, using Schlote's figures, pointed to the high proportion of textiles, especially cotton textiles, among British exports. One might add that iron and steel and coal were also significant and that Britain seemed unable to develop exports of new engineering exports in the same way as America. The range of products sold was too narrow. Equally, Lewis emphasised the tendency for Britain to export to primary-producing countries. Another source of disquiet might be Britain's reliance on invisible exports to make up the deficit on her balance of payments. Ashworth has pointed out that the high volume of invisibles was to some extent a reflection of Britain's large share of the world's mercantile marine and of Britain's maritime bases for imperial defence. It might be questioned how long these features could endure, but to the Victorians they seemed safe enough. By comparison, America achieved an increasing diversity of exports and had the advantage of exporting the larger share of her products to rapidly industrialising western Europe. Hence America did not suffer from the same defects of lack of purchasing power among her customers as did Britain.

With hindsight, all these arguments have substance but the fundamental objection to the approach of Lewis is that he is looking at the nineteenth century to find causes for the obvious defects of British overseas trade between 1919 and 1939. If one treats the period before 1914 as a period in its own right without reference to the sudden shifts engendered by World War I it is not clear that Britain pursued fundamentally wrong policies. Perhaps the principle of comparative advantages resulted in Britain's producing the goods and services which she could do most efficiently. Yet the evidence seems to be that Britain's losses of trade were due to purely competitive factors and that the key to the situation as far as products were concerned lay with iron and steel and machinery, expanding groups in world trade but ones in which Britain's performance was uneven. The geographical composition of Britain's trade which was disadvantageous after 1919 did not show major defects before 1914. 'From 1899 to 1913 world exports of manufactures to semi-industrial countries rose in value by 147%, to non-industrial by 114% and intra-industrial trade in manufactures, where Britain was least well placed, rose by 93% . . . Britain's competitive position was strongest in the markets which were growing fastest, and weakest in the markets growing most slowly.'

Overall, one can say that the impact of overseas trade was more dynamic on the American economy than on the British. The relative American increase in the period was greater but it is not clear that the situation was much more than a combination of historical circumstances. By 1850 America already had an export economy strongly linked with north-western Europe and it was natural in view of the expansion of the Atlantic economy that those links should continue as long as they brought high returns. Britain, on the other hand, already had world-wide links but for historical reasons again had considerable competitive advantages in trade with semi-industrial countries such as India, South Africa, Australia and New Zealand. Nevertheless, Europe was the largest single market area for Britain and remained a remarkably stable one. While there may have been complacent views among contemporaries about the strength of British trade those views had some basis in experience. It seems unwise to be too hasty to condemn British performance or to praise that of America. The one safe generalisation is that the function of overseas trade for the two economies was greatly different as a matter of historical legacy and that America was in the happy position where multiplier effects via overseas trade were probably easier to obtain.

Capital Export and Commercial Policy

Among the possible defects of Britain's overseas trading position were two which merit further discussion: did Britain export too much capital and did she pursue a policy of free trade for too long? Conversely, did America enjoy a better balance between home and foreign investment and did she benefit from a policy of tariffs? Both questions are complex and here a brief mention is made of some issues.

Part of the difficulty in discussing capital is that although investment clearly plays some part in economic development it is difficult to determine how much capital a country can fruitfully absorb at any time because of human factors involved such as quality of entrepreneurship, social and institutional arrangements including the operation of markets and the quality of the labour force. The particular problem here is the extent to which an optimum use of capital was made between the choices open to investors. By any standards the level of British investment overseas was high. Cairncross estimates that between 1875 and 1914 capital in Britain (other than land) increased from about £5,000 million to about £9,200 million or by over 80 per cent whereas foreign investment rose from £1,100 million to some £4,000 million in 1914 or by about 250 per cent. A large part of home investment was merely needed to keep domestic capital per head constant since the number of employed persons rose by about 50 per cent between 1873 and 1913. Out of a surplus of £4,500 million beyond what was required to keep capital per head constant, nearly £3,000 million or 60–65 per cent went to increase British investment abroad. These figures have been revised by Feinstein but their broad emphasis is not seriously questioned. A more recent text-book gives total British foreign investment as £260 million in 1854, £770 million in 1870 and £4,100 million in 1914.[2] Almost 24 per cent of total British capital portfolio investment overseas between 1864 and 1914 was made in just five years (1909–13). Some might argue that between 1900 and 1913 more should have been invested at home and that there was a correlation between the high rate of external capital investment and the disquieting nature of Britain's economic performance during those years.

America's position was different. Between 1850 and 1914 she was a net importer of capital and received funds from Britain, Belgium, the Netherlands and Germany as well as from other countries. In 1854 something like a quarter of British foreign investment was in the United States and to that extent was an important element in the Atlantic economy. By 1870 the proportion of British capital invested in America rose slightly to 27 per cent but by 1914 had declined to 21 per cent. The proportions even of 1914 are a reminder that America continued to receive just over one-fifth of British investment overseas and it is inconceivable that without the sudden and dramatic financial impact of World War I America would have emerged as a major world creditor to rival Britain as quickly as she did. Nevertheless, the United States did make investments overseas which before 1870 were only £15 million ($75 million) but rose substantially to reach £140 million ($685 million) by 1899 and £711 million ($3,514 million) by 1914. The position between 1897 and 1914 was as follows:[3]

America's International Balance Sheet
($ million)

	1897 (Dec 31)	1908 (Dec 31)	1914 (July 1)
Total assets	685	2,525	3,514
Total liabilities	3,395	6,400	7,200
Net liabilities	2,710	3,875	3,686

The table shows that even if America was rapidly increasing her external investment her debts were still substantial. Mira Wilkins has shown that external investment arose largely because of direct investment, some $2.6 billion being direct investment and $0.9 billion portfolio investment in 1914. This direct investment of $3.5 billion amounted to 7 per cent of American gross national product, a proportion as great as in the 1960s. Most of the pre-1914 direct investment was in Canada ($618 million), Mexico ($587 million), the Caribbean Islands and Central America ($371 million), South America ($323 million) and Europe ($573 million). In more distant areas it was small, a mere $120 million going to Asia. The purpose of direct investment could vary according to the area involved. Whereas in Canada secondary manufacturing was important and in Europe a combination of selling, assembling, processing and manufacturing, in Mexico investment was in mining, railroads and oil production and in Central America it was for obtaining sources of supply. The exceptionally sharp rise overall in America in external investment was an associated feature of America's great rise in exports after 1900 and of a rising balance of payments surplus which were the mark of a country with in-

creasing funds to invest. Nevertheless, American foreign investment was lower than that of Britain ($18.3 billion), France
($8.7 billion), Germany ($5.6 billion), and Belgium, Netherlands and Switzerland combined at $5.5 billion. These figures
are a reminder that in 1913 America's influence on the international economy by way of capital export was still small. Even
if in 1913 the burden of lubricating the international monetary
mechanism by capital outflows was becoming somewhat more
widely spread among a number of nations Britain, as already
mentioned, still provided a high proportion of that outflow
with a share of perhaps 43 per cent of world capital export and
without World War I America would not so quickly have become a major world creditor.

Thus it is an open question whether especially between 1900
and 1914 Britain was called upon to bear too great a burden.
Without the war investment of capital would presumably have
led to a new flow of British visible exports on the pattern of previous cycles. In course of time America would no doubt have
come to share more of the total volume of international investment and would have come to develop new relationships with
Britain and other investing countries in the process. Those new
relationships would have needed time to be forged. As in other
spheres changing patterns of international investment were
altered by the war and by its upsets to the international monetary mechanism. Before 1914 and especially between 1850 and
1900 a relatively few countries in western Europe, with Britain
foremost, supplied the capital by which relatively undeveloped
countries could achieve growth and the international economy
could expand.

Hence the function of capital for British and American investors was different. America as a net importer of capital would
probably have had her growth retarded without that capital,
and there was no substantial choice to be made between home
and foreign investment. For Britain the question was somewhat
more complex since, as A. G. Ford has pointed out, the choice
between home and foreign investment was not absolute. It was
true that there tended to be swings in the emphasis between
home and foreign investment so that in the 1890s there was
home boom whereas between 1900 and 1913 there was a relative
expansion in British exports, including export of capital. During
the export boom investment was also made in industries producing for export such as coal or shipbuilding whereas, in the

1890s, home-market industries like the building-construction industry prospered. More than one observer has noted an inverse relationship between the British and American economies whereby an American upward movement sucked in British capital (and labour up to the 1880s) with a corresponding demand for British exports, whereas at other times a British home boom occurred while American activity was relatively low. Nevertheless, the fact previously mentioned that America received only one-fifth to one-quarter of British investment is a warning against undue exaggeration of the importance of the American connection for Britain. The high degree of British external investment was associated to some extent with the cult of British imperialism, with overseas bases and developments associated with the mercantile marine and with general economic 'pump-priming' designed to provide the necessary facilities for general overseas development from which British exports stood to gain. The important changes occurring in proportions of British investment were a decline from 55 per cent in 1854 to 5 per cent in 1914 going to Europe, and a rise during the later part of the period to Australasia and Canada. British Dominions (other than Canada) received 12 per cent of British capital in 1870 and 37 per cent in 1914.

These changes in direction of some investment and the relative stability of proportions of capital export to America are a reminder that capital investment may not be a cause of development so much as an associated feature with other factors or even a result of tendencies induced by other factors. Investment decisions are not, and clearly were not, made in isolated circumstances between 1850 and 1914. There are two ways of looking at them, national and international. From the viewpoint of the international economy, capital borrowed from abroad was the major source of funds in newly developing countries for major construction schemes since income levels were low and financial institutions primitive. The problem might be aggravated by the necessity of the developing country to service loans, which might require more import of capital and hence a higher interest burden. If the flow of funds worked smoothly all was well but sometimes economic crisis and cessation of new investment could cause violent upheaval in borrowing countries. The importance of lending varied, being significant in the transport sector and crucial in the initial stages of development whereas later it could be much less influential in relation to internal savings generated by previous developments. Hence British lending to the United States was probably more important in its impact before 1875 than afterwards. Similarly elsewhere timing was more important than absolute quantities involved. In general the function of British external investment was to smooth the working of the international gold standard which in turn lubricated the international monetary mechanism and rectified the imbalance between rich and poor nations, thus assisting the flow of world trade.

This situation where London was the centre of the world's money market and the leading supplier of international capital did not arise suddenly. Britain's role in the world economy became accepted and institutionalised over a long period of time. The whole complex network of relationships thus produced meant that investment opportunities were not a simple matter of choice between home and foreign investment regarded as separate entities. There were subtle links between trade in some products, in investment and perhaps in political influence. In some areas of the world British investment was low and that of other countries high, witness French and German investment in eastern Europe. Thus although one may follow Cairncross in concluding that British external investment brought satisfactory returns, the problem whether that capital could have been put to better use is unresolved. Most commentators seem to agree that internationally British export of capital was essential, but from a national viewpoint those who argue that external investment should have been lower to the benefit of home industry have to show which industry could have used the capital and what loss of output was involved in its absence. In fact, it seems to be difficult to show that lack of capital was an inhibiting factor. In connection with the emerging motor vehicle industry Saul has shown that lack of capital never seemed to be a stumbling block for that industry. Shipbuilding increased its production by some 59 per cent between 1900 and 1913 with all the capital requirements involved. If, in general, British investors tended to have their sights fixed on external economic trends it was surely that historical experience of British industrial development suggested that stimulus tended to come via the export sector. Unless a radical restructuring of the British economy could occur it was difficult to believe that their judgement was essentially wrong.

Yet condoning Britain's export of capital need not lead the

historian to accept the policy of free trade which was followed for nearly a century, 1846 and 1932 being convenient dates to mark its period of acceptance. That policy became such an article of faith that it was still accepted by politicians and voters as late as 1924. While it benefited industry during the heyday of Britain's industrial supremacy between 1850 and 1873 it is difficult not to believe that, once German and American competition in some products became serious, Britain could not have extracted valuable bargaining concessions from her trading rivals of a kind which could have reduced the amount of the import bill from the high level which it came to reach in the years before 1914. The question is a complex one because the imposition of tariffs does not lead to any one set of automatic effects. Price elasticity of demand, the possibility of substitution of materials and products or of altering consumers' tastes, alternative sources of supply or of markets may all be imponderables which affect the situation yet may not be correctly analysed by policy makers. Opinion among historians would now be sceptical about accepting the optimism of contemporaries concerning the benefits of free trade and tariffs in each country.

Relatively unchanging policies operated on fairly rapidly changing economies. Only an emotive interpretation in terms of assumed rather than real benefits can explain why governments and peoples were prepared to go to such great lengths to maintain those policies. It might be held that free trade was a policy playing on national emotions proud of British industrial supremacy and sensitive to maintain cheap bread. Equally, tariffs could appeal to a chauvinistic sense of American economic independence allied with high profits for particular individuals. In the American case the high tariff of 1864 was hasty and ill-considered, brought about by the urgent need of revenue for war, the wish to offset internal taxes imposed on domestic producers and the protectionist leanings of financial policy makers. It was obviously not intended that the tariff of 1864 should become the foundation of a permanent economic policy, but it is worth noting that the tariff issue was a matter of continuing debate after the lowering of duties in 1846 by the Democratic party. The whole issue can be written largely in terms of local interests, politics and personalities. Conversely in Britain a fully fledged policy of free trade took a very long time to achieve and the lowering of customs duties was a slow and sometimes painful political process.

The merit of free trade was that it provided an easy formula by which Britain imported cheap food to supply a growing proportion of her people while earning the means to pay for those imports by a growing volume of manufactured exports. Since ordinary people could be persuaded to believe that their standard of living depended on it and that the price of foodstuffs would rise if it were abandoned it was not difficult to raise spectres of disaster if there were any tinkering with it. It was a rigid approach which contrasted with the more flexible two-party debate conducted by Americans towards tariffs. The level of the tariff became a matter of some discussion not only in the 1870s but in the late 1880s and early 1890s. The sequence by which even higher tariffs such as the McKinley tariff of 1890 and the Dingley tariff of 1897 were adopted was, as Taussig has shown, a combination of special pleading and of political accident.

Recent writing like that of Hawke is inclined to argue that tariffs did not make very much difference to the American economy. While the general emphasis of the argument may be sound there were surely occasions when tariffs affected imports of British products into America, the most noteworthy being pig iron in the 1870s and tinplate in the 1890s, and one can hardly dismiss all the complaints of British producers as figments of the imagination. At other times, as in the early 1880s, demand for British steel was so great that imports continued despite the high level of duties. In view of the passionate devotion of some Americans to tariffs, however, it is certainly feasible to suggest that there was an element of make-believe in their justification of the system.

Much depended on people's interpretation of the general functioning of the economy. The Dingley tariff of 1897 lasted unchanged for twelve years because of general prosperity and partly because Republicans were continuously in power. The criticisms voiced were largely those of particular interests just as particular interests such as steelmasters raised warnings about free trade in Britain. The Conservative party in Britain came to be interested in protection after 1900 largely because the colonies were relatively united in regard to trade at the Colonial Conference of 1902 and passed three resolutions in favour of imperial preference. Yet Conservatives were divided on the issue and since Liberals held power from 1906 to 1914 free trade remained.

In retrospect, the general support given for continuing with a policy of free trade by Britain after 1875 seems to have been misguided. The fact that relatively high American and German tariffs were operative severely hindered the competitive position of the British iron and steel industry and in particular made exports to the American market difficult at particular times. At the very least the modest programme of retaliatory duties proposed by Balfour in 1903 might have brought some small relative advantages to Britain, and duties on imports of American corn in the early 1880s might have avoided the rapid relative decline of some sections of British agriculture. The exact balance of advantage and disadvantage is a complex one which can still be a matter of historical controversy. What is undeniable is that discussion on free trade and tariffs at the time tended to be conducted in simple terms. At least it was a matter of merit in America that fashions could change and that some flexibility over precise rates of duties could be retained although in practice given the growing strength of the American economy it was doubtful if tariffs served any very great purpose other than to prop up monopoly prices for particular products after 1895. Equally, the tenacious espousal of a free trade policy in Britain was clearly not the outcome of close study of its actual effects. It was easy enough to pour scorn on the complaints of particular industrialists without examining the relevance and truth of their arguments. Such scorn was part of the unwarranted complacency referred to in other sections of this book which beset thinking about the British economy between 1900 and 1914. Men tend to live in the past and to accept the ideas formulated a generation or so previously. It is only by consideration of the psychology of economic beliefs that one can explain why unalloyed British free trade and high American tariffs should have lasted so long.

The Banking Structure

What constitutes a sound banking structure? Historical experience suggests that there is no easy answer to the question. The function of banking is to regulate the money supply and to bring depositors and lenders of money into contact with borrowers of money. As long as depositors and lenders have no loss of confidence in the banker's ability to safeguard their money from undue risk they will continue to use banking services. Confidence, however, is a tender plant and what engenders confidence may vary from one environment to the next. Banking can thus become a facet of the total culture of a nation rather than merely a technical device to ensure that deposits and loans are properly used.

Hence banking, like politics, becomes the art of the possible. It was not possible either in America or in Britain at the very commencement of the nineteenth century to prevent the rise of numerous small banks serving a local industrial or agricultural region. No one would wish to do so since the main requirement in times of expansion was to obtain funds for the needs of commerce and industry in Britain and to a large extent to advance money for agricultural investment and consequent marketing arrangements in America. The great defect, of course, was that small banks tended both to over-issue notes and to over-lend, with the consequence that in periods of downturn in the trade cycle a number of banks failed. The difference between the two countries was that in Britain the situation became increasingly questioned with the merits firstly of joint-stock banking and then of a strong central bank with considerable influence over the whole banking system being progressively accepted. In time the advantages of a few large banks with considerable numbers of branches were appreciated. In America, by contrast, the advocates of a strong central bank were regarded with suspicion by a great body of American opinion and branch banking was regarded with equal hostility. Hence, on the eve of World War I the American banking system seemed in British eyes ramshackle in organisation and suspect in its ultimate soundness.

Yet at the beginning of the nineteenth century the disparities in the banking services of the two nations were not so marked. The great expansion of economic activity during the Napoleonic Wars saw the rise of numerous small banks in Britain with a porportion of them being managed imprudently. After significant banking collapse in the period 1814–16 and in 1825 two acts passed in 1826 strengthened the joint-stock banks which were given power to issue notes outside of a circle of sixty-five miles radius with its centre in London, and the Bank of England was enabled to open branches in the provinces. A further act of 1833 removed any doubts about the legality of joint-stock banking within the sixty-five mile radius and at the same time made Bank of England notes legal tender in England and Wales for amounts over £5. Although significant further measures had yet to come there was already a trend by the authorities to favour joint-stock banks and the Bank of England, because those institutions represented sound banking practice. In America, however, one could detect opposite tendencies in the twenties and thirties with the destruction of the Second Bank of the United States. Chartered soon after the war of 1812, it became a feature of importance in the American economy with the arrival in 1823 of Nicholas Biddle as one of its directors. His great contribution was in developing the control functions of the bank as an agent of the government and the bank came to be a lender of last resort of the state-banks. Furthermore, Biddle tried to influence the general economic situation by manipulating the expansion and contraction of the bank loans. By 1829 its position seemed dominant and even those who opposed it admitted that it had been a good influence for business. Yet within eight years the bank was virtually ruined because of the arrival of Andrew Jackson as president when an all-out attack was launched against it. Jackson questioned the bank's constitutional position and pointed out that there was too much foreign ownership of its shares and that there was too much concentration of American domestic shareholding in the East. Hence an institution of such power and so little responsibility to the people was a threat to democracy. After considerable controversy the government discontinued making deposits with the bank and Editor Greene of the *Boston Post* wrote its funeral piece as 'Biddled, Diddled and Undone'. Despite the fall of the Second Bank there was no movement towards larger banks generally in the United States. The number of small state banks for example rose from 307 in 1820 to 1,601 in 1861 when the Civil War began.

The American situation meant that banking practice varied widely. There were numerous instances, for example, of falsifying the amount of specie held by filling kegs with coals, lead and nails and topping the assignment off with a layer of silver. Another example was when examiners found packages of specie very similar in different banks and found that a sleigh drawn by fast horses went before them as they went from bank to bank. Moreover, the large number of banks in operation each issuing, on average, six different notes, created favourable conditions for counterfeiting money since there were some 10,000 notes in circulation by 1861. The one element of hope in America was that bankers themselves were becoming anxious for reform and some states such as Louisiana and Massachusetts required reserves to be kept against note and deposit liabilities. Those two states with their important maritime trade were exceptions rather than the rule and the amount of reserves held varied widely from state to state. It was not until the National Banking Acts of 1863–4, measures occurring significantly during the Civil War, that a thorough-going attempt was made to remedy the situation. The Banking Act of 1864 provided the legal framework of a national bank system by providing for federally chartered or national banks which bought government bonds and were then to receive standard notes in exchange for the bonds to be deposited with the treasurer of the United States. The act also contained provisions about reserves to be held. In addition, another act made note issue by state banks unprofitable by placing a prohibitive tax of 10 per cent per year on the circulation of such banks. The intention of legislators was clearly that federally chartered banks would be in the majority and, with influence being wielded over them by the larger banks in or near reserve cities, there would be some element of uniformity in the situation.

Yet their hopes were to be disappointed because from the middle seventies state banks began steadily to increase and by the early nineties outnumbered the national or federally chartered banks. By 1914 there were about 17,500 state banks compared with 7,500 national banks. The American situation was in direct contrast with experience in Britain where bankers themselves formulated their own rules about co-operation and at the same time came to regard the Bank of England as a lender of last resort. Hence it was subsequent practice rather than the provisions of legislation which made the celebrated Bank Charter Act of 1844 the great landmark in English banking history. Of course, some provisions of that act were important in their own right. The note issue problem was resolved by separating the Bank of England into two departments, the banking department and the note issue department. The note issue department was required to hold gold and silver equal to the amount of £5 notes issued, with silver being not more than one-fifth of the specie content. In addition, further notes could be issued against cover of government bonds and securities. This was the so-called 'fiduciary issue' which was at first £14 million in amount. In contrast to America, however, it was not necessary to tax previous note issuing banks out of existence. The Bank Charter

Act provided that no new private notes could be issued and that in the event of any note issuing bank losing its existence either by failure or amalgamation then the Bank of England could issue notes in amount up to two-thirds of the lapsed issue. In this way private notes issued gradually disappeared until the last of them went out of circulation as late as 1921. Much more important, however, the act said nothing about the co-operation of the banks with the Bank of England. It was the attitude of the bankers themselves, especially symbolised by the admission of joint-stock banks to the London Clearing House in 1854 and by the clearing house requirement that all member banks must keep deposits with the Bank of England which clinched the matter. During the financial crises of 1847, 1857 and 1866 the Bank of England acted decisively by issuing extra notes as occasion required and then subsequently recalling them. Thus, by the middle seventies the Bank of England was formally established in its supremacy as the central bank and the growing tendency to concentration in banking had already begun.

The opposite tendency towards the growing number of smaller banks in the United States meant that in each successive financial crisis there was little that the American authorities could do to remedy the situation. Some measures to remedy the situation were attempted, especially the National Bank Act of 1887 which attempted to establish more reserve and central reserve cities, but this measure did not really detract from the prestige of New York which remained the most important banking city in the country. The trouble was that New York bankers had to put their funds to some profitable use and they often ended up by financing stock market speculation in varying degrees. Consequently, in times of crisis there was no agency to co-ordinate counter measures. It needed the severe commercial depression of 1907 to evoke the demand for substantial reform which came by 1913. The Federal Reserve Act of 1913, drawn up after the National Monetary Commission Report of 1912 had pointed the weaknesses of the banking system, attempted to create a central institution. That institution was the Federal Reserve System. The United States was to be divided into a number of districts in each of which there would be a federal reserve bank; the number finally decided was twelve. At the head of the system was a Federal Reserve Board of seven members including the Secretary of the Treasury and the Comptroller of the Currency plus five others to be appointed by the President. In the districts, each federal reserve bank was to be organised by a board of nine directors, three of which were to be appointed by the Federal Reserve Board and the remaining six were to be elected by the particular banks of the district. Of the six locally elected directors, three might be bankers and the remaining three were to represent business, industry and agriculture.

Thus, on the advent of World War I, the Americans had only just created a questionable central banking institution with branch banking throughout the country virtually undeveloped, whereas in Britain by the same period, not only was there an undisputed central bank, but the emergence of what came to be known as the 'Big Five' was already well under way. To take just one example, the fifteen Quaker banking firms which combined in 1896 under the leadership of Barclay, Bevan & Company to form the joint-stock firm of Barclay & Company Limited expanded the number of its branches to 606 by 1914. There was nothing comparable in America and the future working of the Federal Reserve Act would be a matter of some doubt because there was still real fear of a central bank in the public mind. Moreover, the federal reserve banks were to be owned by the banking institutions which had the privilege of membership, contrary to experience in most other countries where central banks were owned either by independent private individuals or by governments. Only time and the attitude of bankers themselves would show whether American banking practice could move nearer to the British model. The events of the 1920s and the Great Depression of 1929–33 were to provide a decisive negative answer to those who cherished hopes of a sounder system.

CHAPTER SIX

FROM WAR TO DEPRESSION, 1914–33

The War and Its Immediate Consequences

In a previous chapter the point has been made that in the two decades before 1914 the contrasts between the British and American economies were becoming magnified with signs of slackening or retardation in the one case and growth with increasing diversification in the other. If, with reservations over matters of detail, the broad contrasts can be accepted, it is an intriguing problem to enquire how far the contrasts were accentuated by World War I. To what extent did the war produce harmful dislocation for Britain and beneficial economic expansion for America? Can the war be seen as a cataclysmic event which placed both economies in a new context and thereby created what was essentially a new situation? Alternatively, did the war essentially accelerate existing tendencies? While the two last questions are not necessarily mutually exclusive if applied to different features of the economy rather than overall, the interpretation offered here is that World War I created something of a new situation. While the effects of any war cannot always easily be disentangled from policies and changes occurring after the war, especially if one is trying to analyse long-term changes, the standpoint of the years 1922–3 gives some indication of a postwar situation in which a number of circumstances were now operating which were largely due to wartime change.

Among those new circumstances were the international monetary situation, the state of international trade and the productive capacity of the various nations to meet market demand both at home and abroad. On any reckoning the new situation by which Britain was now a major debtor and America an important international creditor was of far-reaching importance. From being a major creditor in 1914, perhaps the lynch-pin of the international monetary system, Britain had become within little over half a decade a major debtor. The total British national debt at its maximum in March 1920, stood at £7,830 million. In addition, there was a substantial adverse trade balance with the dollar countries (America and Canada). The long-term capital position of the United States, by contrast, changed from a net debit of between £400 million and £600 million in 1914 to a net credit of about £1,200 million by 1922. The smooth flow of international trade was thus to some extent dependent on America assuming the role of international banker and lender which Britain had played in the years before 1914. Although it was true that America did, in fact, invest overseas in unprecedented proportions in the twenties with $11.6 milliard long-term capital and $81 milliard short-term capital being sent abroad as against only $13.3 milliard repaid or invested by foreigners in the USA, much of that investment did not come until 1924 or after when the folly of the reparations policy towards Germany had become apparent. Furthermore, the passing of the Fordney-McCumber tariff in the United States in 1922 with its upward revision of duties ensured that the ability of the Allies to repay war debts to America or to earn dollars by achieving a reasonable level of exports was rendered far more difficult and another barrier to the smooth flow of trade had been created. The outlook for international trade in 1923 was far from bright.

Quite apart from the existence of monetary difficulties and the restrictions of commercial policy the postwar trading situation was aggravated by the legacy of wartime production. An all-embracing war naturally acted as a stimulus to a number of industries or activities and among the most important of them being agriculture, textiles, iron and steel, shipbuilding and coal. The basic postwar situation was that overall production had been substantially increased with the result that there was either world over-capacity in some items or a new supply situation in which the balance of production as between various countries had been greatly changed compared with 1913. Once again a great deal would depend on how postwar policies could act to remedy the situation but the existence of major problem areas was not helpful since these problem areas represented investment in human and material resources which were not easily scrapped. The uncertainty surrounding activity in those areas provided one more problem in international trade.

A good example is provided by agriculture. From early 1915 onwards substantial efforts were made to expand agricultural production in both Britain and America. Wheat was a good example of wartime food production for the simple reason that wheat contains a high proportion of calories per acre of production and becomes a highly efficient crop in terms of feeding potential once the emphasis is placed upon maximum feeding capacity of the soil rather than on market price of the crop. Since land in Britain was limited and the essential exercise was to save as much as possible on food imports the task involved was for government to persuade farmers to convert substantially from livestock or dairy production to grain crops. The ploughing policy of 1917 and 1918 was achieved by compulsory powers being given to the Board of Agriculture and by a minimum price guarantee for wheat, oats and potatoes. In America, however, although some government assistance was given to farmers the main agency of expansion was simply the increased demand from Europe for American agricultural produce. Expansion took place with substantial new capital investment by small individual farmers many of whom were persuaded to undertake expansion by the free play of market forces. The demands made on American food supply by the Allies were shown by the fact that whereas the food exports of the United States for an average of the three years 1914–17 were 6,959,000 tons they rose to 12,326,914 tons in 1917–18 and to 18,667,378 tons in 1918–19. Those figures emphasise the fact that increased food production made a particular impact when the war was already over, and increased world production was a factor in the sharp fall in world commodity prices which occurred in 1921–2. Since individual farmers were reluctant to sell their farms and to suffer substantial losses on their original capital investment American agriculture entered on its long period as a depressed sector of the economy from which it would not emerge until the new upturn engendered by World War II. Of course, hardship occurred to British farmers as well but adjustments back to livestock farming with decreased grain production could be made. The government, after all, had borne a substantial share of the cost of wartime adjustments in Britain whereas for America the essential point was simply that over-commitment resulting from wartime changes in a rather large section of the economy where supply was inelastic brought peacetime difficulty. Agriculture was not the only sector where a long-term disequilibrium situation resulted from wartime expansion. Steel and shipbuilding were in a similar category. World expansion in productive capacity in those industries was especially harmful to Britain since both industries in Britain before 1914 had a substantial export content. New competitors were now in existence and world demand was at a reduced level. Although these same industries had difficulties in America the fact was that shipbuilding was still a small industry recently expanded in wartime and its downturn did not have the same proportionate effect as in Britain while the American steel industry was cushioned, not only being protected by tariffs but having the benefit of demand resulting from the expansion of new industries like automobiles and electrical supply. The vulnerability of Britain's position was further emphasised by the changed position of her coal and textile industries. Substantial increases in production in the Japanese and American textile industries in wartime brought incursions into markets on which Britain could once rely, especially in the Far East. Nor were Japan and America the only countries to expand their textile production: the fact was that a number of countries expanded their textile industries and now relied less than formerly on British textile imports. The coal industry faced an equally tenuous position with diminished exports, competition from newly opened foreign coalfields and from the greatly increased use of oil for ocean-going shipping. The fact was that the war had caused some distortion of the British economy because of the high priorities given to wartime production whereas America was in a more favourable position in the sense that it had been partly possible to expand wartime and more normal peacetime production alike. Hence it might be argued that war played its part in enabling America to enter the twenties with a more balanced economy than Britain. In spite of some curtailing of house building, wartime had put virtually no stop to the expansion of the American motor vehicle industry, for example. As A. D. Chandler points out, Du Pont was able to diversify extensively during the war and its adoption of the form of a multi-divisional corporation in 1920 was due not a little to wartime diversification adding a great many activities to its original gunpowder production. Similarly with the steel industry America was able to let wartime demand induce expansion overall whereas Britain found herself in the position of having to give priority to special steels needed for shells and armaments.

Hence by 1919 there was substantial over-capacity in Britain of electric-arc furnace steelmaking.

Of course, it cannot be argued that all wartime expansion in Britain was of no benefit after the war. There was clearly substantial advance in radio, chemical, aircraft and engineering production, whether by way of increased quantity or by development of new processes and products. Yet the difficulty was that new developments were not sufficiently pervasive to soak up unemployment resulting from slackening of activity in the older industries once the immediate postwar restocking boom of 1919-20 came to an end. By contrast, the increased purchasing power available in the American economy as a result of wartime demand was an element in the American home consumer boom. British industry was substantially affected by the uncertainties surrounding world trade.

It can be argued, of course, that disquieting signs of complacency and lack of change could clearly be discerned in the British economy before 1914. While that may have some cogency the fundamental point is surely that wartime change introduced an unexpectedly rapid alteration in the world balance of supply and demand for many important commodities. The point can be illustrated by the British coal industry. Although oil was the subject of discussion by 1900 as a possible substitute for coal none of the leading British experts before 1914 predicted that oil would very rapidly supersede coal as fuel for world shipping. One of the most authoritative contemporary opinions published in 1915 foresaw that a figure of 100 million tons per annum for British coal exports would be the normal rather than the exceptional total or rather higher than the record total of 98 million tons of coal exports attained in 1913.[1] Was it so wildly optimistic? In spite of troubled industrial relations and in spite of manpower difficulties during the war there was enough optimism for labour to continue to flow into the industry to reach its highest figure of 1,230,000 around 1923. Equally, although prewar markets had been shrinking in a geographical sense D. A. Thomas in 1903 had been convinced that expanding coal exports to Europe – especially to France and Italy – were more than buoyant enough to offset declining markets elsewhere and movements in coal up to 1913 proved him largely correct. The impact of war was to destroy some 40 per cent of Britain's merchant fleet and to destroy large proportions of other nations' prewar merchant fleets as well. During the replacement process for the destroyed ships a number of new ships were oil-burning rather than coal-burning. Since a ship constitutes long-term fixed capital – a life of twenty-five years is not unreasonable – without the impact of war a number of ships in existence in 1913 would have endured a further decade or more. Hence the substitution process of oil for coal would have proceeded somewhat more slowly and it is arguable that the coal industry would have been able to adjust to its mounting problems at a somewhat more orderly pace.

Yet if the coal industry symbolised the problem of unemployment induced by changes in international demand, such a problem was not necessarily insoluble. An essential difficulty was surely that governments, policy makers and the public at large, had not appreciated the extent to which distortions had occurred or, if they did, they assumed too easily that a return could be made to the arrangements of 1914 without overmuch difficulty. One good example would be in the monetary field where the influential Cunliffe Committee of 1919 recommended that Britain should pursue a deflationary policy to prepare for a return to the pre-1914 gold standard. Other examples would be in the readiness to abolish wartime economic controls as rapidly as possible with somewhat reckless disregard for the consequences, or in the reaction of American public opinion away from international commitments to isolationism with resulting difficulties for international commerce. Hence the effects of wartime change depended a good deal on the nature of policies adopted in the postwar situation.

It may be surprising at first sight that a war which had involved so much carnage and suffering should not have been accompanied by greater flexibility of mind and approach to the problems arising. The explanation must surely be that it was a unique war by comparison with any previous conflicts, the first modern war in which ability to produce industrial equipment was a decisive factor in the outcome of hostilities. Somewhat painfully governments learned the rudiments of economic warfare and in so doing involved themselves in massive intervention in economic life. The process of intervention became extremely rapid in Britain once the Ministry of Munitions was set up following the great shell scandal in May 1915, and it was found that securing adequate supplies of armaments involved government control over labour, shipping, supplies of raw materials and production and distribution of most goods. Although the degree of intervention was not quite so thoroughgoing in America it was still considerable by any previous standards. In November 1918, there were 4 million men in the American armed services and 9 million persons (or about one-fourth of the civilian labour force) engaged in war industries in America. What is so remarkable, therefore, is that so massive an experiment in government intervention should apparently have produced so little change in economic thinking. There was no doubt a psychological reaction against such throughgoing interference in economic life and it seems to have been automatically assumed that the play of free market forces would remedy problems left from the war and that government intervention need be only peripheral in the peacetime world.

In retrospect, the failure to adjust to the problems of the new situation is difficult to understand. It was fairly plain that 'the delicate framework of international economic and financial organisation' was smashed. It was also plain, as Ashworth points out, that many economic and social changes already in progress were accelerated. Among such changes could be counted some redistribution of income marked by the advent of something like a mass consumer society in America and the realisation of political democracy with the vote for women and a wider range of social service provision in Britain. There was the growing influence of trade unions and the need to secure workers' consent. Equally, there was the increasing complexity of new technologies like chemicals, electricity and aircraft which did not fit easily into an orthodox framework of theories of perfect competition. Yet the war, by its emphasis on old-style nationalism and by the reaction of old-fashioned individualism which it encouraged, stimulated wrong diagnosis of many problems. One can agree with Ashworth that 'its influence ran deep much later than it need have done. And it is there that the true tragic element in the economic consequences of the war is to be found'.

Contrasts in Prosperity, 1922-9

Compared with the low level of economic activity in 1921, there was recovery in both countries by 1922 and until the commencement of a new major downturn in 1929 it is possible in general terms to treat the twenties as a decade of prosperity. The notion of prosperity is induced by reference to national income figures which for Britain show a rise from 66 in 1921 to 70 in 1922 with a figure of 84 at the end of the decade in 1929. In the United States income per unit of the population grew from \$522 in 1921 to \$716 in 1929. On such crude figures there was a 37 per cent increase in the United States compared with a 27 per cent increase in Britain. Average figures of national income, however, often turn out to be average liars. Although by common consent America is recognised to have achieved more rapid economic development overall than Britain in the twenties the difficulty of commenting upon that decade is to give the correct measure of importance to the peculiar sectoral points of strength and weakness in each country. Furthermore, to take the terminal dates – 1921 and 1929 – may be misleading. According to Prest's index, the index figure of 74 in Britain in 1923 remained almost stationary at 75 in 1924 and at 76 in 1925 and 1926. Only from 1926 to 1927 was there a marked upturn in Britain with a rise from 76 to 83. Fluctuations in America were more erratic but from year to year, especially from 1922 to 1923 and again from 1925 to 1926, were much steeper. It was the heady expansion of some years which seemed to contemporaries to epitomise the buoyancy of America.

By contrast, contemporary opinion in Britain was particularly focussed on the unemployment problem. The best year of the twenties – and indeed the best year for the whole inter-war period – for unemployment was 1927, when 9.2 per cent of the labour force was out of work. For most of the twenties and thirties the percentage remained obstinately and significantly above 10 per cent. In retrospect, unemployment may have been an obsession, obscuring for contemporaries the very real achievements which were being made in some sectors of the economy. Yet the high level of unemployment was a situation about which no one could afford to be complacent while particular regions showed such a high incidence of unemployed with resulting social distress. Such unemployment symbolised in very real measure the difficulties which were being experienced in the 'older' industries of coal, textiles, iron and steel and shipbuilding. The common feature of those industries lay in their vulnerability to over-production or competition in world markets. The nineteenth-century export pattern was no longer buoyant enough to support the greatly inflated labour force which had emerged above all in coal and textiles by 1914. Whereas the year 1924 saw manpower in the coal industry at its highest point of 1,230,000 men, exports in that year at 85 million tons were already down on the 1913 figure of 98 million tons. The decline in British coal exports was a feature of the 1920s with exports in 1925, 1927 and 1928 running at 72 million tons. Only in the prosperous year of 1929 was there an upturn to 82 million. For such an area as south Wales, some districts of which were heavily dependent on coal exports, the whole basis of economic life seemed to be in jeopardy.

Yet those 'old' industries fared little better during the same period in America. 'The mining of Bituminous coal was one of the more prominent of the "sick" industries of the postwar decade . . . The net income of the bituminous coal industry as a whole shrank steadily from 1.7 per cent of the national income in 1920 – a year of high coal prices, shortage, and tremendous profits – to 0.73 per cent in 1929.'[2] The same complaints were heard about the industry in America as in Britain – too many producers, too great a labour force, potential supply continually exceeding demand and ineffective government measures to reform the industry. The textile and shipbuilding industries were similar sufferers. 'The net result of the combined building and sinking losses of the United Kingdom and the United States, the two chief maritime powers, was an increase of the ships of 100 tons and upward of both nations from 24,750,000 gross in 1914 to 34,327,000 gross tons in 1920. Meanwhile, there had been an actual decline in ocean freight, and the extraordinary war requirements for shipping space had disappeared. The result was an excess capacity that depressed freight rates and had a ruinous effect on the shipbuilding industry in both countries.'[3] Only perhaps in the iron and steel industry did America see better performance mainly because of the demand arising for sheet steel from the rapidly growing automobile and electrical industries. Because of that demand the American steel industry was able to invest and re-equip in a way which hardly seemed feasible to British steelmasters. It was the 'new' industries which created the buoyancy of the American economy and, in turn, created demand for the output of the American steel industry.

The expansion of 'new' industries producing for the most part consumer durable goods was a principal feature of the American economy in the twenties. Whereas between 1919 and 1929 a growth of 64 per cent occurred in the output of all American manufactures there was a rise of 255 per cent for automobiles,

156 per cent for petroleum products, 86 per cent for rubber products and 89 per cent for paper products. The output of rayon, of refrigerators, and of radios all increased markedly and so did canned milk, canned fruit and vegetables. Such increases symbolised a new way of life in America: the American people were increasingly becoming a nation of urban or suburban dwellers, a feature shown by the decision of Montgomery Ward and Sears Roebuck to move away from their traditional mail-order businesses to concentrate increasingly on retail outlets in or near the growing towns and cities. The policy of Sears Roebuck to open retail stores on the outskirts of towns on relatively cheap land near main highways showed an appreciation of the extent to which the automobile had become a significant element in American life. Yet the automobile was not for most families the first priority of existence but the second. As always shelter was paramount and it is not surprising to find that the industry figuring in the highest place for new capital investment in the twenties was the building construction industry. The revival in house building was a major factor in the upturn of 1922 following the recession of 1921. One estimate of the amount spent on residential house building between 1921 and 1922 indicates an increase of slightly more than $1 billion compared with a lower increase of $500 million in business construction over the same period. Construction was the main outlet for savings and after 1923 savings found an outlet not only in residential building but in capital investments of business as well and the building boom remained a powerful factor of expansion for five years. 'The federal reserve index of value of construction contracts awarded (1923–25 = 100) rose steadily from 56 in 1921 to 135 in 1928. A similar index of residential construction increased from 44 to a temporary peak of 124 in 1925, dropped slightly in the next two years and finally attained its high point for the period at 126 in 1928.'

Consumer goods industries also made progress in Britain. In proportionate terms the increase in motor vehicle production was more rapid than in America. Whereas American passenger cars increased in annual production from 2,205,000 in 1920 to 4,794,898 in 1929, British cars increased from 32,000 in 1920 to 71,000 in 1923 to 182,000 in 1929. Nevertheless, the relatively low absolute British figure meant that motor vehicles were still a small if growing element in the British economy. Similarly, the chemical, rayon, petroleum, rubber, electrical and building construction industries all achieved expansion in Britain. Although their development was promising it failed to solve Britain's major economic problems because those problems were rooted in the difficulties of international trade. The new industries did not achieve a significant performance in exports, a feature revealed in exports of motor vehicles. The United States exports of cars and commercial vehicles (excluding vehicles exported in parts for assembly elsewhere) amounted in 1929 to 536,000 – more than twice the total British output. In value, the motor vehicle exports of the two countries (including their exports of parts and accessories) were 107 million and 11 million respectively. Such comparative figures showed that America was now gaining a useful export increment from at least one of her new industries.

In fact, the international economic position of the United States was now extremely influential. In 1929 the United States bought 12.2 per cent of the total imports of the world, the only nation buying more being the United Kingdom. In 1927 and 1928, American consumption of nine principal raw materials and foodstuffs was 39 per cent of the total for the fifteen most important commercial nations. Hence the export trade of many foreign nations was dependent on economic conditions in the United States. In turn, the United States remained herself a prominent exporter but from the viewpoint of the international economy a disquieting aspect of American performance was the highly favourable balance of trade, with an excess of exports over imports ranging between $375 million in 1923 and $1,037 million in 1928. Although America imported some invisible items, especially shipping services, the excess of exports over imports remained high year after year. In view, however, of the monetary situation where America was now the world's principal creditor nation, the ways in which foreigners could obtain enough dollars both to pay their debts and to buy what they needed were to sell goods and services in American markets or to borrow from America on capital account or to ship out gold. The first choice of larger exports to America was substantially ruled out by the emergency tariff of 1921 and the definitive Fordney-McCumber tariff of 1922. In practice, American foreign lending – the second choice – was heavy. With the exception of 1923, new foreign issues increased every year between 1919 and 1927. Between 1925 and 1929 about $5.1 billion of foreign loans were sold in the United States.

Many of these loans helped to increase productive capacity and were beneficial both to American interests and to the international economy. There were enough risky ventures, however, for some doubts to be thrown upon the ability of American investors to deploy their resources with optimum efficiency. Equally disquieting was the insistence of the American government on debt repayments, imposing a burden on Britain – especially making it difficult for Britain to play a greater part in promoting the smooth flow of international trade. The conclusion is inescapable that American influence to foster increasing international trade in the twenties could have been wiser and less narrowly conceived than, in fact, it was.

Already in the twenties American commercial policy was having a rebound effect on America herself. Europe had long been the principal consumer of American agricultural exports. In 1921–5 Europe absorbed 53 per cent of the total exports of the United States as against 62 per cent just before World War I. By 1929 the percentage had fallen to 45 per cent. In part the fall reflected the efforts of European industrial nations to grow as much of their own food as possible. Hence agriculture remained a permanently depressed sector of the American economy of the twenties. This relative depression was partly due to the enormous increase in production during the war as a result of international demand which could not be sustained in time of peace. Nevertheless, it is reasonable to suggest that a more liberal external trading policy would have acted as a cushion to the decline of agriculture in the American economy. The extent of that decline in relative terms was measured by the share of agriculture in the national income which had been 16 per cent in 1919 and had fallen to 10.3 per cent in 1921, finishing the decade with 8.8 per cent in 1929.

By comparison with America, Great Britain did not have the resources to restore the institutional framework of the international economy to something resembling a prewar pattern. While the policy of deflation between 1919 and 1925 leading to the restoration of a gold standard (or more correctly, the inauguration of a gold exchange standard) was the subject of much criticism both at the time and later, it might well be contended that monetary policy had become an obsession with British thinkers. In view of the peculiar situation of Britain's export industries it is arguable that a 10 per cent downward shift in prices would not substantially have relieved the difficulties of those industries. World steel and shipbuilding, for example, suffered from over-capacity, and lower British prices would merely have intensified world competition. The British export position was a difficult one. Compared with a share of world exports amounting to 14.15 per cent in 1913 Britain's share declined to 9.86 per cent by 1931. By contrast, Britain's share in world imports remained at rather higher levels, constituting 16 per cent in 1913 and 15.4 per cent in 1929. Hence Britain's balance of payments was only marginally in surplus in the twenties because of an increasingly adverse balance of trade. The visible trade gap averaged £225 million in 1921–4 and then rose to an average of £396 million in 1925–31. Nevertheless, in spite of this disquieting merchandise trade gap, 'invisible' exports still continued in the twenties to fulfil their pre-1914 function of creating a surplus on current account. Although the surplus was small, running at something between £50 million and £100 million per annum, the cumulative effects of such surpluses were relatively considerable since they were used for the main part in overseas investments and so helped in the flow of international trade.

Nevertheless, with a national debt of the order of £7,000 million and with the United States insisting on periodic repayments of British war debts, Britain just did not have the resources to function as the world's principal centre of currency in the way that she had done before 1914. Furthermore, with both the United States and European countries pursuing a tariff policy, the ability of Britain to raise her export levels substantially except to Eire and Commonwealth countries was open to question. In such circumstances the degree of economic growth which Britain did achieve in the twenties was perhaps reasonably gratifying.

As J. A. Dowie has hinted in a recent article, previous statisticians may have under-estimated the degree of growth which did in fact occur in Britain in the twenties. The switch from older exporting industries to newer home consumer based industries was already taking place but, as Dowie again observes, to pose too great a contrast between new and old industries may be false if pushed too far. A good case in point would be textiles where there was clearly a relationship between the new man-made fibres on the one hand and the older industries of cotton and wool on the other. The older textile industries were, in fact, beginning to show some signs of increasing productivity. Clearly, however, the man-made fibres section had not by 1929 brought full returns on the heavy capital investment which had been made earlier in the decade.

Such a situation was in contrast with that prevailing in America where there is some foundation for the view that the boom really came to an end in 1927. In that year there was a slight recession with a $4\frac{1}{2}$ per cent fall in wholesale prices and 1 per cent fall in physical production. The most striking element in the decline occurred in the purchases of durable goods such as automobiles. The output of passenger automobiles in 1927 fell 22 per cent below the previous year. Although production and sales increased again in 1928 the average increase of the two years, 1927 and 1928, together over previous annual output was small. The increase of 1928 provided the most questionable period of the whole long American boom. As Soule points out, the real question is not why the Great Depression began in 1929 but why it did not begin in 1927.

The boom of 1928–9 has become famous in economic literature as the episode of runaway stock market inflation. No writer has described that episode more vividly than J. K. Galbraith who spends something like three-quarters of the space of his book *The Great Crash, 1929* in dealing with the stock market and the tendencies of share investors, and yet in the same book Galbraith sees the stock market episode as merely one minor item causing the ultimate depression. The essential question is why so many funds were available for stock market investment which could not be channelled elsewhere and the explanation seems to lie in the monetary policy of the federal reserve authorities. Conflicting motives were at work among the authorities and the view prevailed that on account of the mild recession of 1927 an easy-money policy should be favoured. A further factor was the desire to support the gold standard in England. Between the middle and the end of 1927 rediscount rates were lowered from 4 to $3\frac{1}{2}$ per cent and purchases in the open market by the reserve banks totalled $435 million. At the same time the loans and investments of the member banks of the federal reserve system increased by $1,764 million although only 7 per cent of this increase consisted of commercial loans. Part of the money sustained speculative business building but much of the credit flowed into stock market speculation. In 1928 and 1929 the movement gathered pace and loans by the banks were augmented by over $2 billion during the first half of 1929. Although some members of the banking authorities knew that the speculation had gone too far it was difficult to bring it to a check without undermining business confidence.

In other words, the final phase of the great American consumer boom rested on extremely shaky foundations and brought into question the nature and effectiveness of government management of the economy. It highlighted the fact that American prosperity rested primarily on demand for consumer durable goods and once that demand had been saturated it was difficult to find new sources of dynamism in the economy given the American government's policy towards external trade. The uneven distribution of purchasing power and the permanently depressed state of agriculture meant that there was relative lack of cushioning sectors in the economy should any downturn occur. By contrast the British government was itself taking decisions from 1926 onwards which were quite accidentally to provide such cushioning. For example the passing of the Electricity Act of 1926 was a measure which would provide cheaper electricity to a wide part of the country just when the depression was beginning to bite in 1930. Similarly, the creation of the great chemical combine of ICI in 1926, which could not have been effected without government approval, was again to yield returns by the early 1930s. Hence in spite of the appearance in Britain of the great depressed sectors of the economy which had their massive toll of unemployed, there were signs of change and development in Britain which had not yet reached their full potential and which provided a foundation for the argument that in spite of America's apparently higher growth interpreted merely in terms of arithmetic, in reality Britain's lower measure of prosperity was more soundly based.

The Great Crash, 1929-33

The Great Crash of 1929 and the subsequent depression lasting until 1933 constituted such a momentous episode in international economic history that it is not surprising if a vast literature exists about it, much of it partisan or controversial. Three problems emerge in the discussion: (1) why did a depression occur in the first place? (2) why was the depression so long and so severe? (3) why was the impact of the depression more severe in some countries than in others? For present purposes, the relevant latter question is why America suffered more than Britain.

Any list compiled by students of the depression would probably include all or nearly all of the following:

Stock market speculation leading to the Wall Street crash of October 1929

Falling world commodity prices

Falling demand for industrial and consumer durable goods

Imbalance of purchasing power between primary producing and manufacturing countries

Unequal distribution of consumer purchasing power, especially in America

International monetary and trading difficulties

National monetary difficulties which for America might be linked with:

The American banking system

Two further general headings might be:

Business confidence

Government policy

The mere list is sufficient reminder of the complexity of the episode. Most controversy centres around the attempt to pinpoint one or two factors which were of prime importance and to establish the relationship or causation between those factors and the rest. In the absence of a definitive generally accepted interpretation it seems best to treat the years 1929–33 as a series of waves in which first one factor and then another seemed to operate either to deepen the depression or to maintain its impact.

The commencement of the depression is often held to be the Wall Street crash of share prices in October 1929. For example, in Galbraith's already mentioned entertaining book *The Great Crash, 1929*, if the importance of the episode has any correlation with the number of pages which the author devotes to stock market speculation one might be forgiven for thinking that the use of funds for share purchases was of immense significance. In the last chapter of the book, however, he tells the reader that the role of the stock market crash has to be seen in the light of the weaknesses of the American economy. What the crash did was to destroy a mood of exuberant confidence. Yet we have always known that stock markets are as much a guide to business confidence as anything else. The relevant question, therefore, is to ask why confidence which so clearly existed in 1928 and much of 1929 should have been so deeply eroded subsequently. The first part of an answer must be to look at those features both of the American economy and of the international economy which already in 1929 could give rise for concern. Most writers are agreed that the relationship of America with the international economy was significant because of America's importance as an international creditor and as the world's leading manufacturing nation which meant that in 1927–8 she accounted for the purchase of 39 per cent of the world's nine principal primary products consumed by the fifteen most important nations. Any downturn in America was bound to have repercussions on the rest of the world.

It is arguable, however, that the international economy was poised for a downturn in any event in 1929. International lending began to contract in 1928 when the stock exchange boom began to divert American funds from foreign investment to domestic speculation. The nation most immediately affected by withdrawal of foreign funds was Germany which was peculiarly susceptible to foreign capital movements because of the large amount of foreign deposits she held. Foreign capital had been an essential element in German economic recovery since 1924 and while one could hardly claim that Germany was the lynchpin of the European economy, the sharp upward trend in German exports associated with the inflow into Germany both of imports and capital meant that Germany's trade was now of international significance. Not long after American foreign lending began to contract there began in 1929 a fall in agricultural and other raw material prices. In most commodities the fall in prices was due to over-investment since some like wheat and sugar had been unduly expanded during the war and others like tin, rubber and coffee had expanded rapidly in the twenties beyond the level justified by demand even at the height of the boom. The fall in primary commodities emphasised what was already known, that primary producing countries were in a vulnerable position and that an imbalance of purchasing power existed between primary producers and manufacturing countries.

Before 1914 that imbalance had been corrected by an international monetary mechanism depending on a gold standard centred on the London money market. Britain's large external capital investment in 1914 was part of an arrangement by which primary producing countries were enabled to borrow relatively easily. The decision of Britain to return to gold in 1925 – albeit with some restrictions compared with 1914 – can be seen as an attempt to return to the arrangements existing before the war. In the late twenties, however, Britain was far more vulnerable than before the war and external confidence in the British economy on which the inflow of foreign funds depended was not so great as it had once been. The export difficulties of Britain's staple industries, the burden of Britain's debt accruing from the war and the attractions of alternative countries for loan deposits were all factors which prevented Britain from building up reserves adequate for the requirements of a major international banker. The structure of international indebtedness with too much hot money involved was a major weakness of the international economy. Loans were contracted rather too sharply and with too little concern for the burden of debt servicing: in 1927 and 1928, for example, Germany increased her debt by over £2,000 million, almost equal to the whole of Great Britain's foreign lending from 1924 to 1930 inclusive. The difficulty of debt servicing was not made easier by America's high tariff policy which hindered exports to America and by the inability or reluctance of most debtors to reduce their price levels. While America and other rich countries were able and willing to lend overseas the international economic system could operate and expand after a fashion, but towards the end of 1928 American willingness to lend overseas fell away and at much the same time the stabilisation of the French franc (the *franc Poincaré*) brought money flowing back into France. Hence there was a reduction of international liquidity and debtors attempted to cut down their imports and to expand their exports. In this situation raw material prices began to decline.

It was in this vulnerable international context that America experienced the stock market euphoria of 1928 and 1929. Presumably the impact of the international situation must be given more emphasis than in many interpretations, since if one looks at the American economy in isolation a number of the criticisms made of that economy to account for the stock market downturn of October 1929, could apply before that date. The agricultural sector had been depressed for most of the decade; the banking system had experienced a disquieting number of failures; there was a considerable amount of purchasing power in the hands of a relatively small proportion of people who would thus tend to be more volatile in their saving, investing and spending habits than if consumer purchasing power were more broadly based; the corporate structure tended to be unsound since firms financed their own expansion and money or credit available from the banks tended not to be utilised for productive purposes and hence was made available for speculation; and economic advice and intelligence were not notable for sober realism. While Galbraith may be right in saying that the stock market collapse was implicit in the speculation that went before it, the various weaknesses in the economy had not arisen in a short period of time except for the stock market euphoria of 1928 and 1929. Even if many commentators at the time thought that share prices had risen too high they did not anticipate that much more would be involved than a necessary shake-out of prices, and they looked forward to a stabilisation of the American economy in 1930 or 1931. They would have been horrified to foresee the extent and duration of the American downturn.

Perhaps the timing of the Wall Street crash was unfortunate since it launched an industrial depression at a time when a world agricultural crisis was already commencing for somewhat different reasons. It was little wonder that business confidence was jolted and that international lenders were uneasy about the whereabouts of their funds. Nevertheless, for both America and Britain 1930 was by no means a disastrous year even if levels of activity were lower than previously. It was certainly true that unemployment levels rose sharply in Britain from 9.7 to 16.2 per cent but in America, although the relative rise in unemployment was sharper than in Britain, the rise was possibly because the low level of 3.2 per cent in 1929 climbed to 8.7 per cent in 1930. Britain's difficulty lay in the vulnerability of her traditional export industries which were immediately affected by the new downturn in world trade, the quantum of world trade falling by about 7 per cent between 1929 and 1930. In spite of such difficulties, Britain's national income held up surprisingly well in 1930. As Richardson has shown, a cushioning effect was already operating in the form of the remarkably good performance of some of the new industries which suffered very little decline in production, and at the same time the purchasing power of those in regular employment was rising because of the fall in the cost of living in monetary terms so that real wages tended to rise. Already the fall in America's gross national product from $104.4–$94.4 billion – a fall of some 10 per cent – was steeper than the fall in Britain between 1929 and 1930, presumably because of the greater loss of business confidence in America and because of the uneven distribution of consumer purchasing power and high level of indebtedness. At that point in the situation, according to Romasco's account, President Hoover was by no means complacent about the fall in stock market prices and called presidential business conferences to ensure that businessmen did not retrench. Perhaps mere talking may be scoffed at but the conferences were possibly an indication that the business climate in America was not yet over-despondent. In retrospect, the most gloomy features of the year 1930 were the downturn of world trade and the unstable financial and political situation in Germany. Germany's policy of sharp deflation under Chancellor Bruning was in part an attempt to restrict imports from other countries, thus tightening the circle of international trade.

Nevertheless, it is a matter of controversy how far the American government and American investors were helping to make the situation worse by unsound actions. In the second half of 1930 American new foreign security issues were lower than in the first half (a normal seasonal feature in any case), but since the total of the issues was higher in 1930 at $2,180 million than in 1929 at $1,417 million it cannot be said that the United States helped significantly to aggravate the financial situation for most of 1930. On the contrary, many central banks like those of Britain, Germany, Italy, the Netherlands and Sweden were able in 1930 to relax the restrictive policies which they had followed by raising interest rates late in 1929. What was disquieting was the uncertain position in international trade and the new restrictions on the flow of trade. America herself was a leader of restrictionism by exacting the Hawley-Smoot tariff in mid-1930, 'which imposed the highest rates in American history and among the highest in the world'. The year 1930, then, experienced a downturn in international trade which no one seemed able to counteract; but financial disasters on any major scale were yet to come even if the German and Austrian financial situations were disquieting. It might be argued that the second half of 1930 was a turning-point since in a fluid situation there could be an attempt either to revive international trade or to pursue strictly nationalist policies which would create further uncertainty and restrictionism. Unfortunately, international business confidence received a further blow when in the elections to the German Reichstag of September 1930, the number of National Socialist members rose from 12 to 107. There was panic among foreign creditors and a massive recall of short-term credits. Although the panic abated when it seemed likely that the Reich government would withstand the opposition of the National Socialists, the German financial situation was basically uncertain since exactly one-half of the credits that flowed into Germany from abroad up to 1931 (RM 10.3 billion out of RM 20.6 billion) were short-term credits which were never consolidated into longer-term investments.

Hence the international financial situation remained uneasy while world trade continued to drift downward. British exports, for example, declined by 18.4 per cent between 1929 and 1930 to be exceeded by a fall of 23.5 per cent between 1930 and 1931 while American exports fell from an index base of 100 in 1929 to 77 in 1930 and 51 in 1931. An uneasy situation was hardly improved by the news in May 1931 of the difficulties of the Austrian Credit Anstalt, news which precipitated a run on the German banks and severely aggravated financial uncertainty. In a sense one might say that every major financial centre had a spotlight thrown on it and major governments and central bankers were alive to the dangers threatening the structure of the entire European credit system. Thus the support given to the Reichsbank by the central banks of Britain, France and the United States and by the Bank for International Settlements to the extent of RM 420 million in June 1931, and the reparations moratorium proclaimed by President Hoover again in June 1931, were substantial attempts to alleviate the situation. Yet the general atmosphere was one of gloom. France, with a relatively strong currency linked to gold, received substantial inflows. Again, from mid-1930 the Federal Reserve failed to pursue an aggressive monetary policy in America itself in spite of the fact that new gold inflows left it free to pursue a more expansionary policy if it so desired. Policy confusion prevailed and some American officials looked only at interest rates on the safest short-term securities and at excess reserves in big city banks, concluding that credit conditions were already so easy as to be 'sloppy'. Because their views prevailed, the money supply in America had by September 1931, fallen about 10 per cent from its level in mid-1929.

Hence many would argue that in the crucial turning-point

between June 1931 and September 1931, the real contributory factor was the prevailing nature of economic ideas as expressed in government policies. Maybe with resolute international monetary co-operation and with the will of various governments to resist internal policies of retrenchment the tide of depression could have been halted. To make such a statement is to ask for the general acceptance of economic ideas which could not easily have been held by any policy maker in 1930 (that is, by anyone born before 1900 and probably before 1880). The intensity with which partisan national standpoints were espoused requires some effort of imagination to grasp two generations later. Hence after the Austrian and German financial troubles of May and June, it was an unfortunate coincidence in timing, to say the least, that during the month of July the reports of the Macmillan and May committees should be publicised in Britain. 'Suspicion of Britain as a safe repository of money grew. On 14 July the *Report of the Macmillan Committee on Finance and Industry* was published, and this report, although in general sensible and reassuring, drew attention to the large volume of London's short-term liabilities. This feature of Britain's position was not new, but was an inheritance from the stabilisation policy of 1925 and its aftermath; on the other hand, Britain remained unable to increase her short-term assets, and increased international illiquidity and uncertainty made this position unusually precarious. There was also the Royal Commission on Unemployment Insurance, critical of the "unsound finance" of the Unemployment Insurance Fund. And lastly there was the Committee on National Expenditure, the so-called May Committee, which reported on 31 July. It forecast a government deficit of £120 million at the end of the financial year in April, and recommended increased taxation and reduced expenditure especially in the field of unemployment payments.' The report of the May Committee, advocating financial retrenchment, implied that the limits of prudence had been overstepped. A further implication which could be read into the findings was that the existing Labour government had mismanaged the situation. It was certainly the case that attempts to reduce expenditure on unemployment insurance were extremely distasteful to some members of the Cabinet and, while they were hesitant to act, credits made available from foreign sources were being exhausted. In short, notwithstanding the fall of the Labour government the months of August and September saw immense pressure building up on sterling and, on 21 September 1931, Britain went off gold.

It was ironical – perhaps a comment on the poverty of prevailing economic thinking – that 'a turning-point in modern economic history', an act of policy which Britain had been loth to implement because of the repercussions which it would have on international trade, was within a relatively short space of time beneficial to Britain since with the pound devalued British exports tended to rise. Equally ironically America and France, the two countries whose monetary policies had been in major part responsible for the general situation leading to Britain's abandonment of the gold standard, now felt the repercussions of increasing uncertainty. The loss of international liquidity put increasing pressure on all countries, but especially on debtor countries, to export. Receiving countries naturally resisted these exports since payment for them drained reserves of foreign exchange and tended to increase unemployment. The resort to tariffs became general and Britain joined in with a temporary Abnormal Importations (Customs Duties) Act followed by the Import Duties Act of February 1932. Britain's definitive tariff policy for the thirties was worked out during the course of 1932 with the report of the Import Duties Advisory Committee in April recommending that duties on manufactured goods in general should be 10 per cent *ad valorem* and with the Ottawa Conference in July and August attempting to create an imperial preference system. Britain's actions were symptomatic of the way in which the world was increasingly divided into economic and political blocs.

Hence in international terms a new situation had been created after September 1931. The repercussions of the new situation on Britain and America were partly a reflection of their relative involvement with international trade before that date. One argument is that by mid-1931 Britain's exports had fallen almost as far as they were likely to fall, whereas American exports still had some way to go. This might be true to some extent but it might also be true that Britain's much heavier relative commitment to exports in the twenties with their emphasis on the so-called older industries, retarded to some extent the advance of the new industries. The linkages might be complex and indirect but there is some justification for Richardson's view that the advent of cheap money and the conscious realisation that investment in the older industries was unprofitable

brought an acceleration to the switch away from older industries to newer industries. Nevertheless, monetary policy
takes time to work through the economy and in any case, for
technical reasons, a thoroughgoing policy of cheap money was
not completely in being until June 1932, with the conversion of
5 per cent War Loan to 3½ per cent. By that time the bank
rate was down to 2 per cent. Equally important, however, was
the general business sentiment that stability in prices, in interest
rates and in exchange rates had been or were being achieved,
the last through the setting up of the Exchange Equalisation
Account established in April 1932. Yet monetary policy was not
the total explanation. The revival in business confidence so
early in Britain compared with that in other countries has still
not been altogether satisfactorily accounted for. Part of the explanation might be business confidence in a 'National' government with a Conservative political flavour, and part might be
the soundness of British banks compared with the collapses and
defaults elsewhere. The relatively low level of indebtedness
might also be advantageous compared with the situation in
America and it is noticeable how British banks were reluctant
to foreclose on debtors compared with their American counterparts. There is also a possibility that rising real wages among
those who were in employment – which was, after all, nearly
four-fifths of the labour force – generated savings which could
be utilised for consumer durables and especially for new housing.
The plain fact is that although the industrial depression in
Britain was at its worst in the third quarter of 1932 the rising
demand for new housing had already made a tentative appearance. For whatever reasons, one may adduce Britain had
contrived to avoid the worst repercussions of the crisis in the
international economy.

In America, however, the situation between September 1931
and March 1933 deteriorated. Monetary economists can no
doubt be satisfied that the different performance of the two
economies was related to differences in the money supply.
Milton Friedman, for example, points out that 'from the
cyclical peak in August, 1929, to the cyclical trough in March,
1933, the stock of money fell by over a third . . . The monetary
collapse was not the inescapable consequence of other forces,
but rather a largely independent factor which exerted a powerful influence on the course of events . . . The contraction is in
fact a tragic testimonial to the importance of monetary forces . . .

it is hardly conceivable that money income could have declined by over one-half and prices by over one-third in the course of four years if there had been no decline in the stock of money.' Friedman points to inept monetary policies in the United States, and associates them particularly with the absence of Benjamin Strong, Governor of the New York Bank and the dominant figure in the Federal Reserve system until his death in 1928. Strong's successor, Harrison, was not able to exercise his personal authority against opposition or inertia on the part of other bank governors. In the spring of 1932 when they agreed to a large open-market operation to pump credit back into the system they were only half-hearted about it. The key failure, Friedman argues, was in the lack of vigorous action to stem the first liquidity crisis late in 1930 and he points out that the failure of the Bank of the United States in December 1930, with over $200 million deposits was of exceptional importance since it was the largest commercial bank as measured by volume of deposits ever to have failed up to that time in American history. He argues that if there had been restriction of convertibility of deposits into currency as there had been in 1907, the Bank of the United States might have been able to re-open since it ultimately paid off 83.5 per cent of its adjusted liabilities at its closing on 11 December 1930, despite having to liquidate so large a fraction of its assets during the extraordinarily difficult financial conditions that prevailed during the next two years. The next two major banking crises were a result of indecision in 1930 with a resulting lowering of confidence in the Federal Reserve system. Altogether Friedman's interpretation of events in America constitutes a powerful case for the contraction in the supply of money as the major difference between the levels of depression in Britain and America, and Britain's early commencement of recovery late in 1932 can be seen in that light.

Nevertheless, a total monetary explanation is not the whole story, and an interesting comment by Alfred Hettinger, jr, at the end of the Friedman and Schwartz volume is that psychological and political factors were of greater importance in 1929–33 than the authors are prepared to allow. Hettinger believes that 'business is simply decision making and calculated risk taking'. In the final analysis, monetary policy acts on men whose conduct is not predictable. J. M. Barker, a senior official of Sears Roebuck & Co said in 1936 that the force of unreasonable, emotional mob psychology could sometimes have dire economic effects. During the depression 'a citizen fearing devaluation could choose gold rather than paper and the international flow of gold, seeking safety, was as unpredictable as that of a gun loose on a battleship pitching in heavy seas'. Neither the British nor the American economies operated as a closed system, and the extent to which the level of their national income declined was to some extent conditioned by the operation of world market trends and of the uncertainty engendered by international monetary flows. There was no clear forecast of demand, and businessmen were reluctant to risk new investment unless they could be reasonably convinced of the possibility of an upturn. A number of theories are adduced for Britain's ability to 'weather the storm' and for America's tendency to 'panic'. Equally certainly, psychological and political factors constitute only part of the explanation. In 1932, for example, it would be a gross exaggeration to say that Hoover's government was totally inept and Ramsay MacDonald's government in Britain provided a prime example of economic wisdom. On the contrary, both seem to have been to a large extent in the grip of forces beyond their control. It was rather that the structure of the two economies was different and that the total influences on demand in America all seemed to work one way whereas the imbalance in the British economy left powerful pockets of demand relatively unaffected. Building construction provided the extreme example of different behaviour during the depression and it may be a significant example: by 1929 the great American construction boom of the twenties was largely over whereas British building construction was turning strongly upward and the years 1930 and 1931 by their uncertainty halted a large volume of potential demand. In that sense potential demand gave a stimulus of new opportunity in Britain whereas the belief in over-production and satiated demand provided a powerful disincentive to new investment in America. Failure tends to breed failure and success to breed success. That may be a trite remark to end a survey of a still highly controversial episode, but in 1932 and 1933 contrasts of mood in the two countries had become apparent. They were not altogether explicable in purely economic terms.

CHAPTER SEVEN

CONTRASTS IN ECONOMIC RECOVERY, 1933–40

Terms like 'depression' and 'recovery' are obviously relative, not only to each other but to some more normal equilibrium state with which they are compared. This somewhat obvious point has special relevance to the 1930s and to the statistical table assembled by H. W. Richardson comparing real national income in seven countries between 1929 and 1937. With the index at 100 in 1929 for both Britain and the United States, in 1932 the British index had fallen a mere point to 99 whereas the American index was down to 63; by 1937 the British index was at 118 and the American index at 96.[1] The point at issue is whether one uses 1929 or 1932 as a yardstick by which to assess recovery in the thirties. If 1932 is chosen then American recovery from 63 to 96 was proportionally steeper than British recovery from 99 to 118. The majority of economic historians would disagree with such a view, probably on the ground that the low point of such an extraordinary depression as that of 1929–33 is hardly a valid stage at which to begin a measurement of economic dynamism. By implication, most writers tend to use 1929 as the more useful criterion even though it might be argued that inflationary tendencies had pushed the American index rather high by 1929 and that the relatively low point in 1932 showed the converse situation. The discussion is merely a warning once again that crude national income figures need to be interpreted with caution. Richardson himself uses a number of other economic indicators to measure British recovery, three important ones being gross domestic investment, production and profits, all of which showed striking increases between 1933 and 1937. Elsewhere he points to the increases in employment and production in industries such as electrical engineering, building materials and building construction and in vehicles. Overall, his interpretation is clear: '. . . there can be little doubt about the strength and vigour of Britain's recovery after the depression of the 1930s. The upswing was a very long one when compared with previous recoveries.' Although Richardson's optimism is by no means universally shared – witness, for example, B. W. E. Alford's relative pessimism about Britain – even the most gloomy British interpretations seem cheerful by contrast with the vast majority of views about America which are summarised by Broadus Mitchell's title *Depression Decade*. According to Lester V. Chandler, 'in the United States, the grinding deflation of employment, output and prices continued until March, 1933, the nadir of the depression. The Roosevelt administration, which assumed office at that time, made almost frantic efforts to restore prosperity, but the economic recovery was tragically slow, halting and incomplete. Not until mid-1941, sparked by America's mounting rearmament programme, did employment and output again approach full-employment levels. Thus, America's greatest depression lasted about a dozen years, from mid-1929 to mid-1941.'[2]

The general tenor of these views which contrast economic performance in the two countries in the thirties is not in too great dispute although some writers would say that the extent of recovery or depression has been over-stated. Variations in emphasis reflect the extent to which commentators judge an economy by its social defects or by the level of productive activity. There was still misery and unemployment in Britain and in the case of chronic long-term unemployment the situation seemed as hopeless as ever. Average unemployment in Britain continued to run at levels of over 10 per cent except in 1937 when the level was 9.5. Comparative movements of unemployment percentages between 1932 and 1937 were: Britain, 22.8 to 9.5; America, 23.6 to 16.4. The question at issue is the extent to which fall in unemployment is a genuine index of recovery. It is true that British unemployment began falling rapidly in 1933 and by 1935 was down to 14.4 per cent, whereas in America the rate remained above 20 per cent for both 1934 and 1935. The relatively early fall in British unemployment is in line with other economic indicators of recovery. Nevertheless, the difficulty about relying on unemployment as a measure is the unevenness of its incidence. It varied from industry to industry and from age group to age group. Particularly in the United States, unemployment figures tended to be swollen by two factors – an increase in the total labour force brought about by an increasing number of juveniles as a result of a rising birth-rate and technological unemployment. Even in Britain technological unemployment was in considerable evidence. Between 1929 and 1937 output per head increased by 23 per cent in shipbuilding and total employment decreased by 13 per cent. Output in vehicles during the same period increased by 66 per cent whereas employment in that industry increased by only 23 per cent. The new industries, and even older industries with an emphasis on increasing production through capital investment rather than by addition of labour, could not soak up the chronic unemployment existing where the labour force was associated with the older industries.

Nevertheless, despite all the warnings about the unreliability of using unemployment figures as an index of economic performance there seems little doubt that the crude contrasts between British and American unemployment in the mid-thirties were important and that British recovery was more pronounced than American. The grounds for such an interpretation are the relatively high level of capital investment in British industry contrasting strongly with the unwillingness of private entrepreneurs to invest in industry in America, the rising levels of consumption in Britain associated with rising average living standards, and the ability of Britain to effect changes in her economic structure to the extent that the home market was the focus of recovery and international trade came to play a proportionately less dominant role than in the past despite its continuing importance. The main areas of emphasis seem to be clear enough: the new industries such as electrical engineering, motor vehicles, man-made fibres, oil and chemicals were among the more vigorous elements in industrial performance; inasmuch as they were associated with a housing boom and with increased demand for consumer durables they reflected the growing importance of large urban markets especially in London and Birmingham, but to a lesser extent elsewhere. In America the consumer durable boom seemed to have played itself out in the twenties, and during the thirties the way out of an economic impasse was difficult to achieve. Despite the valiant efforts of 'New Deal' administrators to inject a degree of pump-priming into the American economy most commentators seem to agree that the results of New Deal efforts in purely economic terms were disappointing whatever other benefits may have accrued.

It is one matter to state the contrast between the two economies in such broad terms; it is another to explain exactly why the contrast should now seem so marked and precisely what factors were dominant. There are a number of controversial points and even when apparently satisfactory explanations are given for them one cannot dismiss the historian's last ploy which is to draw attention to the working of accidental and unforeseen circumstances. For example, why should electricity in Britain have exhibited quite such a marked upturn in the thirties? It is true that the housing boom associated with a financial policy of 'cheap money' from 1932 generated demand for electrical supply and electrical appliances. Nevertheless, it might also be partly an example of supply creating its own demand simply because the increasing availability of electricity in the early thirties was a chronological accident. The Electricity Act of 1926 created the legal and administrative outline for the setting up of the regional electricity boards providing standard voltage and, since the necessary arrangements took time, the actual provision of standard voltage was being made in increasing quantity during the years of depression. How otherwise than by this accident of timing does one explain the extraordinary performance of the radio industry which almost doubled its production from 506,000 to 1,000,000 sets between 1930 and 1932? To some extent electricity provides an example of the application of a new technology whose economic performance (supply and demand) was independent of general economic patterns prevailing at the time. The problem arises how far it was a special case and how far it was a somewhat extreme example of the general application of new technologies which provided new shifts in demand and supply curves, examples of Schumpeter's phenomenon of lumpiness. Nevertheless, there is no necessarily pre-ordained extent of demand for a new technology: it might be true that by 1929 nearly every household in America possessed a motor vehicle in average terms, but the question to ask is why there was not subsequently a trend, however small, to increase possession towards two motor vehicles per household. One may argue that new technology requires social and psychological digestion: the difference between one and two motor vehicles per household connotes a radical change in family life and in the environment. Schumpeter's argument that producers determine the level of demand by influencing tastes and habits may be accepted for some moments in time but rejected for others, since producers seldom influence tastes and habits totally and there may well be a reaction against their more extreme claims for the benefits of the innovations they introduce. Put more simply, few writers seem to suggest that America could continue to expand the economy by way of the new consumer durable goods industries; but if such expansion could not take place then presumably those who argue that over-production had occurred and that new demand could not arise in those industries have a substantial point.

In any event, a comparison of the so-called new industries in the thirties accentuates the contrast between the two economies in striking terms and so distorts interpretation. The motor vehicle industry declined markedly in America in the thirties but expanded in Britain: it was, however, one industry among many. Hence a total economy does not consist of one group of industries, however much their growth or lack of growth may be an influence on overall economic performance. If some writers have been obsessed by industries symbolising technical change in the twenties and thirties they have perhaps underestimated change which was occurring in other industries and activities; that change, of course, was not necessarily for the better. It is in looking at the balance of economic activity as between different sectors that one has perhaps a better view of overall functioning. Granted that 'new' industries were expanding in Britain even if they were stagnant in America, what was happening to primary production, to service industries and to older or less publicised industries than those which Richardson emphasises? Surely an essential point is that both economies were engaged in a fundamental readjustment in their relationships with the international economy. In the primary sector, for example, it was the war and the external market rather than domestic demand which had stimulated American agriculture to new levels of production. Falling world commodity prices and the stagnation of the international economy in the thirties seemed to offer little hope for the American agricultural sector. In Britain, by contrast, the new policy of tariffs, of Commonwealth preference and of agricultural subsidies which commenced operation from 1932 brought virtually a 50 per cent increase in wheat production by 1938 and a rising demand for home-produced eggs and milk. No doubt subsidised agriculture operated on a base of higher prices for the domestic consumer, but the point was that Britain did achieve a transfer of resources from production for export to production for the home market. 'The importance of foreign trade in the economy was declining, the ratio of net exports to national income falling from 17 per cent in 1929 to 11 per cent in 1937 while the ratio of retained imports to income fell from 23 per cent to 18 per cent in the same years . . . in the period 1932–38 capital repayments from abroad exceeded new overseas issues by over £60 million. The recovery in Britain after 1932 was thus a home market recovery *par excellence*.'[3]

Such a situation can be looked at in two ways. It was no doubt fortunate that Britain could achieve a shift in resources which brought a rise in national income, but the virtual stagnation of the international economy clearly involved limits to the potential expansion of the economy. Britain's gloomy overseas trade situation, particularly the fate of invisible exports which fell by about £200 million from some £450 million per annum in the late twenties to some £250 million in 1932 and which for some years in the thirties did not perform their former role of covering the deficit on the balance of trade is a point emphasised by the pessimists. A buoyant economy, they might argue, could not endure for long if the international economy did not achieve a substantial upturn. In fact, of course, the situation was not quite so clear-cut and world trade did achieve some revival between 1933 and 1937. Nevertheless, despite a 41 per cent expansion in British exports between 1932 and 1937 those exports were still only 71.5 per cent of the 1929 figure in 1937 because of the slump in exports between 1929 and 1932. Despite a favourable movement in the net barter terms of trade the external situation was not promising. Both Richardson – an optimist – and Pollard – a pessimist – agree that the relative switch away from the older export industries was a striking feature of the thirties. America, by contrast, appeared to be in an impasse since, with the home market at a low ebb, the international economy by the measure of 1929 levels seemed to offer little scope for expansion. A crucial question is to what extent American difficulties were created by her own monetary and commercial policy. It is true, of course, that in 1934 the extreme duties imposed by the Hawley-Smoot tariff of 1930 were revised and the Secretary of State was empowered to remit duties by generous amounts if bilateral trade agreements could be concluded. Such trade agreements, however, tended to be made with countries with which America normally had significant trade and with the revival in the international economy those were the countries with which America would trade in any case. If bilateral agreements, however, did not provide any great stimulus, the reason might rather lie in psychological barriers to more liberal trade arrangements – economic nationalism having become a tenaciously held attitude of mind – and in the flow of money. As Robertson points out, a massive repatriation of American loans took place between 1934 and 1940. There was a capital transfer of $7,400 million supplemented perhaps by another $3,700 million for errors and omissions. In addition, gold flowed into the country to the order of nearly $15,000 million. Hence the total inflow was of the order of $25,000 million. It was little wonder that international illiquidity persisted when so little American external investment took place and when capital was being repatriated to Britain. H. W. Arndt, who during World War II undertook a study of the economic problems of the thirties, criticised American external commercial policy to an extent which no American commentator in the thirties seemed prepared to do. Altogether there seemed little hope for any decisive upturn in the volume of world trade when monetary and commercial barriers were still so influential.

That being so, the years between 1933 and 1937 may constitute a special situation for Britain in her relative switch to home-based production, an adjustment which perhaps could not continue at the momentum of 1933–5 for very much longer. By 1937, for example, radio production was not so much for new sets as for replacement ones, showing that a new demand situation had been reached. Again, by the late thirties it is arguable that bottleneck problems were being created by the concentrated allocation of resources in the London and Birmingham areas to the neglect of the so-called older industrial areas. Such problems might be symbolised by the numbers standing on suburban trains from London's south-eastern outer districts during peak hours or by the traffic crawls of vehicles from London to Brighton on a fine weekend summer day. No doubt the bottleneck problems can be exaggerated because even in the South East unemployment remained high in the thirties relative to its incidence in the decade before World War I. Yet it was clearly much lower than in other industrial regions in the thirties and while expansion lasted, even if it was uneven in its incidence, it brought hope where there could otherwise have been despair. Richardson says that 'there were sound economic reasons why the depression should end when it did. Thus, there is no need to advance psychological explanations in an analysis of the recovery, for its causes are comprehensible in economic terms.'[4] Nevertheless, even if economists do not take kindly to psychological factors those factors do have an influence on investment decisions and on decisions of workers where to seek employment. Anyone who lived in the thirties had to take account of the two faces of England, the prosperity symbolised by the mock Tudor housing of the London suburbs and the despairing poverty symbolised by Orwell's *Road to Wigan Pier*. Yet the despair associated with the older industrial regions did at least show some signs of lifting. It is not often stressed that the performance of the coal, steel and textile industries was really rather creditable between 1932 and 1939 compared with the years 1924 to 1932. In the coal industry there was a rise in production from 209 million tons in 1932 to 240 million tons in 1938 and output per man tended to rise; if performance was not better the real difficulty lay in the export sector where British coal exports continued to decline. Similarly, the textile industry probably became a more efficient industry and the steel industry more than doubled its production between 1932 and 1939, benefitting both from the imposition of tariffs in 1932 and from the general stimulus provided by an expanding home economy.

By contrast, the symbolism of America in the thirties was perhaps that of Steinbeck's *Grapes of Wrath*. The general gloom surrounding the American economic scene seemed impossible to dissipate in spite of the valiant efforts of the New Deal administrators to remedy the situation. The problem is to decide why their attempts to prime the pump of the economy seemed so disappointing. Some writers say that the experiment in deficit financing, even if novel in the extent to which it was undertaken, was insufficient to meet the requirements of the situation. The word 'requirement' conveys a subjective appraisal since what is usually meant is that a hypothetical amount of additional investment should have been undertaken to generate further economic activity in order to reduce the level of unemployment. As is well known, the establishing of a socially acceptable level of unemployment and an acceptable definition of poverty can vary from one generation to the next. To

American contemporaries of the thirties the levels of unemployment and of poverty were unacceptable by the standards of anything known for a generation previously, yet ingrained habits of mind suggested that such a situation would automatically correct itself when prices fell and when the cost of new private investment was low enough to convince entrepreneurs that new risks could profitably be undertaken. In other words, confusions and divisions in social attitudes existed and the efforts of the New Deal administrators reflected that confusion. On the one hand in a political democracy there was considerable pressure on them to promote measures to alleviate unemployment and social distress, and on the other hand there was inevitable resistance to policies which seemed to flout accepted canons of economic behaviour. The New Deal could by no means avoid the slur of a stigma.

There is, therefore, justification for a view which sees the thirties in America as a decade in which psychological barriers to economic adjustment were crucial. Whatever the deficiencies in the quantity of money available between 1930 and 1933 there could be no doubt that the reserves of banks rose considerably between 1933 and 1941. There was a huge rise in the monetary gold stock coupled with a rise in member bank reserves in the Federal Reserve system. Taken with the virtual 40 per cent devaluation of the dollar against gold in 1934, the trend of policy meant that the Roosevelt administration could hardly be accused of pursuing a deflationary policy. On the contrary, by 1936 federal reserve officials began to worry about the inflationary potential of huge amounts of excess reserves which were available for lending. Hence measures were taken to raise reserve requirements on all types of deposits with effect from August 1936. Again in 1936 or early in 1937 federal government expenditure was decreased and taxes rose. It was assumed that the banks 'would meet the increased requirements by drawing down their excess reserves, that virtually none would respond by selling securities or restricting loans, and that interest rates would not be affected. In fact, however, interest rates began to rise . . . Also, bank credit and the money supply, which had been increasing since early 1934, ceased to rise and actually declined about 5 per cent in the following year. The Federal Reserve had again made the mistake of underestimating the banks' demands for excess reserves for liquidity purposes.'[5] Federal reserve officials were wrong in their judgement that the very large volume of excess reserves in 1936 and 1937 was serving no useful purpose. On the contrary, they served to satisfy the banks' continued high levels of demand for liquidity and to bring pressures on the banks to expand their loans and investments. The federal government had to take steps by 1938 to increase money supply. The short slump of 1937-8 was instructive in that the disappointing part of the equation was that private entrepreneurs did not take great advantage of credit which was available and the level of private investment, especially in residential and non-residential construction, remained disquietingly low. Thus increased money supply did not have the effect of stimulating sectors of the economy where chronic difficulty appeared to exist. Hence America, like Britain, suffered to some extent from structural problems.

The nature of the structural problem, however, was somewhat different from that of Britain since different industries were affected. Between 1929 and 1933 the percentage decline in real output had been only 7.4 for gasoline (petrol), 7.7 for woollen and worsted cloth production and 11.4 for cotton consumption. By contrast, among the industries experiencing a 50 per cent decline or more were the following:[6]

Shipbuilding	53.1
Furniture production	55.6
Non-ferrous metals and products	55.9
Lumber production	57.9
Iron and steel	59.3
Machinery	61.6
Cement production	63.1
Non-ferrous metal smelting	63.5
Transportation equipment	64.2
Automobile production	65.0
Railroad car production	73.6
Copper production	78.0
Common and face brick production	83.3
Locomotive production	86.4

A number of these activities were associated with building construction or with consumer durable goods industries and their performance, even though improving during the thirties, remained disappointing. No doubt part of the explanation could be that during the twenties considerable structural change was taking place in any case with a shift away from any agricultural employment and residence in rural areas to urban employment and residence. There were presumably limits to such a shift given the relative proportion of work available in towns and given that demand and prices for industrial goods were turning down by mid-1929. With the onset of the depression particular areas were hard hit, among them being Jefferson county, Alabama, with its coal, iron and steel; Oregon with its lumber mills; Detroit with its automobile production; Pennsylvania with its coal mines; and Chicago and Cincinnati with canning and other activities. While the industrial measures of the New Deal might help to some extent to deal with the situation in a macro-economic context it could hardly be said to have done very much to alleviate the problems of particular industries. From this point of view one might argue that the relative lack of government intervention was to some extent an advantage in the British economy since macro-economic measures relieving unemployment in the most distressed areas could help to sustain a labour force which from the viewpoint of structural balance was in need of some reduction. Of course, governments in Britain were not under quite such pressure to intervene since unemployment declined relatively sharply between 1933 and 1937 whereas in America the continuing high incidence of unemployment brought pressure for government intervention on social grounds alone. Governments with little or no experience of economic intervention – planning would be far too sophisticated a concept for the decade – could hardly be expected to review the situation in any detail. Without any clear guidelines on what should be done the Roosevelt government fell back on attempting to please all sections of the community at once and measures concerning industry revealed the general dilemma. The National Industrial Recovery Act of 1933 symbolised the situation. One part of the act authorised the Public Works Administration, the purpose of which was to provide direct employment and to raise overall purchasing power. The other part of the act authorised the creation of the National Recovery Administration which was an experiment in industrial co-operation by arranging for each industry to set up a code authority and to formulate a code of fair competition. The mere fact that the act could be passed showed that doctrines of perfect competition were unpopular even among some businessmen because of the low ebb which competition appeared to have brought in its train. On the other hand, it was a little too much to expect businessmen to discard their established habits of control and individual decision-making, especially when the act was also attempting to cater for the interests of workers. Under the codes both employers and workers would exert pressure for price increases. However, there would be some inevitable disagreement about the distribution of returns from those increases. In the process, the interests of consumers tended to be neglected. 'It should have been evident from the beginning that in each industry there would be sharp conflicts of interest among employers, workers and consumers of the products. However, many were surprised by the bitter controversies that developed within industries as firms disagreed on price policies, output quotas and various trade practices.'[7]

If difficulty occurred over plans dealing with industry there were equally problems in measures concerning agriculture. The basic aim of agricultural policy seemed to be to raise the money incomes of farmers by increasing the prices of their products. There were, however, serious problems in implementing collective or co-operative schemes. Farms varied greatly in size, the very large number of farmers meant that each individual farmer could hardly believe that restricting his own output really made much difference and, with the basic situation that most important agricultural commodities produced a surplus over possible home use, the real key to the situation lay in the ability to export agricultural surpluses. Attempts to introduce a 'two-price system' by which domestic prices could be kept above world prices by means of quotas, subsidies and import tariffs were fraught with difficulty not least because with the large number of farmers it was difficult in practice to prevent domestic buyers or processors evading taxes or enforced prices by collusion with farmers and, secondly, because of retaliation by other countries who were large agricultural producers. Other more technical problems were related to the changing productivity of various farms and to soil conservation. All that one can say by way of summary is that the Agricultural Adjustment Act of 1933 and its successor of 1938 were associated with a rise in farm incomes as the table on p 144 shows.[8] Hence it is difficult to say how much of the improvement was due to the specific measures of the acts and how much was due to increased demands generated by a rising national income. In any event, it is clear that agriculture remained very much a problem sector of the economy, rather more so than in the

Farm Incomes and Farm Parity Ratios
(price indexes: 1909–14 = 100)

Year	Realised net income of farm operators	Net income to persons on farms from farming	Prices received by farmers	Prices paid by farmers	Parity ratios
1929	6,264	7,024	148	160	92
1932	1,928	2,510	65	112	58
1933	2,767	3,012	70	109	64
1934	3,871	3,428	90	120	75
1935	4,605	5,858	109	124	88
1936	5,138	4,954	114	124	92
1937	5,232	6,754	122	131	93
1938	4,273	5,101	97	124	78
1939	4,394	5,189	95	123	77
1940	4,289	5,299	100	124	81
1941	6,153	7,455	124	133	93

The striking feature of these figures is that they seem to follow general trends of other economic indicators particularly in the impact of the short slump of 1937–8.

twenties, and its plight was the occasion for revolutionary changes in the relationships of the federal government to agriculture. Once the federal government took steps to influence prices, output and the relative supplies of various types of products, uses of land and even the production patterns of individual farmers it proved impossible to return to the non-interventionist policies of the twenties. Agriculture, then, was a striking symbol of the difficulties existing in the American economy which led to massive government intervention.

Despite that intervention there seems little reason to question the general verdict that the New Deal was a disappointment as a recipe for economic recovery. Despite massive public works programmes and despite the operation of deficit financing, the high level of unemployment was unacceptable for an advanced industrial nation. Perhaps the truth is that America's long period of economic growth under conditions of apparent competition to 1929 had left her a nation divided in herself and hence the necessary co-operation to achieve a sufficient upturn in national income for general living standards to rise was lacking. Alternatively, the impact of the international economic situation was greater than many writers have been prepared to allow. In any event, the experience of the New Deal seems to confirm the theme of contrast between the two economies with which this chapter began. Even the rearmament boom in its early stages seems to have been pursued with more vigour in Britain. No doubt that was so partly because of Britain's greater possible military danger, but one has also an impression of greater vigour and determination in the pursuit of changing production. The thirties ended as they began, with the British economy showing striking advances in certain sectors and with considerable restructuring still under way. No doubt to some critics this chapter will have exaggerated Britain's performance relative to that of America, but in the long span between 1850 and 1950 it was so unusual to find a decade where contrasts between the two countries could be interpreted to Britain's advantage that those who tend to assume that America always provided the superior model might ponder it with some attention.

CHAPTER EIGHT

AGRICULTURE, INDUSTRY AND THE LABOUR FORCE, 1914–39

Agriculture

In this chapter the problems of agriculture, industry and the labour force between 1914 and 1939 are considered in relation to their adjustment to changing economic trends. For the economic theorist agriculture is especially intriguing in raising the question of state intervention. In both countries three broad phases can be distinguished: firstly, a wartime phase when state influence over agriculture became increasingly important; secondly, a relative relaxation of state influence during the 1920s; and thirdly, a renewal of interventionist measures in the 1930s to solve the severe problems caused by restrictions on international trade and the impact of the world depression.

In wartime the state may be in a position to influence both demand and supply yet the actual measures taken depend on the degree to which governments feel obliged to regulate the market. Because of received economic ideas there was no thoroughgoing reappraisal of the economic forces at work until the war was already well under way. In Britain there was little attempt to interfere with normal market forces until well into 1916 although demands on shipping space had some effect on the ability to import food. Hence pressure to produce as much food as possible within Britain itself was inherent in the situation and the setting-up of County War Agricultural Committees in 1915 to examine the possibilities of increasing the output of food and to organise the supply of agricultural labour, fertilisers, machinery and feeding stuffs was as much a portent of change as a real influence. In America rising demand from

Europe was experienced by early 1915, due to the need to make good food production losses caused by the spoliation of agricultural land in northern France. Additionally, the internal prosperity in America and consequent buoyant demand for food stimulated an increase in production and the year 1915 saw the first billion-bushel crop in American history. This increase owed little to state intervention and the main problems lay in distribution and transport. These problems were accentuated by the German submarine campaign against Allied shipping and it was no accident that a vigorous food production policy was launched in Britain only with the increase in shipping losses late in 1916. A Food Production Department of the Board of Agriculture was formed in 1917 and in each county an Executive Committee of the War Agricultural Committee was given extensive powers to tell farmers what crops to grow and to require farmers to plough up grassland. The Food Production Department allotted quotas of the increased arable acreage to be secured, and became the central source of supply for the industry by providing labour, machines, fertilisers and seeds on a large scale. State intervention on such a vigorous scale in America was not necessary but the increasing concern over adaptation to the wartime situation was shown by encouragement and directions to farmers emanating from the federal government. The result of these wartime policies was a substantial increase in production. The wheat crop in Britain amounted to 11,640,000 quarters compared with an average of 7,090,000 for 1904–13. Both oats and potatoes achieved an increase of 50 per cent on prewar figures. In America wheat acreage increased from 47 million as an average for 1909–13 to 74 million in 1919, or about 50 per cent, but because the increase was achieved partly by ploughing up meadows and wild grasslands in the Great Plains states and in Minnesota and Montana, land not necessarily best suited for wheat, and partly because harvests fluctuated with relatively poor years in 1916 and 1917, wartime wheat production was on average 38 per cent greater than the 1909–13 average. Other American items to increase were hogs, cotton and tobacco.

This wartime situation was clearly not expected to last indefinitely yet wartime circumstances could influence the approach of governments to possible peacetime eventualities. In Britain the realisation that home food production was a strategic requirement in time of future possible hostilities was mixed with some regret that agriculture was now a relatively minor part of the economy in national income terms and that the rural way of life was declining. Hence the Corn Production Act of 1917 guaranteed minimum prices to farmers for wheat and oats and at the same time agricultural labourers were assured of minimum wages. This emergency measure was followed in 1920 by another Corn Production Act which embodied permanent peacetime policy in which guaranteed minimum prices and guaranteed minimum wages were retained. Yet in putting forward such a policy governments presumably failed to appreciate the extent to which wartime conditions were abnormal and the likelihood of violent price fluctuations as international transport improved in peacetime with supply of agricultural products remaining at a high level. By 1921 the brief postwar boom collapsed and agricultural prices fell drastically. In 1920 the British wheat harvest attained an average price of 86s 4d per quarter whereas in 1921 it was 49s, and in 1922 40s 9d. Oats declined similarly. At these levels a continued policy of guaranteed prices would have involved subsidies of such an amount that governments would have found it impossible to justify them. Hence the whole policy was apparently swept away with the Corn Production (Repeal) Act of 1921 and the adjustment to the peacetime conditions of the 1920s was a painful one.

Nevertheless, British farmers were operating under less painful circumstances than their American counterparts. In the year beginning July 1919, the value of American agricultural exports reached a peak of \$3,861,000 whereas in the year beginning July 1921 the amount was about half that figure at \$1,915,000. Most of the years in the 1920s were even lower than that with the exception of year beginning in July 1924 when the total rose to \$2,280,000. American farmers were badly hit because of the level of their indebtedness. Total farm mortgages in the United States rose from \$3,300 million in 1910 to \$6,700 million in 1920 and \$9,400 million in 1925. In 1925 indebtedness represented about 42 per cent of the value of owner-operated farms. Then, as Kindleberger points out, 'from 1925 to 1929 a process of what might by analogy be called structural deflation occurred in the world primary product economy. Instead of excess demand, there was excess supply. A few countries tried to meet the situation by absorbing the excess supply in stockpiles. Without an adjustment in production, this only stored up trouble. Other countries, one by one, found it necessary to evade the consequences of the excess supply by keeping it out of the domestic market, or selling the crop for what it could bring, perhaps cushioning the consequences at home by depreciation, which forced prices down abroad. The excess supply imposed a kind of structural deflation on the system.'[1] America with her important involvement in the international agricultural economy could not escape repercussions from the situation. Farming accounted for a quarter of total employment in the United States in 1929 and farm exports for 28 per cent of farm income. Even if net income of farmers rose during the 1920s, presumably because of the prosperity in the United States as a whole, it was not surprising that the share of agriculture in the national income, which was 16 per cent in 1919, fell to 10.3 per cent in 1921 and continued falling to 8.8 per cent in 1929. As one might expect, not all products were equally affected by the decline in exports. Cotton had suffered during the war and showed relative gains in the 1920s. Tobacco held its levels reasonably well because of the growth in consumption of cigarettes.

In contrast to the United States, Britain experienced the repercussions of the international economy by way of imports and import prices rather than by way of exports. In a sense the difficulties of Britain post-1875 repeated themselves, and once again there was a relative switch away from grain crops to pasture, livestock rearing, fruit, vegetables and market gardening. It was not surprising that the acreage of wheat reached a record low level of 1,247,000 in 1931. Nevertheless, the situation was in some ways different from the later nineteenth century. Firstly, in the immediate postwar period there was a substantial change in British landownership. At the end of 1921 the *Estates Gazette* believed that one-quarter of the land of England must have changed hands during the last four hectic years of land sales. In 1955 Sturmey estimated that in 1914 owner-farmers constituted 11 per cent of total farmers whereas in 1927 they were 36 per cent. Between 1918 and 1921 something between 6 and 8 million acres changed hands and such an enormous and rapid transfer of land had not been seen since the English Civil War. There was a social revolution in the English countryside with the dissolution of a large part of the great estate system and the formation of a new race of yeomen. The great landowners were affected by the sharply rising costs of domestic servants and of estate management. Farms could be sold at prices based on their current annual value and not on their existing rents which were low at the end of the war. Sellers capitalised this difference and took their share of increased land values as an untaxed profit. Smaller net incomes from land simply confirmed that the low return in relation to capital value imposed a price on landownership which was no longer balanced by social advantages. Nevertheless, the new owners were by no means a class of newly rich. Their difficulties increased both because of the general problems of agriculture but also because the burden of wages was much heavier than before the war. This relative improvement in wages was largely due to the Wages (Regulation) Act of 1924 which restored state regulation of agricultural wages. Nevertheless, these burdens were to some extent compensated by the fact that the general price level fell rather more steeply than agricultural prices so that the purchasing power of agricultural produce in terms of other commodities was greater in 1933 than in 1913. Overall, both in America and Britain agriculture in the 1920s showed paradoxes. The international economy created grave problems but a rise in internal living standards in both countries tended to raise farmers' overall income. The burden of debt and the fear of bankruptcy was undoubtedly greater in America. Nevertheless, the pressures on profitability created an incentive to better farm management and in both countries there was a substantial increase in the productivity of the average farm worker. It has been estimated that in Britain the volume of output per worker rose by nearly 40 per cent in the ten years 1925-34. This was achieved by the use of tractors, combine harvesters, milking machines and better practices in general. In America the output per worker increased by 26 per cent between 1920 and 1930.

Yet in spite of increased productivity in general and prosperity in specialised regions or products, the general sentiment was one of gloom and depression. Especially in America those who were burdened with mortgages and other fixed charges were extremely vocal and great interest was taken in various schemes of relief. Both in America and in Britain governments in the 1920s placed the main reliance on self-help or co-operative action, with governmental policy strictly supplementary or incidental. One exception was the British sugar-beet industry which owed its rapid development to generous financial assistance from the state, a result of difficulties in sugar supply experienced during the war. A subsidy was granted for a period of ten years starting in 1924. Between 1924 and 1933 the subsidy cost the taxpayer about £30 million and with this encouragement the acreage under sugar beet in Britain increased from 22,000 in 1924 to 404,000 in 1934; in the latter year the home output of sugar was nearly a quarter of total consumption. Otherwise, government assistance included relief of agricultural land holdings and buildings from local ratings burdens under the derating scheme of 1928; encouragement to small holdings; the establishment of an Empire Marketing Board in 1926; and assistance given by the state for the provision of agricultural credit. Equally in America the Federal Intermediate Credit Act of 1923 provided for twelve intermediate credit banks and other lending agencies with agricultural paper maturing within three years. They were to provide at moderate rates the finance necessary between the planting seasons and the actual marketing of crops. Another important American development was the encouragement of co-operative associations. The Capper-Volstead Act of 1922 freed farmers' co-operatives from the threat of prosecution for the violation of the anti-trust laws. Reasonably continuous success was enjoyed by associations controlling the selling of milk and citrus fruit but, in general, co-operative associations did not fulfil the farmers' hopes that they would remedy the excess of supply over demand in the staple crops. The inability of voluntary organisations to control output in so wide a field and with such a large number of individual producers was especially shown where the market was international. Even the larger and better financed associations could not make headway against a production trend that rendered supplies continuously larger than demand at the prices they would have liked to maintain. Hence government concern was reflected in the important Agricultural Marketing Act of 1929. It committed the federal government to a policy of stabilising farm prices, even though it worked as much as possible through non-government institutions. The act established a Federal Farm Board with the primary function of encouraging the formation of co-operative marketing associations. The board was also authorised to set up 'stabilisation corporations', to be owned by the co-operatives, which would use a $500 million fund to carry on price-support operations.

The failure of the Federal Farm Board to cope with the difficulties occasioned by the economic depression of 1929–33 showed the extent to which the depression itself brought a new dimension to the situation. The years 1930-3, like those of 1920-3, brought a further sharp fall in world commodity prices occasioned by the surplus of supply over world demand. In this situation American agricultural exports could hardly be buoyant. With the coming of the major impact of the depression in 1930, the Federal Farm Board strove valiantly to support farm prices through its stabilisation corporations. Between June 1929 and June 1932 the corporations bought surplus products only to suffer losses as prices continued to fall. The board itself took over the operation and accepted losses, in three years spending some $676 million in stabilisation operations and loans to co-operatives yet the individual farmer, faced with falling prices, maintained or even increased his output. A new measure was called for and it came with the major agricultural measure of the New Deal, the first Agricultural Adjustment Act of May 1933, which sought to raise prices. The means of raising prices consisted of a combination of production controls, benefit payments, government purchases and marketing agreements. Production controls were to apply to farm commodities which were 'basic'; at first only seven products were named but by August 1935 eight others had been added. Roosevelt insisted on decentralisation of administration with production allotments or quotas being made by local, county or district production associations. There is some controversy about how far it was an exercise in grass-roots democracy and how far power was largely concentrated in an agricultural hierarchy dominated by prosperous farmers and by the Farm Bureau. Less prosperous farmers and minority groups suffered discrimination. Nevertheless, farm incomes and farm prices rose markedly from the low levels of 1932. Net incomes to persons on farms from farming more than doubled between 1932 and 1935 and the parity ratio (prices received by farmers: prices paid by farmers) rose from 58 to 75. The parity ratio, which had been 92 in 1929, rose to 92 and 93 in 1936 and 1937 but then fell back to 78 and 77 in 1938 and 1939. Chandler's conclusion is: 'It is impossible to say how much of the improvement of farm incomes and prices resulted from the specific programmes to control production and raise farm prices. A considerable part of the improvement resulted from the general rise of national income, which increased demands for farm products.' The basic approach of the act of May 1933 continued through the 1930s although the

Supreme Court in January 1936 declared the processing tax under the act unconstitutional on the grounds that its proceeds were destined for the purpose of control of farm production which was beyond the constitutional power of the federal government. A new Agricultural Adjustment Act of February 1938 retained measures to support farm prices and incomes but it provided that measures were to be used more flexibly to adjust supplies to demands and to maintain an 'ever normal granary', a favourite concept of Secretary Wallace. 'To take into consideration the effects of prices not only on the size of farm incomes but also on quantities demanded and on amounts supplied was an important change. It was a step forward toward allowing flexible prices to equate demand and supply.'[2]

In fact, the extent to which it was legitimate to interfere with the functioning of a free market economy, and for what purposes, was at the heart of the problem of government intervention in agriculture in the thirties. For economic theorists the paradoxes involved were nowhere more apparent than in Britain. As Tracy points out, as late as the autumn of 1931 a committee of eminent economists came out uncompromisingly against protection in any form. '[Their] book was one of the most forthright and closely reasoned statements of the free trade position ever produced in Great Britain. Yet within a few months all its recommendations had become a dead letter, as the Government resorted to protection and Imperial Preference. It would be hard to demonstrate more conclusively the futility of abstract economic reasoning when the livelihood of much of the population is at stake and strong political forces are at work.'[3] The case for protection was to secure food supplies in case of threat of war and to use import controls to give the British farmers first claim on the home market with the ultimate aim of reaching new self-sufficiency in food. The problem was that it was impossible in a highly industrialised country to give up the traditional policy of cheap food very quickly and, in any event, Britain could not ignore her considerable interests in the British Empire. Nevertheless, measures had to be taken to avoid large-scale dumping like that experienced in October 1931 when the volume of food imports was 35 per cent above normal. Emergency measures of protection inaugurated in November 1931 were replaced in 1932 by the Import Duties Act which has remained the basic legislation of the British tariff. It imposed a general tariff of 10 per cent *ad valorem* but some food stuffs and raw materials were exempted. An Import Duties Advisory Committee could recommend changes in the duties. In the same year, 1932, the Ottawa agreements made between Britain and Empire and Dominion countries gave exemption from duty or preferential duties for Empire products and undertook to control imports from competing foreign countries. These measures gave little benefit to British agriculture since British farmers were still exposed to the full blast of competition from the Empire while farmers in most other European countries were sheltering behind high tariffs and strict import controls. Measures to help British farmers involved a mixture of subsidies, marketing schemes and import restrictions on a commodity by commodity basis. The schemes have been criticised for their piecemeal nature and for not amounting to any coherent policy as a whole. Marketing schemes or subsidies or a combination of both were brought in for wheat, sugarbeet, milk, hops, potatoes, beef, cattle and bacon. Marketing schemes were based on the Agricultural Marketing Acts of 1931 and 1933. After the introduction of import duties, Britain began tariff negotiations with a number of countries and in subsequent years several trade agreements were signed. Overall, however, one cannot say that the measures introduced brought profound results. The market prices of most important foodstuffs remained low and in 1933 the overall agricultural price index reached its lowest point at 76 per cent of the pre-crisis level. It then recovered sluggishly and even in 1938 was only at 88 per cent. The inclusion of subsidies raised the overall index by only a couple of points. Subsidies, however, were important for wheat where the market price remained very low, but the subsidised price approached the pre-crisis level. Between 1932 and 1938, the wheat area in the United Kingdom as a whole expanded from 1.3 million acres to 1.9 million while the area of most other crops declined and the total arable area fell from 13.6 to 13.0 million acres. The most striking result of intervention was a shift in the pattern of food imports away from foreign countries in favour of the Empire. 'By 1938, as compared with 1927–9, total food imports from foreign countries had fallen by 17 per cent in volume, while those coming from the Empire had risen by no less than 43 per cent ... British trade policy ... succeeded in ensuring a larger market for the Empire while bringing total imports down to nearly the level which prevailed before the crisis.'

The overall conclusion, therefore, is that governments in both countries could not insulate their agricultural sector from the international agricultural sector as a whole. Historians seem to have been rather more critical of measures taken in America than in Britain, possibly because rather more public interest was aroused there because of the greater importance of agriculture to the economy as a whole. As so often, historical judgement depends upon an appraisal of the feasibility and correctness of aims proposed. In any appraisal, one must not forget that disequilibrium often occurs between supply and demand in agriculture because of the long time taken for investment decisions to be realised in higher or lower levels of production. Intelligence or knowledge about the market was, and is, often extremely defective. One can say that the measures taken in the 1930s were well-intentioned but not extraordinarily effective. One can only be sympathetic with British and American governments in their difficulties, difficulties which could only have been surmounted by much greater and more determined international co-operation.

Industry

As with agriculture so with industry the years between 1914 and 1939 constituted a period of fluctuation presenting considerable problems to governments, entrepreneurs and workers alike. Yet on any long-term view the period must be counted one of considerable advance, with a substantial rise in overall production and with new technology being introduced at an increasing rate. Technology had both merits and demerits since it connoted progress and yet helped to pose problems of industrial structure in the balance between 'new' and 'old' industries. Structural problems, however, were induced as much by changes in demand as in supply and the general problems of world trade were bound to affect industry. Relative orientation towards home or export markets was an important influence on firms. Equally, changes in technology and in markets affected the size of firms with a tendency to large-scale organisation leading to important new concepts and practices in management. Again, as with agriculture, a changing ethos resulted in a reappraisal of the relations of particular firms or particular industries with the state.

Optimism about industrial progress may seem slightly misplaced in view of the unemployment which occurred in both countries especially after 1929. Yet the rise in national income experienced between 1914 and 1939 was due perhaps as much to production rises in industry as in any other sector. An index of British production compiled by the London and Cambridge Economic Service shows that from an index number of 65 in 1913 and 68 in 1924 there was a rise to 80 in 1929, a fall back to 68 in 1931 and 1932 and then another rise to 105 in 1937 with a slight fall to 100 in 1938.[4] This index included mining and quarrying, manufacturing, building, gas, electricity and water. Trends in America tended to be slightly different with a steeper rise between 1914 and 1929 and greater sluggishness in the 1930s. The indices of industrial production (those of Kuznets and the Federal Reserve Board) show the trends. The first index reveals a fairly steep rise in wartime from 100 in 1914 to 137 in 1918; the second different index shows a rise from 58 in 1921 to 110 in 1929, then a steep fall to 58 in 1932 with a recovery to 113 in 1937 and lower levels at 88 in 1938 and 108 in 1939.[5] As one might expect, these production indices broadly follow trends in the national income.

Nevertheless, overall indices tend to conceal substantial changes in the composition of industry and in the performance of particular industries. Two main considerations arise: firstly, there was the impact of new technology which reflected developments in consumer durable industries and, secondly, the changing balance of the international economy with many different nations undertaking particular kinds of industrial production for the first time. The second feature resulted from two main causes: the relatively short-term though important effects induced by World War I and the more long-term quest of undeveloped nations to achieve a higher standard of living by undertaking new industrial activity. During the war both short- and long-term considerations operated. The short-term effect consisted of a production stimulus for old industries like steel and shipbuilding and for new industries like radio, electrical equipment and aircraft. These influences might lead to substantial benefits in peacetime with consumer appreciation of technical progress resulting in increased demand, or might lead to overproduction and the installation of excess capacity which would be a more or less permanent peacetime disadvantage. The wartime legacy of difficulty for some industries in Britain has led some writers to draw a distinction between old declining industries and new expanding industries. Yet, as Dowie and Alford have insisted, it is a mistake to draw too sharp a contrast between two groups of industries as if they were quite separate features of the economy. There were important linkages between the two groups and even in the 1930s the old industries were still substantial contributors to the economy whether in terms of men employed or of capital invested. It is more realistic to draw attention to the changing balance of industry and to the possible reasons for change.

Among the older industries steel and shipbuilding showed the fluctuations engendered by swings in international demand. Both were inevitably expanded during the war but America was in a far more favourable position to achieve that expansion. The world's production of shipping was twice as great in 1918-19 as in 1913-14, chiefly because of the great increase in American building, and it is likely that the capacity of the world's merchant shipbuilding yards doubled during the war whereas British capacity increased by only 25 per cent. Britain's share of the world's total merchant fleet fell from 39 to 33 per cent. During the fluctuations in international trade in the 1920s and 1930s the British industry was in a difficult position. The change effected by oil burning is shown by the fact that in 1927-30 Britain built 65 per cent of the world's tonnage of steamships but only 41 per cent of the tonnage of motor ships. The industry was very much affected by the world depression and British mercantile tonnage launched fell from just under 1,500,000 in 1930 to 468,000 in 1931 and to only 131,000 in 1933, a year which began with unemployment among insured shipbuilding workers amounting to 63 per cent. If there was some revival in the 1930s the British share of launchings remained much lower than in pre-depression years and in 1936-8 it was only 36 per cent of total world launchings. This decline relative to other countries can be attributed mainly to the autarchic policies pursued by many governments. In spite of change and adjustment in British shipbuilding Britain was in a vulnerable position compared with foreign competitors. Yet shipbuilding was a problem industry in many countries including the United States. Artificial expansion from 5,323,000 tons to 15,997,000 tons under the American flag between 1914 and 1920 brought peacetime difficulties and shipping-line losses were met by government subsidy. In the general atmosphere of expansion and competition of the decade it was not surprising that subsidies should be strongly criticised.

Indeed, it is often forgotten that there were several problem industries in America in the 1920s. Railroads were hit by the new services offered by motor buses and commercial vehicles. Coal experienced a relative decline and its net income shrank steadily from 1.7 per cent of the national income in 1920 to ·73 per cent in 1929, with manpower rising from 639,300 in 1920 to 704,600 in 1923 and then falling to 502,800 in 1929. Cotton textiles and steel also suffered from a mixture of over-capacity, changing national or international demand, and the complexities of technological change. From the gloomy impressions conveyed by contemporary observers it is often assumed that these were industries with special problems primarily because of their export difficulties. Yet both coal and steel showed that the problems were highly complex in each country. This complexity was shown in America by the United States Steel Company. By 1913 US Steel came to dominate the industry in the production of heavy products such as rails, plates and structural shapes. With demand shifting to sheet and strip steel consequent on the relative shift from railroads to automobiles, the old works of US Steel around Pittsburgh became obsolescent. American Rolling Mill became the leader in the continuous rolling process. New plants closer to markets were built by both the National and Republic Companies. At the end of the 1920s US Steel was still a huge firm but its problems showed the painful consequences of economic growth. Steel remained a vital industry, but in servicing newer industries such as aircraft, automobiles, engineering and electricity it had to adapt to a world requiring new qualities and shapes of metal. It was little wonder, therefore, that major reorganisation should be required, especially in Britain where too many small and inefficient firms existed and where steel exports now had to meet the resistance offered by foreign tariffs and cartels. Nevertheless, the final picture of the British steel industry was one of expansion, even if it was accomplished in the end fairly rapidly in the 1930s by the formation of a production and marketing organisation (in the guise of the British Iron and Steel Federation), by substantial government intervention and by the boost given to demand by the rearmament programme.

Coal was equally a problem industry in both countries and was also a complex one. Britain was especially affected by the decline in coal exports with the high point of 98 million tons exported in 1913 falling to 46 millions by 1938. There was conversely an increase in demand for coal for firing electrical generating stations although even in 1938 electricity works consumed only 14.9 million tons out of 227 million tons produced overall in that year. In America 35.1 million short tons were consumed by electric power plants in 1919 and 41.9 million in 1927. If power generation did not bring a great boom to the coal industry in America it was either because of the replacement of coal by petroleum and natural gas or because of greater technical efficiency in producing power which led to economies in the use of fuel. British coal production fell from 287 million tons in 1913 to 267 millions in 1924 and to 227 millions in 1938. In terms of millions of dollars (1954 values) American bituminous coal and lignite production rose from 565 in 1913 to 2,130 in 1920 and then fell to 1,030 in 1927, 407 in 1932 and rose to 864 in 1937. The social and regional problems associated with the difficulties of the coal industry were, especially in Britain, a symbol of the problems of structural adaptation.

That symbol has often been exaggerated by the contrast between coal, an older industry with great incidence of unemployment in the coal-producing regions, and the growth of the new glamour industries. Those glamour industries are symbolised by the 'prosperity decade' of the 1920s in America and usually include motor vehicles, electrical supply and manufacture including radios, chemicals, man-made fibres, petrol and oil, rubber and glassmaking. Changes in the building construction industry and in methods of retail selling sometimes bring those activities into a classification with new developments. Overall, new activities tended to be marked by a high application of technological research, by a substantial increase in the size of firms because of the high degree of capital investment involved and by important changes in industrial location.

Perhaps the most noteworthy industry in terms of its social effects was the motor vehicle industry. It seemed to be the symbol of industrial advance in the America of the 1920s. 'In 1913 462,000 vehicles were sold by all American manufacturers. By 1919 the figure had risen to 1,658,000 and ten years later 4,587,000 were sold. There were some 7,577,000 vehicles registered in 1919; in 1929 there were 26,705,000. By 1925 motor vehicles ranked first among all American industries in value of product.'[6] In Britain production of 34,000 vehicles in 1913 had risen to 95,000 in 1923, became 238,000 in 1929, fell slightly to 226,000 in 1931 and climbed to 511,000 in 1937. The industry's comparative rate of growth in the 1920s in Britain was thus higher than in the 1930s, a feature which applied also to electrical supply and to man-made fibres. Yet many of the new industries were in a relatively early stage of development in Britain by 1929, and most of the technical and organisational advances seem to have been made in America. It is claimed that the radio, motion picture and motor vehicle industries not only dominated the growth sectors of the American economy but altered American life and tastes as well. Yet in a sense some of these growth sectors were still a small section of the economy even if they were growing fast in their own absolute terms. For example, in 1919 electric light and power produced .48 per cent of the American national income and paid .38 per cent of total wages and salaries, whereas in 1929 it produced 1.6 per cent of the national income and paid .84 per cent of the total wages and salaries. In Britain, even if the number of consumers of electricity rose from 730,000 in 1920 to 2,844,000 in 1929 and to 8,920,000 in 1939 there were still substantial pockets in Britain where electricity had not been installed even in 1939. Electricity was important because it went along with a whole range of new consumer tastes and fashions, a feature of the rise of a new high-mass-consumption society which seemed to symbolise America in the 1920s and Britain increasingly in the 1930s.

These developments seemed to be new. Yet as always the question is whether history has not been written by the most articulate sections of the population, those who benefited most from new trends. The warning is important because it highlights the dangers inherent in presenting some tendencies as if they were complete breaks with the past, and in no field is the warning more necessary than in industrial management. America, the business society, can be presented as a contrast with Britain, a more conservative environment, with the implication that America led the field in new ideas. In particular these considerations apply to the Chandler thesis of the multidivisional corporation. The solution to management problems arising in very large firms was to break up the old hierarchical line management into autonomous divisions with central coordination being achieved by some overall policy-making body which rigorously eschewed interference in detailed administrative actions in the divisions. Chandler uses the four case-studies of Du Pont, General Motors, Standard Oil and Sears Roebuck to prove his point.[7] Yet one must be careful in postulating overall generalisations about management since the crucial question arises whether any given management structure is really the cause or effect of a particular firm's economic situation. It can be argued that by 1920 Du Pont and General Motors had become unwieldy because of the proliferation of their activities and that the multi-divisional arrangement was largely a response to their organisational difficulties. In relative terms growth in size of firms was a common feature in both countries and some large firms in Britain such as ICI or Unilever adopted a form of organisation which was in effect multi-divisional. Moreover, Sears Roebuck spent a great deal of effort trying to find a viable form of organisation and during the 1930s adopted a more centralised form of this. Alleged superiority of management ideas did not save American industry from a long period of depression in the 1930s and the response to the situation by management was essentially short-term. Nevertheless, the inter-war years in both America and Britain induced more discussion about management problems even if, as John Child shows, ideas about the social psychology of work were confined to a relatively small body of men in Britain without overmuch influence on works' management practice.[8] Perhaps what was more important was the realisation by managers and entrepreneurs that traditional economic notions were not of much help in the difficult situation confronting them in the early 1930s. Free enterprise solutions to problems did not appear realistic when there seemed no easy way by which the market could be induced to expand. Since scientific methods and rational planning had contributed to productivity in individual firms, there was a case for applying them to a whole industry or even an entire economy. It was against this background that the National Recovery Administration was launched in 1933.

The essential motivation behind the NRA, as it was behind various forms of state intervention in Britain, was the tacit realisation that blockages had occurred in the free market system. In Britain those blockages were apparent immediately after World War I with the emergence of unemployment in the older industries. Yet the feasibility of state intervention was shown by the experience of wartime itself when co-operation between private enterprise and the state achieved production targets. During the inter-war years the debate shifted to the question of the right levels of employment, output and profits. In doing so it became a political question since there was room for disagreement about what those levels should be. The classic example of an industry which became a political question was, of course, the coal industry. Even those who were opposed to full-scale nationalisation of the industry criticised the large number of units and technological backwardness. The dilemmas involved are to be seen in the Coal Mines (Reorganization) Act of 1930 which, passed by a Labour government, attempted to achieve mergers and amalgamations but remained largely a dead letter because of the opposition of employers. It is probable that contemporary opinion was not very sympathetic to coal employers because of their apparent indifference to workers' suffering and because of their obstinate clinging to rights of proprietary possession over mines whose economic viability was suspect. In that sense belief in the play of free market forces was being eroded and it is noteworthy how few economists of fame really sprang to the coalowners' defence. It is equally interesting to note that recent researches on the British coal industry are far more inclined to justify the actions of entrepreneurs of the inter-war years on economic grounds than would have been the case a generation ago. In other words, they are inclined to see a measure of unreality in the debate during the 1930s about the correct role of the state.

The uncertainty about what should be done was equally evident in the steel, shipbuilding and cotton industries. The last two showed the dual features of employers' co-operation to attempt to meet difficulties and of government measures which granted loans and encouraged reorganisation. The British Shipping (Assistance) Act of 1935 and the Cotton Industry (Reorganization) Acts of 1936 and 1939 attempted to minimise competition and to achieve modernisation of equipment. In other words, state intervention in Britain could hardly be imposed from above but rather was effective within the limits of employers' willingness to co-operate. In the steel industry the Scoby-Smith Committee as early as 1918 had spoken of the industry's need for government help. The committee abhorred state management of the industry but pointed to the government's future role as one of providing the right environment within which the industry could effectively operate. The industry itself accomplished significant mergers and amalgamations in the 1920s and one prominent industrialist, Sir William Firth, advocated increased rationalisation and modernisation including a new plant at Redbourn in Lincolnshire. The granting of a tariff on imported iron and steel in 1932, the formation of the British Iron and Steel Federation in 1934 due in large measure to government action, and the existence of a consortium (for investment in steel) headed mainly by the Bank of England necessarily made the industry something of a political issue. Firth's plans for Redbourn were thwarted and on social grounds the new plant was built on a restricted valley site at Ebbw Vale in south Wales. At the same time steel prices during the 1930s remained high behind a tariff wall, and some critics felt that the opportunity to bring down costs through improvement and modernisation was largely lost. Duncan Burn was one writer who expressed the view that Firth was the man to lead the industry to achieve a better structure but that he was frustrated by the industry's old guard who had the ear of government officials and advisers.

In the same way, one might say that NRA in America was a mixed blessing. There were some, like Henry Ford, who remained vigorous exponents of free enterprise, resisting passionately all attempts to enforce the NRA codes. Most employers avoided extreme attitudes and attempted to co-operate even if the whole operation remained controversial. Under the National Recovery Act each industry was both permitted and urged to set up a code authority and to formulate a code of fair competition: the code would usually include fair conditions with respect to output, prices and competition and fair practices concerning wages, hours and conditions of work and collective bargaining. Obviously, the interests served by the NRA codes were essentially those of employers and workers with consumers being left largely out of consideration. By the spring of 1935 the NRA was widely criticised and friction between entrepreneurs in many industries had grown. Some critics opposed the extension of the National Industrial Recovery Administration after June 1935 but the issue was settled in May of that year when the Supreme Court declared the NRA unconstitutional in the Schlechter Case. Yet although the NRA was under attack, some of its functions were transferred to other government agencies and its provisions were important for labour relations and for the oil and bituminous-coal industries. In one sense it was a relatively short-lived experiment and it is hardly surprising if judgements about its usefulness have differed widely. Roosevelt himself stressed the short-term aim of promoting recovery and Schumpeter emphasised the improvement in business morale. Nevertheless, optimism faded as recovery proved slow to appear and it was probable that code provisions limiting plant use, production, and expansion of capacity served to limit employment and income. Caution was the order of the day.

Hence because of the hostility or lukewarm approach of employers, state intervention in America was tentative and liable to failure. Despite much controversy, intervention can still be seen as more constructive and positive in Britain. The infant airline system owed much to government subsidy, and the creation of Imperial Airways in 1924 with government backing showed an appreciation of the flaws in private enterprise philosophy in a new high-technology industry. Equally, the creation of the British Dyestuffs Corporation during World War I and the blessing given to its fusion into ICI in 1926 as well as the creation of the sugar-beet industry in 1925 were attempts to promote activities in which Britain was defective. As early as 1923 the government intervened in the cotton industry by levying 6d per bale to continue the finance of the Empire Cotton Growing Corporation which had been established to reduce dependence on outside cotton. It may be argued that the setting up of the Tennessee Valley Authority in America was equally a positive attempt at industrial development but it did not come until 1937 and was the only project accomplished among a dozen or so envisaged. The evidence suggests that in spite of the difficulties of mental adaptation industrialists learned to live with 'a mixed economy' in Britain sooner than they did in America.

The Industrial Labour Force

It was only to be expected that rapid changes in the fortunes of the economies as a whole would be reflected in the fortunes of the industrial labour force. Labour historians are apt to see the years from 1914 to 1939 as a period of wartime gains with erosion after it. The inter-war years are seen as a period of ebb and flow in the struggle between employer and employed with trade unions being involved in the traumatic experience of the General Strike of 1926 and struggling to avoid the possibility of punitive measures afterwards. In America the prosperity of the 1920s brought little need for forceful action by trade unions but the experience of the depression and the need for reappraisal of labour's position in the 1930s led to changes both in the law and in more militant action by the unions. Yet just as before 1914 the traditional picture of the institutional fortunes of the industrial labour force needs to be tempered by an appreciation of the way in which those fortunes corresponded with the deeper social and economic changes which underlay them.

One of those deeper trends was a rising standard of living. Most interpretations of the period agree that wages and income per head grew during the period. Rising money wages were noticeable during the war and after. Phelps Brown gives money wage-earnings in 1924 compared with 1913 as 193 per cent for the United Kingdom and 213 per cent for the United States. It may be true that in Britain real wages between 1914 and 1917 declined because prices rose faster than wages, but by the mid-twenties the situation was upward for those who were in employment. According to Paul Douglas, the average annual earnings of employed wage earners in the United States in terms of constant purchasing power (1914 = 100) stood at 8 per cent above the base year in 1921, 13 per cent above in 1922, and 19 per cent above in 1923. Real wages also rose in Britain although the rise was fitful, downward between 1920 and 1924 and then upward to produce a rise of possibly 10 per cent in real wages during the 1920s. The depression of 1929-33 clearly had a marked effect in America and Phelps Brown shows how, among five countries, it was in Germany and the USA that money wage-earnings fell most from their average of 1925-9. The level of money wage-earnings was 71 per cent in the USA and 95 per cent in the United Kingdom in 1932 as compared with 1929. Since wages were stagnant in America in the 1930s, a decade when they rose substantially in Britain, the rise in real wages was faster in Britain during the inter-war years as a whole. Two sets of figures given by Phelps Brown are as follows: (1) between 1920 and 1938 the average annually compounded rate of rise of wage-earnings in composite units of consumables was 1.37 per cent for the United Kingdom and 1.25 per cent for the United States; (2) the average annually cumulated percentage change in real wages was 1.68 per cent for the United Kingdom (1924-38) and 0.65 per cent for the United States (1920-38). These figures are in some contrast with those for 1895-1913 when real wages in Britain tended to fall. Nevertheless, they tally with the statistics on productivity which show that the depression experienced in America was so marked that, in spite of the rise occurring there in the 1920s, the subsequent depression was so severe that the overall rise from the end of 1923 to the end of 1938 was very small. One estimate is that the average annually compounded rates of rise of real national income per occupied person between 1923 and 1938 were 1.8 per cent in the United Kingdom and 0.2 per cent in the United States.

No doubt the figures are subject to caution since they are complicated by unemployment and by working hours. There is also the fact that the United States made up ground very sharply between 1939 and 1941. Nevertheless, even if they are explained to a significant extent by general economic trends they still raise the question whether wages were not safeguarded from more drastic falls during the 1920s and the depression by superior trade union organisation in Britain. Did the relative weakness of American trade unions prove a long-term disability during the period? The question how far trade unions were important in influencing earnings is difficult, but there are pointers to show how union action corresponded with broader social trends to produce wage rises.

Firstly, union action coincided with a growing appreciation of the importance of manpower in the economy. During the war it was possibly the other way round with wartime circumstances making it necessary for governments and employers to consult and to co-operate with unions. Nevertheless, it is possible to exaggerate the degree of power actually gained by unions in Britain during the war. The 'Shells and Fuses' agreement of March 1915 demanded sacrifices from engineering unions in their consent to using unskilled labour including women to do work hitherto reserved to skilled men. The Munitions of War Act of July 1915 gave the government enormous powers over the munitions industry and its workers. Yet the reality of the situation demanded more conciliatory gestures than a display of force, particularly in view of the hostile attitudes shown by Clydeside engineering workers and south Wales miners in 1915 and 1916. It was partly the realisation of the importance of union and Labour party co-operation which led Lloyd George late in 1916 to invite three Labour MPs to become government ministers. Pelling believes that these appointments did not prevent industrial unrest but helped to keep it within bounds. George Barnes, Minister of Labour at the time, believed that there were 'psychological' conditions causing unrest which included beliefs of inequality of sacrifice, the breaking of government pledges, the unreliability of union officials and the general atmosphere of uncertainty. This atmosphere of change was given a new twist by the occurrence of the Russian Revolution in 1917 which was to be the occasion for the creation of many myths – both left-wing and right-wing – for a decade or more to come. Since the Coalition government of 1918 was dominated by the Conservatives and since the tone of industrial relations was determined largely by dealings between the government and the workers directly under its control, the situation was a fluid one. It was, perhaps, a determination not to be forced into too easy an acquiescence of unfavourable terms which led the miners to be as stubborn as they were. Two royal commissions, the Sankey Commission of 1919 and the Samuel Commission of 1925, which went into the organisation and conditions of the coal industry in some detail, were both appointed against the impending background of a miners' strike. The militancy of miners in Britain between 1919 and 1926 was legion and it is a major problem to explain why the miners should have come in those years to dominate British trade union politics. While there were certainly the usual arguments about wage levels, hours and working conditions there was also a background of questioning of the old order of hierarchy and power in industry which became more pervasive. Since miners seemed to have taken the lead in this questioning, for they had substantial representation in Parliament by the criterion of Labour MPs with links with any one industry, they provided a symbol of social change and aspiration to a fairer distribution of wealth. It is not controversial that the General Strike of 1926 was occasioned largely by the problems of the mining industry and that the response of workers in other industries who were called out on strike by the General Council of the TUC was virtually total. All the features of the period up to 1926 suggest an economy and society in considerable convulsion over the direction and purpose of social and industrial change. In that sense the miners seemed to represent a progressive social force, yet at the same time the economic basis of their arguments was profoundly conservative. In seeking to keep up wage levels in an industry whose export markets were seriously weakening, they were tending to fly in the face of the facts. The paradoxes of the situation were scarcely appreciated at the time.

A possible line of argument is that in any event the broad features of trade union action and organisation in a free market economy will reflect the general ethos of the business and industrial environment in which it operates. Whereas in Britain industry was uncertain of its balance and its direction, in America the main lines of advance in the 'prosperity decade' of the 1920s seemed to be well defined. There was an incentive for unions to co-operate with employers since the trend of wages was upwards. The theory of a high-wage economy was taken up by some businessmen, not least Henry Ford. Yet the picture overall was hardly one of enlightened action but rather of the hostility of public opinion against unions, which made it difficult often enough for unions to press their claims. Even if wartime membership increased, bringing AFL membership to 4,078,000 in January 1920 and, together with 1,032,000 members in other unions, the total membership of unions to 5,110,000, that situation was not to last for long. Firstly, there was a drive against left-wing unions and one verdict is that by 1924 'for all practical purposes the IWW was dead, victim of the most systematic campaign of extermination in American history'.[9] Secondly, in 1920 the 'American Plan' was launched to restore allegedly traditional rights, among which was the right of every American to accept employment under conditions satisfactory to himself without interference from a union business agent. Lastly, the leadership of the AFL tended to be conservative. It was true that John L. Lewis, President of the United Mine Workers, challenged Gompers's re-election to be AFL president in 1921 and received one-third of the votes cast, a show of support which alarmed AFL leaders. Nevertheless, with the death of Gompers in 1924 the new president, William Green, had to contend with the conservative reaction to labour in the Coolidge period, loss of effective control in some industries and the general hostility of government and the courts. In this situation membership of the AFL remained fairly static in spite of growth in the occupied labour force as a whole. Overall union membership declined from 3,600,000 in 1924 to 3,400,000 in 1930 while AFL membership dropped to 2,770,000 in 1930. Nevertheless, it would be an exaggeration to describe labour as completely quiescent in the 1920s. There were obviously great differences between various industries and strikes occurred in the older industries of coal and textiles. Discontent in the coal industry, as in Britain, reflected the relative economic difficulties of the industry. With demand for coal declining, there were closures of 3,300 bituminous-coal mines between 1923 and 1929 and some 250,000 men lost their jobs in consequence. Additionally, rapid advances in technical efficiency led to hardship for those workers made redundant.

Yet the contrast of the 1920s obscure the fact that between the wars in both countries the underlying trend was a search for a new definition of the place of unions in modern industrial society. Although employers in both countries might seek at times to discredit organised labour, the problems involved in the organisation of large numbers of men in large-scale industries could not be resolved by slogans or by simple political formulas. In that sense the long-term significance of the General Strike in Britain might well be considered the generation of new attitudes to industrial problems despite the apparent victory of the Conservative government of the day in defeating the strike and in spite of the apparently punitive clauses of the Trade Disputes Act of 1927. The act contained clauses declaring sympathetic strike action illegal, and the contracting-in clauses reduced the Labour party's income from trade union affiliation fees by a third since the party lost the subscriptions of those who did not bother to contract in but who had not previously bothered to contract out. Nevertheless, the clauses against sympathetic strikes were never invoked and informal contacts were made between businessmen and union leaders partly as a result of the Mond-Turner talks which took place in 1928 and 1929. Mond was the chairman of ICI and Ben Turner the chairman in 1928 of the TUC General Council. The 1930s thus became a decade of what Pelling has described as 'sturdy constitutionalism'. Between 1934 and 1939 the number of working days lost as a result of disputes only once exceeded 2 million whereas between 1919 and 1926 it had never been less than 7 million. This moderate approach meant that the TUC took a cautious attitude to the problem of unemployment for fear of becoming involved in left-wing agitation. As was to be expected from the general economic trends of the time, membership of unions in older industries like coal and textiles declined absolutely even if in those industries the proportion of members to the total work force remained much the same. Problems arose in expanding industries like motor vehicles where demarcation problems arose between unions. Nevertheless, the Amalgamated Engineering Union between 1933 and 1939 and the Electrical Trades Union between 1929 and 1939 doubled their membership. General unions grew considerably and by 1937 the Transport and General Workers Union was larger than the Miners Federation with a membership of 654,510 which made it the largest union in Britain. The General and Municipal Workers Union increased its membership from 269,357 in 1934 to 467,318 in 1939. Overall, the approach to the problems of the 1930s brought about a good deal of employer-worker dialogue and it can be argued that, in a situation where the main influences causing average wages to rise were the general economic trends of recovery, the unions had little to gain by being recalcitrant.

Except for particular unions or left-wing groups in the 1920s recalcitrance was not a general feature of the labour scene in America. Yet the coming of the depression and the general questioning of economic and social organisation which occurred during the depression decade of the 1930s led to a fundamental reappraisal of the place of unions in American life. The plight of the unemployed and the decline in income of those who remained in work were causes of an increasing disillusionment with the working of a free market economy. After all, by March 1933 unemployment was estimated at more than 12 million workers, a phenomenal figure which was bound to raise questions. One estimate is that between 1929 and 1933 labour income declined from $51 million to $26 million, a fall of 48 per cent. Already in 1932 increasing sympathy with the cause of labour and an appreciation of its vulnerability to employer pressure was shown with the enactment of the Norris-La Guardia Act. The act showed congressional recognition of the fact that under prevailing conditions the individual worker was unable to protect his freedom of labour. The courts were denied the right to issue injunctions which would uphold 'yellow-dog' contracts or prevent the joining of unions. Nevertheless, in the period of depression in which the act was passed it did little to improve unions' bargaining power. That point was shown by the experience of labour in the aftermath of the National Industrial Recovery Act of June 1933. That act contained clauses especially designed to safeguard labour in Section 7 (a). It provided that every individual code made under the act must allow workers the right to organise and bargain collectively through their own chosen representatives and to be free from interference or coercion by employers. After the act was passed there was a revival of labour unionism, particularly among unions like the United Mine Workers and the United Textile Workers. Unionism appeared among unskilled and semi-skilled workers. Nevertheless, industrialists resisted the principle of Section 7 (a) of the act and some firms prohibited union organisation while others formed company unions. Between 1933 and 1935 some 400 company unions were created. Complaints from unions became vocal and although a National Labor Board was appointed by government in August 1933 to be replaced by a National Labor Relations Board, it was felt that big business virtually had its own way. When the act was declared unconstitutional in May 1935 a new solution was called for. It came in the Wagner Act (after its sponsor Senator Robert F. Wagner) or National Labor Relations Act which was passed in July 1935. The passage of the act, which had first been sponsored in 1934 with President Roosevelt showing a somewhat hostile attitude to it at that stage, revealed that the government had come to understand that labour's right to organise was only theoretical in the face of management's hostility. The act provided for a new National Labor Relations Board of three experts empowered to enforce the right of employees to join a union. The board was given power to prohibit unfair employer practices. Nevertheless, even if industry remained hostile, the years 1936 and 1937 have to be considered as marking victories for labour. This was so because public opinion was swayed by the revelations of the La Follette Civil Liberties Committee during those years. The committee found that the use of labour spies, of systematic denunciation of labour leaders, of propaganda campaigns to promote law and order and of weapons adapted for use in disputes such as submachine guns, tear gas and grenades, had all taken place. Both as a result of changing public opinion and of the Supreme Court's decision in April 1937 in the case of the National Labor Relations Board v Jones & Laughlin Steel Company something of a revolution occurred in management-labour relations. Yellow-dog contracts, black lists and other forms of discrimination were outlawed. Labour spies, anti-union propaganda and company unionism effectively became features of the past. At the same time, the emergence of the Committee (afterwards Congress) for Industrial Organization under the leadership of John L. Lewis created a breakaway organisation from the AFL and since it organised successful strikes in the steel and automobile industries in 1937 it can be said to have made union organisation more dynamic.

In 1939 when the war began in Europe there were still many employers both in Britain or America who had not fully accepted the unions' place in collective bargaining arrangements. Nevertheless, the bitterness and suffering experienced by workers in the 1920s and 1930s had not been without their effect on many features of industrial management. There was an overall feeling that the worst forms of punitive employer attitudes in the past must be avoided. The productivity in high-capital-intensive industries meant that the importance of the contribution by workers was more fully appreciated. Changes in social attitudes and changes in the structure of industry reinforced each other. Union activity can be seen largely as a reflection of these broader trends, trends which tended to benefit workers unless industrialists could exert enough power to prevent workers' gains. Hence in a defensive role the unions' activity was still crucial.

CHAPTER NINE

FINANCE AND MARKETS, 1914–39

International Trade and Tariffs

It has been implicit in previous sections that monetary and institutional difficulties prevailing between the wars were associated with serious problems in the flow of international trade. The question is to know to what extent trading difficulties arose from institutional difficulties – monetary arrangements, tariffs and so on – and to what extent trade was impaired by maladjustment arising from changes induced by World War I. As we have seen, world over-production of certain items like steel and ships brought problems for Britain. Over-production of food – especially wheat – brought problems for the United States. The balance of international trade was upset by the war but between the wars it was impossible to restore the prewar balance of trade and the search for a new balance was slow and painful.

The problem was thus essentially one of establishing some new kind of international trading structure to take account of the diminishing importance of Britain and the increasing importance of America, Japan and other nations. Unfortunately, shifts in relative trading importance were not fully appreciated until late in the period and this lack of understanding was shown in the commercial policies of the United States. Once the restocking boom of 1919–21 was over and the possibility of severe international competition emerged, the United States imposed the Fordney-McCumber tariff in 1922 with import duties generally higher than in any previous American measures. Both France and Germany imposed tariffs in the 1920s, the emphasis of policy being to prevent American imports with their threat to French and German farming. Even Britain, still nominally wedded to free trade, had in practice developed policy changes through the Safeguarding of Industries Act in

1921 with its important protection for new industries such as motor vehicles, dyestuffs and the like. Hence one may accuse some of the countries involved of 'economic nationalism', but accusations do not help one to arrive at a satisfactory interpretation of what was actually happening. Tariffs may be seen also as helpful braking mechanisms to stop abrupt changes in supply and demand conditions from being abnormally harmful. At times of sudden shifts in demand or supply, established trading interests may well try to hold the position as before.

In the light of these considerations the vicissitudes of the international economy become understandable. Between 1919 and 1925 the position was abnormally uncertain because of the need to adjust from wartime to peacetime conditions with restocking and reorganisation being important considerations; then between 1925 and 1929 with Britain's return to gold the international economy ran more smoothly and during those four or five years the quantum of world trade increased by some 20 per cent. This increase in trade during the later 1920s was in line with a world rise in industrial production of between 23 and 27 per cent. From this viewpoint the performance of Britain and America was not quite in line with world trends. In terms of total gold, silver and merchandise exports and imports there was a sharp drop in American exports between 1919 and 1921 from $8,528 to $4,560 million; then from 1921 to 1925 the position was fairly stable, but the latter year of 1925 saw some improvement to $5,272 million. Until 1929 the rise in exports was not spectacular but in 1928 a high point was reached for the inter-war period at $5,776 million and in 1929 the level was $5,441 million. Between 1921 and 1929 imports followed a similar trend to exports but there was always a surplus of exports over imports, 1928 being the highest year with an excess of $1,448 million. Britain's performance was even less exciting. Once again 1919–21 was an abnormal period with the high level of imports of 1919 and 1920 at £1,464 and £1,749 million being brought down to £987 million in 1921. Physical exports running at £822 million in 1921 rose to £940 million in 1925, then fell to £790 million in 1926 (the year of the General Strike) and were stable in 1927, 1928 and 1929 at £839, £853 and £848 million respectively. Britain's modest benefit from the upturn in world trade in the 1920s came mainly from invisible exports which rose from £250 million in 1922 to £362 million in 1929. Except for 1926 when there was a small deficit of £15 million there were modest surpluses in the balance of payments ranging from £47 million in 1925 to £173 million in 1923. The two late-decade years of 1928 and 1929 saw surpluses of £123 and £103 million respectively.[1] This performance meant that Britain's share of total world exports declined from 13.9 per cent in 1913 to 10.8 per cent in 1929. Perhaps even more disquieting was the comparison between the rise in volume of world exports of 27 per cent between 1913 and 1929 and that of Britain's exports which fell by 19 per cent in the same period.

A great deal of British writing has concentrated on Britain's vulnerability in terms both of products and markets. The important prewar exports goods were declining sectors of world trade and a fair proportion of her exports went to primary producing countries whose incomes were easily hit. Nevertheless, too much should not be made of particular factors in a highly complex situation. As we have seen, American performance in the 1920s was not remarkably buoyant and in the 1930s British performance was rather more creditable than that of America. Part of the difficulty for both countries was that rapidly changing technology brought both a demand for new products and substantial alterations in the markets for old products. Beyond a certain level there was high elasticity of demand for some products. Thus American exports of automobiles, including engines and parts, were valued at $84 million in 1921 and became $541 million by 1929; they fell to $76 million in 1932, recovered to $347 million in 1937 and finished the decade in 1939 at $254 million. This highly volatile performance in a new industry urges caution about easy assumptions that the nature of the overseas trading problem remained unchanged throughout the two decades.

The differences in performance both for Britain and America between the 1920s and the 1930s suggest that in spite of difficulties over tariffs and international monetary arrangements the reorganisation of an international trading system proceeded not too badly in the 1920s. The world economic depression of 1929–33 created a different scale of difficulty. The problem is to know whether causality lay from the monetary situation (with a breakdown in business confidence due to financial factors) to the general economic situation, or whether increasing maladjustments in the trading situation were already causing difficulties quite apart from monetary factors. The statistics of British and American exports suggest that apart from a few items where export demand was inelastic there was a sharp fall in export levels between 1929 and 1931–2. Thus American unmanufactured leaf tobacco exports fell in value only from $146 to $110 million between 1929 and 1931. Fruits and nuts equally held up well. American unmanufactured cotton remained fairly stable in quantities exported (3,982 to 3,667 million lb) but falling price levels meant a drop in value from $771 to $326 million between 1929 and 1931. Automobiles, petroleum and related products, iron and steel mill products, and machinery – all experienced severe falls. Exports of machinery, for example, fell from $604 to $131 million between 1929 and 1932. Richardson has suggested that falls in British exports were not so catastrophic partly because the previous sluggishness of those exports meant that something nearer a floor in demand had been reached, yet the fall in visible exports and re-exports from £848 million in 1929 to £422 million in 1932 was serious enough. Even more serious for Britain was the sharp decline in invisible earnings which fell from £362 million in 1929 to £166 million in 1932. This decline was a reflection of the general decline in world trade. It was this inability of invisibles to perform their traditional function of covering the deficit on the balance of trade which led Britain to run fairly continuous deficits in her balance of payments in the 1930s. The largest was a deficit of £105 million in 1931 and the other large ones were £51 million in 1932, £56 million in 1937 and £54 million in 1938. It has been argued that this deficit in the balance of payments was the price paid for a recovery in the home market and in domestic manufacturing where any upturn was bound to suck in imports given Britain's insufficiency in raw materials. Import levels were lower in the 1930s than in the 1920s but apart from the high years of 1937 and 1938 (£945 and £846 million respectively) they were running between 1931 and 1936 at levels between £618 (1933) and £780 million (1936) which were some £350–400 million lower than the levels of 1924–9. Granted that at these lower levels expressed in value terms there was not a corresponding fall in quantities imported because of Britain's improving terms of trade, the fall in imports was still relatively substantial and suggests that the real impact of 'economic nationalism' (if expressed simply as a policy of reducing imports as far as possible) was considerably more effective from the beginning of 1932.

Nevertheless, the proportionate fall in British imports was minor compared with the substantial falls registered in the United States where merchandise imports fell from a level of $4,399 million in 1929 to levels of $1,323 million in 1932 and of $2,047 million in 1935. The high American import point was in 1937 at $3,084 million. American exports fell in corresponding fashion although America continued to register a surplus on her merchandise trade. It has often been held that America's reduction of imports was an important obstacle to any major improvement in world trade because of the repercussions which it induced, those countries which exported to America being unable to earn sufficient to buy their own imports from the rest of the world. Yet were the blockages induced by tariffs alone or by monetary factors? One of the important features of the period 1934–40 was the enormous inflow of gold into the United States. This was because, with an undervalued dollar from mid-1933, export surpluses and payments due to America were not offset by capital movements and the balance had to be paid for in gold. It is estimated that 'for the seven-year depression period, gold flowed into the United States in the astronomical amount of nearly $15 billion'.[2]

In this situation the greatly reduced levels of trade persuaded the American government to attempt a remedy by pursuing a policy of 'freer world trade' associated from 1934 with Cordell Hull, Secretary of State. The policy consisted largely of arranging trade agreements with America's principal trading buyers and sellers. This was done by securing the passage of the Trade Agreements Act in 1934 which empowered the president to enter into trade agreements with foreign countries for the reciprocal reduction of tariffs and other trade restrictions. By 1938 Cordell Hull had succeeded in bringing some 60 per cent of the total foreign trade of America into the scope of trade agreements. Yet in view of the much lower levels of American trade – both imports and exports – in the 1930s compared with the 1920s, the success of the policy was doubtful. Some would argue that the level of American exports could have been increased only if America had been willing to allow substantial external credits to stimulate trade. Yet if one assumes that the low levels of international trade were due to a general lack of confidence and to maladjustments in the international economy then the extent to which any one country could unilaterally alter the situation was problematic.

From this point of view the fundamental change of commercial policy adopted by Britain from 1932 onwards appears more as a response to world trends than any very thoroughgoing attempt to alter the balance of trade in Britain's favour. To contemporaries the abandonment of the policy of free trade which had been a tenet of faith since 1846 could appear as a major change, yet the fact was that the issue of protection which had seemed so profoundly controversial in 1923-4 seemed to be unavoidable by 1931-2. The abandonment of free trade came in stages with an emergency levy late in 1931 to check the flow of imports and a general 10 per cent *ad valorem* tariff in 1932 on all imports except food and some raw materials. Higher duties were possible on the recommendation of the Import Duties Advisory Committee. Late in 1932 a scheme of imperial preference was arranged at Ottawa. Whereas in 1930 some 83 per cent of imports had come in free of duty, after Ottawa the percentage was about 25 per cent. Recent opinion suggests that overall the imposition of tariffs made little difference since protection came after the worst losses in exports had been sustained. A great deal clearly depended on relative elasticities of demand of goods imported and of the ability of particular countries to pursue retaliation. Nevertheless, particular industries like iron and steel which had been heavily affected by imports before 1932 had a basis for recovery, and the cutting of imports might stimulate confidence in protected industries. The tariff might also be useful as a bargaining counter especially with areas like Europe where trading conditions were especially difficult. The system of imperial preference erected at Ottawa seems to have benefited the Dominions more than Britain and, while Britain became more dependent on the Empire for exports, most Dominions except Australia reduced their dependence on Britain as a supplier.

Overall, the experience of Britain and America in relation to overseas trade seems to have been one in which their own ability to remedy the situation was subject to severe limitations. It was, of course, true that mistakes were made and there would probably be few defenders today of the Hawley-Smoot tariff of 1930 and of the undervaluation of the dollar in 1934, not at least from the viewpoint of their impact on the international economy. The truth was that the international economy had become more complex even before 1914 and was increasing in complexity all the time. Even between them Britain and

America accounted for only about 25 per cent of world trade in the 1930s. While this proportion was not unimportant a great deal depended on the attitudes and policies of other countries. It was only by a much greater degree of international co-operation than existed, that the international economy could function more effectively and it is doubtful whether greater co-operation could have been achieved given the outlook of the time.

International Finance

One aspect of the inter-war economy which has occasioned major controversy is that of finance. Britain's policy of deflation between 1919 and 1925 leading to a return to gold in the latter year, her abandonment of the gold standard in 1931 and the subsequent series of national devaluations in the 1930s, have been seen as a saga of international monetary breakdown. Not until the Bretton Woods Conference of 1944 with the decisions to create the International Monetary Fund and the so-called World Bank were new arrangements made to remedy the situation. Opinion among economists is still divided over interpretations of the inter-war situation. How far could different monetary policies have been carried out? What were the effects of the policies which were pursued?

Britain's 'gold standard policy' of 1918-31 became controversial only in the course of time. That controversy, stimulated although by no means created by Keynes, centred round the issues applicable mainly to the domestic situation in Britain, especially the effects of monetary policy on prices of British exports and hence on the employment situation in depressed export industries. Yet the essential point about the policy was that it was an attempt to restore an international monetary system which was believed to have worked well before 1914. Probably historians would now be less optimistic about pre-1914 arrangements than the members of the Cunliffe Committee (appointed in January 1918 to consider the post-war monetary situation), and would point to indications that the system could not last indefinitely in the form it had assumed around 1900. Both in 1893 and in 1907 – especially the latter year – the resources of the Bank of England were severely stretched in dealing with financial crises centred largely on the United States. In retrospect it is astonishing how small the Bank of

England's gold reserves were – some £30 million or so – to sustain a complex international mechanism. As with so many financial systems, the essence of the operation was confidence and, as long as there was general confidence in Britain's ability to act as the centre of the world's money market, gold would flow freely in and out of London. What is in doubt is how long Britain could continue to be the world's leading creditor and exporter of capital; sooner or later other countries, especially the United States, would have to assume more of that burden, as they were beginning to do just before 1914, in order to provide international liquidity. Moreover the degree of automatic adjustment of the exchanges to gold was much overemphasised and with hindsight one can see a good deal of 'management' in the system.

The merit of the arguments of Keynes lay in drawing attention to the potential defects of the prewar system and to the relevance of those defects to the situation after the war. Britain's assets were much depleted even if she was still an overall creditor, and since the United States had emerged as the leading international creditor there would have to be much greater co-operation between the two countries which would entail an international outlook which the United States did not seem sufficiently to possess. Yet, as Moggridge has pointed out, the Cunliffe Committee assumed throughout that Britain would return to the gold standard at the prewar par and there was no questioning of the assumption by committee members. Nevertheless, the committee knew that the task would be neither quick nor easy to accomplish.

The difficulty lay partly in immediate postwar uncertainties, especially those of the American economy. Yet by the end of 1922 with the exchange rate at $4.63½, much higher than the low point of $3.40 in February 1920, the possibility of serious consideration of a return to par emerged. The authorities decided to wait upon events because of various continuing uncertainties, especially war debts and reparations questions which upset the exchanges. The probable course of the dollar exchanges was also problematic. Hence a policy of waiting continued early in 1924 and official opinion on the desirability of a return was formed in a series of discussions commencing in March 1924. The correspondence of Benjamin Strong, governor of the Federal Reserve Bank of New York showed that the acceptance of the Dawes Plan for dealing with the problem of

German reparations would remove a major hurdle. Governor Strong was in close touch with Montagu Norman, governor of the Bank of England, and it was clear that American official opinion was in favour of Britain's return to gold as soon as possible. Sterling rose on the exchanges after October 1924 and the time seemed ripe for a return in April 1925.

There seem to have been four main elements in the decision: (1) the lack of any widespread influential opposition and the unanimity of business, financial and political opinion; (2) the apparent disappearance of public antagonism to it; (3) the rise in the dollar exchange in late 1924 which meant that the additional adjustments to achieve parity were small; and (4) the belief that benefits would accrue in terms of trade and employment once the restored system brought smoother flows in international currency transactions. This last point is important since it shows a realisation that Britain with her widely spread commerce could make a substantial improvement of her own trade only within the context of an improvement in world trade as a whole. Opponents of the decision stress that an over-valued pound raised the prices of British exports in world markets and was thus an impediment to export recovery. The whole argument over Britain's trade performance depends, in fact, on how far demand for British exports was price elastic. Since export difficulties of a serious kind had already arisen before 1925 and since it is not hard to show the export market problems existing for coal, textiles, iron and steel and other items, it is likely that those who blame monetary policy virtually alone for Britain's export ills are overstating their case.

Nevertheless, there was surely an element of complacency in the situation. Those who advised the return to gold seem to have been exclusively concerned with sterling in its relation to gold and the dollar and not sufficiently with the importance, or potential importance, of France and Germany in trade and finance. Over-valuation of sterling might affect British businessmen's confidence. In any event, Britain's balance of payments' position was much weaker than before the war and deposits could be attracted into London only by relatively high interest rates. There was also some under-estimate of the amount of 'hot money' which might upset the situation by its sudden movements.

The complacency, however, was general. Alternative policies were not widely canvassed and most of the discussion seems to have centred round how and when Britain should return to gold rather than whether she should do so at all. Alternative long-term policies received little debate and half a century later much of the writing of Keynes in the 1920s seems to have been concerned more with negative points of criticism than with important alternatives. With the acceptance of Keynes's general views on economic policy as expressed in the *General Theory* of 1936 there has been a tendency to accept rather too readily his strictures on monetary policy in the 1920s. If his criticisms warned against complacency those criticisms applied with particular force to America, France, Belgium and all those other countries which tended to assume rather too readily that Britain's return to gold automatically meant a return to better trading conditions.

Yet if complacency begets confidence it may be justified. The return to gold was an event of international importance and was an important background to the expansion of world trade occurring between 1925 and 1929. Yet London was no longer such an important financial centre that it was automatically regarded as the most important money market. New York rivalled London, a feature which was to become apparent with the American stock market boom of 1928 when, with the easy money policy then operating, short-term funds flowed into the United States. The buoyant conditions of 1925–9 also saw a good deal of short-term money being deposited in Germany. Hence London found some difficulty in maintaining reserves at an adequate level and interest rates remained relatively high.

The test of the system came with the depression of 1929–30 and with the financial crisis of 1931. Confidence was obviously affected in the winter of 1929–30 but monetary flows outwards from Germany were counteracted by deflation on the part of the authorities and central bankers were clearly concerned not to allow the position to deteriorate. Declining confidence, however, meant that 'hot money' could become excessively unstable. In the event, instability did not become a major problem until the middle months of 1931. A major new wave of financial uncertainty was begun by the difficulties of the Austrian bank Credit Anstalt in April, which started an assault on the German Reichsbank. Then in July the movement spread to London, partly as a result of the revelations of the May Committee that the British government was possibly running into deficit. By

September the losses of gold reserves were so heavy that on 21 September Britain went off gold.

During the financial crisis central bankers certainly endeavoured to co-operate. Assistance, including that of the Bank of England, was given both to the Credit Anstalt and to the Reichsbank. Towards the end of August the British government obtained credits in Paris and New York amounting to £80 million but these were exhausted within just over two weeks. Youngson believes that there is no evidence that Britain had overlent abroad. To him the situation required a financial centre of enormous strength to maintain liquidity and confidence and London was clearly not such a centre. Internationally the event was disastrous and constituted a setback to international co-operation, giving rise to a new bout of economic nationalism to which British, French and German tariffs bore witness. One may argue that international co-operation was already in ruins before the summer of 1931 but it would be more correct to say that national governments had not appreciated how great the need for co-operation was if the monetary system were to remain intact. There were many villains of the piece or none according to one's viewpoint.

From an international viewpoint a major problem of the 1930s was the lack of international liquidity. This lack of liquidity obliged debtor countries to export, and receiving countries replied with tariffs since the arrival of imports increased unemployment and whittled away foreign exchange. The situation merely highlighted the underlying maladjustments in the balance of world trade. Yet it also showed up the basic differences in the internal financial position of Britain and the United States. Their different financial history was one of the many aspects of paradox in the 1930s.

Once Britain was relieved of the burden of maintaining strong reserves there was no reason why she should maintain high interest rates. The logical consequence of the abandonment of gold was the inauguration of 'cheap money'. A major step in the operation was the conversion of the 5 per cent War Loan to a 3½ per cent basis, the importance of this step being that the War Loan amounted early in 1932 to over a quarter of the total national debt. Interest rates were already falling and the government followed them down. By the end of 1932 general interest rates were of the order of 2 per cent and stayed at that level for much of the decade. Some have seen cheap money as an inherent factor in Britain's recovery in the 1930s. Once again the problem is to distinguish cause and effect. Did cheap money engender recovery or vice versa? Nevertheless, once Britain left gold she had to be careful of managing the pound in such a way as not to repeat the history of German inflation of 1919–23. There was no large-scale expansion of money and from April 1932 the Exchange Equalisation Account operated to fix desirable rates of gold to sterling and hence of sterling to any currency linked to gold. By 1933 with the American bank collapse and with difficulties in other countries sterling was once again considered a worthwhile currency and holders of capital returned deposits to London.

This relatively fortunate experience of Britain was not followed by America. Although America remained on gold until 1933 foreign banks in America and holders of wealth were uneasy and transferred funds abroad. Although American gold reserves were high the New York Federal Reserve Bank raised the rediscount rate in order to raise general interest rates with the aim of stopping the outward flow of gold. At a time when business confidence was low because of the downturn in the economy in 1931–2 this action had an adverse effect since nothing was done to stop the decline in reserves of member banks in the Federal Reserve system. With the third great wave of banking failures occurring early in 1933 the money supply in June 1933 dropped by 30 per cent from the figure of June 1929. When Roosevelt came to power in March 1933 banking reform was clearly one priority but an attempt was made to deal with the gold situation. In March 1933 restrictions were placed on gold and foreign exchange dealings. On 5 April 1933 the order was given for all holders of gold to deliver up their holdings to federal reserve banks. The aim of gold policy was to raise the price level of commodities, particularly those which had sustained important declines. America virtually left the gold standard in 1933 and from 1 February 1934 fixed the official price of gold at $35 per oz. Gold no longer circulated internally and could not be held privately; it ceased to be the basis of the monetary system but became a commodity whose price was officially supported. These arrangements of 1933 and 1934 made possible a period of relatively easy money yet that policy hardly had the same stimulating effects on the economy as in Britain, possibly because of differences in economic structure and of potentiality for change in structure in the conditions of the

1930s. At least monetary policy did not cause a contraction in the economy except during the recession of 1937–8 when the Federal Reserve Board acted with a tighter monetary rein to reduce what it saw as a problem of excess reserves which had grown rapidly from 1935 onwards.

The growth of those reserves in America was due to an inflow of funds, especially from Europe, caused partly by a desire of fund-holders to seek some reasonably safe haven in a somewhat uncertain world. Inasmuch as flows of funds to America meant a shortage of credit and increasing illiquidity in the international system they did not augur well for any significant upturn in world trade and investment. Yet since they showed that the United States was now regarded as the major world financial centre and that any major attempt to revive an international monetary system must be centred on America they indicated the realities which any future reformers must take into account. In 1939 the international monetary scene was still gloomy enough, and the operation of exchange restrictions and of protectionist trade policies were all too common. In spite of these difficulties world trade had improved since 1932 and the major trading countries, including Britain and America, had actively pursued reciprocal trade agreements. Yet it was clear that not until new arrangements could be made to solve the problem of international monetary liquidity could the prospects for the international economy become substantially brighter.

Banking

Banking is an aspect of the inter-war scene deserving special mention because of its vicissitudes in America at a time when American financial instability could have world-wide repercussions. The institutional defects in American banking in 1929–33 had considerable effects on business confidence and therefore by implication on the level of activity in the American economy. It was an episode contrasting strongly with the 'soundness' of British banking institutions where during the uneasy years of the depression virtually no British banks failed. The final amalgamations creating the so-called 'Big Five' commercial banks were over in Britain by 1923 and the strength of the reserves of those banks together with their cautious and prudent management meant that the banking sector was the one aspect of the financial scene where there were few qualms. The main interest of British inter-war banking history lies in the evolving relationship of the commercial banks with the Bank of England and in the banks' role in helping to fulfil monetary policy.

The relationship of the ordinary banks to a central bank (or embryo central bank) provided the vital contrast between the two systems. The absence or near absence of central control in America was a matter for attention in the Federal Reserve Act of 1913. In the system which emerged after 1913 the chief co-ordinating body was the Federal Reserve Board which supervised the working of twelve federal reserve banks in twelve districts covering the country. In each of these twelve banks there was a directorate of nine men divided into three groups of three men. The first group were usually bankers, the second came from industry, commerce or agriculture and the third was appointed by the Federal Reserve Board, one of them being the 'federal reserve agent'. In practice, a division of authority emerged between the first two groups who came to represent bankers and the third group representing the Federal Reserve Board. Since the act had left unclear who should be the executive or operating head, the Federal Reserve Board decided that he could be either a director or come from outside and should be known as 'governor'. Since bankers possessed a majority of votes among directors they chose invariably a practising banker as governor and the crucial choice of Benjamin Strong as governor of the New York Reserve Bank had immense influence on the development of the system. The important point was that the 'agent' had less power than the 'governor' and in course of time the governors became dominant. From the outset a Council of Governors was formed with Strong as chairman and by 1916 it became known as the Conference of Governors. Until 1922 there was a tussle for power between the Conference and the Federal Reserve Board and although thereafter the governors met board members at meetings in Washington the New York bank under Benjamin Strong continued to determine policy.

It was one of the accidents of history that Strong himself died in October 1928. Most authorities seem agreed that he could have provided the firm leadership necessary during the crisis of 1929-32. Nevertheless, speculation about personalities does not alter the unsound nature of the banking system below the level of central policy-making. As we have seen in a previous section, one of the features of the later nineteenth century was the greater growth in numbers of state banks compared with national banks. Hence banks did not have the strength which large banks, operating branches with diverse activities, could have had. Between 1900 and 1930 the number of banks trebled from 9,000 to nearly 30,000. During the 1920s there was a disquieting regularity in the number of bank failures when several hundred banks failed each year. Much of the explanation lay in the depressed state of American agriculture and in the plight of farmers who were often the main customers of small country banks. During the nine-year period 1921–9 as many as 5,411 banks failed. Although 85 per cent of these banks had total assets of less than $1 million, the remaining 15 per cent were national banks of which some were large. There was a suspicion that not all was well with banking practice.

This suspicion was reinforced by the events of 1928–33. During the four years 1930–3 a total of 8,812 banks went down in three waves of failure in which the last wave of early 1933 accounted for nearly half of them. What one wishes to know is whether banking practice was itself at fault, whether there was some desirable weeding out of unsatisfactory elements or whether some banks deserved to be saved but were allowed to go under because of faulty official policy. The simple answer is that all these features were operative but in what proportions remains highly problematic. Much subsequent publicity was given to the involvement of banks in the stock market boom of 1928–9 and the somewhat reckless use of banking funds for stock market speculation. Again there is little doubt that there were too many banks in America and many of them were small with insufficient reserves to withstand a major crisis. Nevertheless, the occurrence of banking failures on such a scale was itself a major factor in undermining business confidence and acted as a powerful deflationary influence because of the consequent fall in the total available money supply, something of the order of a 33 per cent decline in the stock of money, partly because bank deposits became unattractive. Friedman believes that a major turning-point was the failure of the Bank of the United States in October 1930; it was the largest commercial bank, as measured by volume of deposits, ever to have failed up to that time in American history. The withdrawal of support by the clearing house banks from the concerted measures sponsored by the Federal Reserve Bank of New York to save the bank was a serious blow to the system's prestige. Perhaps if the Federal Reserve banking system had imposed a restriction on the convertibility of deposits into currency, as had happened in 1893 and 1907 before the system operated, there might have been an end to bank suspensions arising primarily from lack of liquidity. The Bank of the United States ultimately paid off 83.5 per cent of its adjusted liabilities at its closing on 11 December 1930, despite having to liquidate much of its assets in the difficult financial conditions of 1931-2. Once liquidity became a fashion, 'any runs on banks for whatever reason became to some extent self-justifying, whatever the quality of assets held by the banks'.[3]

Criticism has been levelled also at the Federal Reserve system's handling of the whole crisis. Even in November and December 1930 when the number of failures increased sharply, over 80 per cent were non-members of the system. The influential personalities in the system were big city bankers who viewed the disappearance of smaller bankers with equanimity. There was clearly an underestimate of the psychological repercussions of allowing banks to fail even if the few large member banks which failed at the end of 1930 were regarded as cases of bad management. Once some large banks failed the fear grew that other banks could fail. In this situation of doubtful confidence the role of the central bank was decisive. Yet, as we have seen, the Federal Reserve system was hampered by divided authority. Equally, the governors of the various federal reserve banks were primarily concerned about the solvency of their own banks and they failed to see that since the power to create money lay within the Federal Reserve system they could not fail. Hence they were the one group who could effect a rescue operation for banks in trouble.

It would be unfair to suggest that they did nothing to combat the situation. Nevertheless, the Federal Reserve did allow banks to fail in large numbers and federal reserve banks were the first to collect on loans to failing banks before other creditors could do so. In 1931 federal reserve officials refused to inject reserves into the system by means of purchases in the open market. A reappraisal came only in 1932 when in the course of the year large open-market purchases came to be made, yet the purchases came to an end in August 1932 and did not prevent the numerous banking failures (about 5,000) which occurred early in 1933. Equally, a Reconstruction Finance Corporation was established in January 1932 with authority to make loans to banks and to other financial institutions. By the end of 1932 RFC loans to banks were $0.9 billion. Overall, RFC made loans of nearly $2 billion to banks and purchased nearly $1 billion of bank stock. Yet even if many large commercial banks were saved from failure by the RFC the inclusion of a bank's name on the list of those receiving help was interpreted as a sign of weakness and could lead to a run on the bank in question. The failures of January and February 1933 were a reflection of the continuing lack of confidence. The decline in confidence was checked only with the coming into power of the government of Roosevelt.

Whatever else remains controversial about the New Deal, its measures concerning banking are generally considered to have solved the major problems. A temporary plan of deposit insurance was provided in the Banking Act of 1933. Then the Banking Act of 1935 established a permanent arrangement whereby a Federal Deposit Insurance Corporation (FDIC) was launched with capital loaned from the Treasury and from the federal reserve banks. Thereafter it obtained funds from premiums paid by insured banks. It was provided with substantial powers to act in emergencies. Equally, the ultimate power of the Federal Reserve Board was upheld. During the crisis of 1930–2 the board asserted its authority over control of open-market operations and by the act of 1935 it was to be called the Board of Governors, implying its overall control. The selection of chief officers of reserve banks was to have the board's final approval. Since 1935 the board's authority has been unquestioned. Furthermore, with the reduction in the number of banks between 1920 and 1933 a trend began towards concentration in banking which continued well into the 1950s and 1960s. In that sense the banking crisis of 1929–33 provided a permanent warning about the dangers of small-scale banking.

Controversy still reigns over the extent to which the banking failures of 1929–33 need have been allowed to go. Some banks were not particularly viable concerns and their ultimate disappearance was to be expected. On the other hand, the disappearance of so many banks at once and the consequent reduction in the stock of money was bound to add to the difficulties of the economy. The extent of the banking crisis was a clear sign that both the theory and practice of American banking needed substantial change. No one was encouraged by the lack of confidence revealed in the system yet that lack of confidence was itself a product of previous experience which had shown the potential vulnerability of the banks. Maybe a sound banking lesson had to be learned the hard way and, if so, the banking crisis of 1930–3 was not completely in vain.

CHAPTER TEN

THE CHANGING ROLE OF THE STATE

In this brief survey of economic change no topic provides more interest and paradox than the changing economic role of the state. In view of the vast scope of even this one topic there is only space here to review some of the main issues arising between 1850 and 1939. Perhaps the main question to ask is why the state should have come to exercise so much more influence over the economy in both countries by 1939 compared with a century earlier. The question arises because it has often been assumed that for much of the nineteenth century a *laissez-faire* philosophy prevailed which aroused deep suspicion of state economic involvement and supported private enterprise and initiative wherever possible. Two examples of such a philosophy would be Herbert Spencer's *Man versus the State* (1884) which had considerable vogue in America and *Self-Help* by Samuel Smiles published in 1859. The emphasis of John Stuart Mill's *On Liberty*, also of 1859, was that liberty in general consisted of the absence of restraint and that restraints, especially by governments, should be kept to a minimum.

Yet *laissez-faire* as a coherent doctrine is extremely difficult to define and has been something of a myth of nineteenth-century history. As Robbins has pointed out, classical economists by no means excluded the state from economic activity.[1] In the *Wealth of Nations* Adam Smith postulated three functions for the state: the task of defence; the duty of prescribing and implementing laws; and the duty of promoting community projects which were socially desirable but unprofitable for private entrepreneurs to undertake. It is obvious that these three areas could allow for immense alteration according to changing interpretations. Defence could alter because of changing technology (and higher costs) and because of changing political commitments; laws might alter with evolving views on economic custom and practice; and opinions on desirable community projects could vary with changing social and political fashions. There is also the probability that the state became more important in providing a co-ordinating mechanism as opinions changed and as economies become more complex. It is not too difficult, therefore, to find reasons why state intervention might increase even though some intriguing comparisons arise in reviewing differences in detail between the two countries. One is presumably justified in believing that the scale of increasing state intervention has connoted general public approval, even if the nature and degree of intervention on any specific topic may have occasioned lively debate.

In the mid-nineteenth century the debate over defence reflected the different place of Britain and America in the world economy. Externally, Britain spent a greater proportion of national income on defence than did America and even between 1850 and 1870 defence costs increased considerably with changing technology. Of course, military expenditure incurred a violent short-term rise in the United States with the Civil War. In thousands of dollars, expenditure of the US War Department was $1,031,323 in 1865 compared with $16,410 in 1860, $57,656 in 1870 and $38,117 in 1880. A rapid normal increase came only in the 1890s with a rise from $44,583 in 1890 to $134,775 in 1900, reflecting the emergence of America as a growing world power especially in the Pacific with commensurate military and naval commitments. Equally Britain's commitments in the age of imperialism were reflected in naval expenditure. Ashworth points out that between 1888 and 1913 defence expenditure rose by 138 per cent with the proportion of central government's outlay on defence rising from 33 per cent in 1880 to 41 per cent in 1905. This expenditure had important economic effects, one illustration being the modernisation of the Royal Dockyards after 1886. In 1882 the five yards employed 19,349 men with Portsmouth alone accounting for 6,256; hence one of the largest industrial establishments. In 1897 a rough estimate suggested that the navy, naval shipbuilding and the manufacture of the supplies which they needed gave employment to a million men. In the United States military or naval activities formed a substantial part of federal as distinct from state or local government expenditure in the nineteenth century and in both countries, though at slightly different times, defence expenditure came to constitute a powerful if perhaps half unconscious influence on general economic activity.

In terms of relative growth American defence expenditure grew more rapidly than British expenditure and between the wars usually constituted a higher proportion of total central or federal government expenditure than in Britain. The figures are as follows:[2]

	Britain			America		
	Army and Navy £1 million	Total £1 million	A:B %	Army and Navy $ thousand	Total $ thousand	A:B %
1910	53.0	156.9	33.7	312,997	693,617	45.1
1925	100.4	750.8	13.3	727,123	3,063,105	23.7
1930	96.3	781.7	12.3	839,020	3,440,269	24.3
1935	96.3	784.7	12.3	924,261	6,520,966	14.1
1938	179.9	909.3	19.7	1,240,394	6,791,838	18.2

Only in 1938 when rearmament had already caused a sharp increase in defence spending did British proportions again exceed American ones. Of course, caution has to be exercised in interpretation as proportions of public outlay since the figures do not show spending by local or separate state authorities. Yet they illustrate clearly enough that even in the later 1920s when some pundits bemoaned the deplorable rundown in the armed forces, defence was more expensive than before the war largely because of technical improvements.

Between the wars, if not earlier, there came a growing realisation that defence was not a separate compartment of activity without repercussions elsewhere. For example, while the history of agriculture and of railways between the wars was complex there is little doubt that defence considerations were one element in the operation of subsidies in Britain in the 1930s. Equally important, the British Dyestuffs Corporation set up in 1918 owed its establishment to the state and when the corporation was handed over in 1926 to the proposed firm of Imperial Chemical Industries it is inconceivable that the government of the day would have sponsored the information of such a giant near-monopoly unless defence considerations had been influential. Other areas of activity were sugar and aircraft. The British Sugar Corporation of 1925 established to undertake the production of beet-sugar stemmed from serious wartime sugar shortages while subsidies given to civil airlines came from an appreciation of the links between civil and military aircraft development. Government help for industry, often with defence implications, was forthcoming also for research, whether under-taken by the Department of Scientific and Industrial Research created during the war or by industrial research associations which received some government help.

Thus defence, especially in wartime, involved some inter-ference with market mechanisms. Yet the 'market', as the classical economists and Bentham in particular held, was not a natural feature but an artifact. Government could influence the market by prescribing and implementing laws, but what the classical economists did not emphasise was that the operation of the market could be substantially influenced by current trends in opinion which governments simply reflected. While a good deal of propaganda proclaimed the virtues of a 'free market economy' there were numerous exceptions. An obvious example was in the operation of commercial policy where, as long as the federal government in America depended on tariffs for the greater part of its revenue, there would be some hesita-tion in lowering existing duties. Yet tariffs were supported by trading or industrial interests which believed, rightly or wrong-ly, that they benefited from such a policy. Free trade was abandoned in Britain when a substantial body of opinion came to accept protection, yet it is doubtful if ironmasters or farmers were wholly convinced of the virtues of free trade from the 1870s onwards.

In practice, businessmen and politicians were well aware of the power of governments to influence the environment. The key question lay in whose interest such influence should be exercised. Banking legislation, already mentioned earlier, pro-vides an interesting example of contrasting attitudes before the 1930s. While farmers and rural interests in America resisted changes and others advocated larger banks and a stronger central bank; but the federal government lacked the means to remedy matters until the trauma of the 1930s. This ambivalence – or balance of interests – was revealed also in attitudes to company legislation. As the nineteenth century wore on, so it was appreciated that large-scale organisation was necessary if economies of scale and technical improvement were to be achieved. In America the corporation became a more accepted form of enterprise and the function of the state changed from special chartering of particular corporations to enacting general incorporation laws which were adopted by various American states. Similarly in Britain the limited liability acts of 1855 and

1862 which were at first regarded as something of a 'rogues charter' became generally accepted and the legal distinction after 1908 between 'private' and 'public' companies (those appealing to the general public for funds via the Stock Exchange) were a recognition of new needs in a complex situation. Yet even if the great bulk of industrial and commercial activity was in private hands there was in both countries a continuous debate about the power and influence of private entrepreneurs. In the United States the passage of the Sherman Anti-Trust Act of 1890 showed a recognition that some very large companies or groups might require special surveillance because of their monopoly power. Yet the administrative machinery to enforce the act was weak. In both countries belief in the virtues of private competition remained strong yet there was a recognition that large-scale operations and nationalisation might promote efficiency. It was a nagging suspicion of the backwardness of British industry which was responsible for government encouragement of quasi-nationalisation and mergers between the wars, especially in the problem industries.

Interference with industry showed a growing appreciation that at least some industries had a public as well as a private face. If industry operated within a given environment it reacted with that environment, drawing human and material resources from it and yet shaping the environment in particular ways. Of all activities in the nineteenth century it was the railways which most vividly demonstrated the point that governments could not ignore private economic operations having a major influence on the community, nor could entrepreneurs ignore the community. 'Railroad leaders were necessarily social leaders. The railroad was likely to be the most important enterprise in each of the communities served.' In America as Carter Goodrich has shown, state and federal governments promoted loans and land grants for railroad construction but state provision of social overhead capital, however indirect, implied that there was some notion of communal return from that capital. Even if in Britain capital for railways was privately invested there was a continuing interest from the 1840s onwards in railway safety and in freight and passenger charges. The most important acts on these subjects were those of 1888 and 1894 on freight and passenger charges. No less an advocate of free enterprise than Gladstone believed in the 1840s that railways might be candidates for nationalisation because they had an inherent tendency to monopoly and a monopoly in provision of public service needed to be publicly supervised. The inspectors of the Railway Department of the Board of Trade became a powerful influence on railway practice. In America the enthusiasm of earlier decades came to be tempered by a suspicion of railroad monopoly power in fixing freight charges and in granting rebates to privileged customers. The Inter-State Commerce Act of 1887 was the major landmark in a series of acts like those of 1903, 1906, and 1910 which all attempted to deal with the problem. After the war the act of 1921 in Britain recognised that railways were a monopoly and in return for monopoly recognition to four companies legal duties were laid upon them by government. In America subsidies paid to railroads which were in trouble in the 1920s due to transfer of traffic to the roads and highways was in sharp and apparently distasteful contrast to the prosperity achieved by industry in an environment of free competition. The dilemma was beginning to pose itself: at what point does one cease to regard an industrial or commercial activity as a private matter and at what point does it become a desirable community operation liable to government aid, subsidy or direct management control?

This question was and is difficult to answer in any precise way. In practice, the formula developed in each case depended much on convenience and expediency. Often arrangements made depended on local circumstances and possibilities. It might well be that government intervention was difficult to resist when social rather than economic issues were paramount. Was it on social grounds that in Britain the Post Office operated as a nationalised industry from 1840 onwards? In America much of education was organised publicly but rather by local or state governments than by federal governments and no one seemed to raise an outcry against unwarranted interference with private educational entrepreneurship. The lack of such an outcry might be because private entrepreneurs in education could be notoriously variable in the quality of their output. If in Britain, there was greater acceptance of private education, that might be because some of it was of reasonably high quality, but it was also a reflection of the wider differences between social classes in which private and expensive education could be contrasted with education which was public and cheap. Nevertheless, however niggardly one might regard public education provision, especially in Britain, in the middle of the nineteenth century the essential fact was that expenditure on education in both countries grew enormously. In America expenditure on public elementary and secondary schools was (in thousands of dollars) 63,397 in 1870, 426,250 in 1910 and 2,233,110 in 1938. In Britain in the same period, gross central government public expenditure on education, art and science was £1.62 million in 1870, £17.9 million in 1910 and £63.1 million in 1938 while local authority education expenditure was £2.2 million in 1875, £27.5 million in 1910 and £505.6 million in 1938. Clearly in both countries there was an enormous increase in the first third of the twentieth century.

The reasons for this expansion were complex. Politicians who promised educational expansion hoped to sway votes by their promises, parents welcomed the rising social status which education might bring for their children and in an industrialising society wider educational provision was necessary for the production of highly qualified manpower. The debate is still wide open about the relative importance of these factors and equally there is little agreement on the extent of the return on expenditure viewed as an investment in human capital. One line of thought has argued for the superiority of American education on the grounds that it was less élitist and that it permitted choice of a wider range of subjects, especially technical subjects, to a higher age. Nevertheless, those who have bemoaned Britain's lack of technical education, whether in the 1860s or the 1950s, have to meet the point that no great lack of qualified manpower seemed to emerge and, whether one is studying the steel industry in the 1880s or the so-called new industries in the 1930s, no serious bottlenecks of manpower shortage showed themselves. Olive Banks has stressed that desire of parents for 'grammar school' education between the wars was based on a sound appraisal of vocational opportunity made possible by such education in administrative and service functions. While the relative lack of development of technical education might reflect to some extent on entrepreneurial foresight, one must not underestimate the enormous economic importance of 'learning by doing'. In general, education seems to be able to contribute fruitfully to economic development when it is associated with other factors of development all tending the same way. Conversely, it seems difficult to avoid some misinvestment in periods of substantial educational expansion presumably because manpower planning has either not been practised or has not been especially successful. All that one can say is that the pressures operating for expansion of the public educational system seem to have been irresistible.

If education roused not too great controversy as an activity suitable for considerable government control, industry was a rather different matter. Just as with railroads, so some branches of industry might be deemed a community service. In the United States electrical supply fell especially into such a category and its history paralleled that of railroads. At first public enthusiasm was strong and public loans were floated to aid electrical undertakings. Subsequently suspicion became aroused that profits might be high and pressure grew for legislation to prevent monopoly price-fixing. In Britain the history of public utilities was slightly different but public control began in a haphazard way with the so-called 'gas and water socialism' of the 1880s. Municipalities began to organise utilities such as gas, water, local transport and harbours themselves instead of leaving the initiative to private enterprise. Although this tendency might receive approval from socialist thinkers the essential motives could be found in a mixture of local convenience and expediency, particularly since support of an undertaking from public funds could remove risk and uncertainty. Moreover, municipal authorities found in practice that no overwhelming opposition was experienced to their initiative and, as Ashworth points out, local authority indebtedness for trading purposes grew from £79 million in 1885 to 208 million in 1906. Furthermore, as in the case of gas and electricity, there might be technical advantages accruing from concentration of ownership and control, and the interests of an efficient public service could mean that it was better not to endure too much wasteful and expensive private competition for too long. At least some such considerations explain the passing of the Electrical (Supply) Act of 1926 in Britain under a Conservative government which created regional electricity boards possessing monopoly powers to purchase electricity from private producers at a fixed price. The aim was to eliminate small inefficient producers and to achieve standardised current and voltage throughout the United Kingdom. The act implied a measure of public control over the industry which severely impinged on a 'free market'.

Between the 1880s and the 1920s thinking changed and the test of acceptability of any such measure seemed to be whether the opinion prevailed that government was the best body to supervise the control of the service or industry in question. From this point of view it might be wrong to contrast Britain's creeping socialism in the 1920s with American 'free enterprise'. The historical statistics of the United States show increases between 1922 and 1932 from $1,296 to $1,766 million in highways, from $553 to $794 million in the postal service, from $204 to $349 million on police, from $287 to $462 million on hospitals and from $128 to $445 million on public welfare. Solomon Fabricant has shown how the number of government employees rose substantially. All this was before the major appraisal in America occasioned by the New Deal and may be explained in both countries partly by increasing complexity of the economy rendering some extension of public services inevitable.

Yet since both countries were democracies aiming at the greatest happiness of the greatest number it might be claimed that social change and reform were implicit in their political theory. What was desirable for the community and worthy, therefore, of public expenditure, could alter with time. Certainly in both countries notions of social welfare underwent change. Social welfare involved the administration of poverty, health, employment and housing. They are problems, of course, which tend to be associated with each other but they may each require some specialised expertise for their treatment. The growth of such expertise, however, is fairly recent and during the nineteenth century precise knowledge on such problems was difficult to find. In both countries attitudes in the early nineteenth century towards poverty tended to be primitive and the assumption was that poverty arose from lack of will to work. Self-help was the answer to material affliction. No doubt it was easier in America with its greater opportunities for men and women to avoid the direct extremes of poverty yet there were equally opportunities for unscrupulous employers to exploit workers, and the conditions of female workers in the New England textile mills were scarcely enviable. In both countries voluntary agencies, especially those affiliated to religious organisations, attempted to alleviate hardship but their efforts were essentially piecemeal and perhaps one of their most useful functions was to spread information about the nature and causes of the poverty which existed. Yet the information available to voluntary agencies was essentially localised and unsystematic and in Britain it was not until the methodical researches of Booth and

Rowntree were undertaken that the extent of poverty was revealed. Booth showed in the 1880s that some 30 per cent of the inhabitants of east London lived in 'primary poverty' and Rowntree found comparable figures in York around 1900. In the face of such figures it was difficult to maintain that poverty was solely due to personal deficiencies, and attention was drawn to the social defects implicit in existing economic arrangements.

Between 1895 and 1914 reappraisal of existing arrangements was taking place in Britain but in an *ad hoc* way. Workmen's compensation for industrial injuries (1897), wage boards to fix minimum wages in sweated or dangerous trades (1909), old age pensions (1908), and unemployment and health insurance (1911), all put important principles into operation. Yet the effects until 1914 were small with only a small proportion of elderly people being eligible for pensions, and those eligible for unemployment insurance were confined to the relatively dangerous trades. Equally, the Royal Commission on the Poor Law which reported in 1909 showed an awareness of the complexity of the problem of poverty without fundamentally altering the administrative arrangements for dealing with it. Clearly some persons were 'poor' not through any great fault of their own but because of the imperfections of the economic system via the trade cycle or via sudden changes in demand. The dilemma of the Liberal government before 1914, as it was to be increasingly the dilemma of governments between the wars, was that neoclassical economic theory tended to assume that human problems would be solved by the operation of the market and that long-term instances of over-production or of under-consumption could not occur.

In that sense of questioning the bases of existing economic theory the period between the wars in both Britain and America constituted a new phase. Even so, existing habits of thought could not be altered overnight and if governments came in practice to exercise greater economic intervention they did so largely by way of piecemeal responses to particular problems. Yet by the 1930s some of those problems such as the international monetary situation, the state of the world trade and consequent effects on demand were so great that governments were becoming more concerned about the possible influences of their actions on the general performance of the economy. Nevertheless, because of their different circumstances the problems confronting the two countries presented themselves in different ways.

In retrospect, the myth of *laissez-faire* died hard in Britain since the mood of 1919–21, as Tawney has pointed out, was to abolish wartime controls and to return to the allegedly free economy of 1914. Yet in the 1920s governments in Britain could not avoid intervention in an unprecedentedly large way for peace-time. One feature of this intervention was that whereas about one-third of government expenditure went on defence in 1910 only one-seventh did so in 1925. No doubt part of the explanation lay in a reaction against the priorities associated with World War I but part lay also in a piecemeal redefinition of government's role to encompass much greater concern for social welfare and education. Perhaps no activity is more interesting to study than that of housing. Before the war previous legislation had empowered municipalities or local authorities to use public funds or to raise loans for housing, but not very much was achieved by 1914 because of the lack of will to provide housing. Economic theory provided a good enough justification for non-intervention and as long as no great general public discontent existed on the issue there was no impetus to change the situation. Yet discontent was growing and perhaps in the Welsh mining valleys industrial bitterness around 1910 was as much due to inadequate housing as to wages and mining conditions. By the end of the war the housing shortage was clear. With his slogan of a land fit for heroes to live in, Lloyd George launched a policy of government aid for housing and with the Addison Act of 1919, the Wheatley Act of 1923 and subsequent measures, government influence on the housing situation became important, especially in the stimulus given to reviving the building construction industry. Even if those who benefited from subsidised housing were not at first the most deserving, an important new sphere of intervention became accepted. In the same way governments were obliged to assist unemployment on a much greater scale than hitherto because of the greater scale of the problem. Between 1920 and 1934 there was a series of expedients giving unemployment assistance but the essential point was that the scale of assistance given was far wider than that envisaged in the act of 1911 and in 1931 almost led to a deficit on government accounts for the year. The definitive act of 1934 at last abolished nineteenth-century conceptions of poverty and defined various categories of assistance from short-term unemployment to long-term disabled and infirm.

Unemployment also provided a sharp reminder of the problem of industry. The problem industries of coal, textiles, steel and shipbuilding not only involved the social problem of unemployment but symbolised the poor performance of the British economy and raised the question of the efficacy of monetary policy. Although the coal industry became the political problem industry par excellence in the 1920s and provided a hot debate both about the nature of industrial ownership and control and about the correct level of wages, it was not the only industry which roused public interest. It could be argued that the war brought a realisation that industry was not solely private property to be left to individual fortunes but constituted a valuable national asset. In this sense the Report of the Scoby-Smith Committee of 1918, which stated rather vaguely that government should not control the industry but should ensure that the circumstances under which it operated were not disadvantageous, was a pointer to changing views. By 1934 the British Iron and Steel Federation had been created with implications for centralised buying and selling and for some element of national planning. BISF was not a government agency yet government clearly helped in its formation. Equally, the two royal commissions of 1919 and 1925 with the attempt to cartelise in 1930 showed the government's continuing concern with the coal industry. There was also aid for the cotton industry and an attempt to eliminate surplus capacity in shipbuilding in the 1930s.

This piecemeal pragmatic British approach to economic problems was paralleled in America. If government intervention in America increased in the 1920s it did so largely in response to a need for greater services which government could best provide. Clearly the depression of 1929–33 caused a climate of crisis in which an overall approach seemed to be required. Yet if the New Deal commencing in March 1933 brought a promise of more rational co-ordination to solve economic problems the promise was not fulfilled. The more scholars have examined the New Deal the more they have been inclined to view the solutions proposed as a series of piecemeal attempts to solve particular problems. It was true, of course, that deficits were permitted on current account but the deficits were small in relation to the total amounts involved. Some measures tended to cancel each other out such as those in industry where higher prices enforced by the codes were offset by higher wages made necessary by labour legislation. In a situation of uncertain demand it was a debatable way of ensuring recovery. Nevertheless, the New Deal administration of 1933–40 did have popular support and clearly the measures proposed were generally acceptable except to those businessmen who opposed massive extensions of government economic authority. Yet few would go to the lengths of Henry Ford in opposing by force the authority of the National Industrial Recovery Administration. The fact was that in a difficult and unprecedented situation few had any clear idea of an overall strategy to be pursued.

It is a mistake, therefore, to see in the New Deal any systematic attempt to pursue the ideas of Keynes. It was true that the Roosevelt government practised both deficit financing and large-scale public works. Yet there is little evidence that the ideas of Keynes had been widely studied in America and notions of budgetary management were somewhat rudimentary by later standards. The public works programme was hasty and haphazard and very few public projects had important long-term multiplier effects, the one outstanding exception being the Tennessee Valley Authority. Yet even if much of the New Deal was experimental and different features of it were not well co-ordinated, the inroads made by government into different areas of economic life seemed to hostile contemporary businessmen to be disturbingly exceptional. Yet once the major work of Keynes had been published in 1936 and became known in America it became enthusiastically received by some economists because it seemed to justify the practices of the New Deal and to provide a recipe for the future in avoiding the extremes of boom and slump such as those which had been experienced between 1927 and 1933.

In Britain likewise the climate of opinion changed considerably even if government continued to balance budgets. This change in opinion was due to a growing realisation of the human waste arising from unemployment, the concern of teachers about the malnutrition of their pupils – their success in securing free milk being one example. There was a general, if vague, consensus that unemployment must be cured as a social problem. Because of the scale of unemployment the time was ripe for the ideas of Keynes to be well received. Both his writings and the practical realisation that only government action could overcome the inadequacies of the market system which had led to unemployment meant that the society of the mixed economy with its quest for full employment had arrived. World War II both confirmed and strengthened the aspirations which it embodied. Yet by 1939 the search for an economy of full employment was still groping and hesitant. Nevertheless, it embodied a concept of escape from the human misery and hopelessness of the inter-war years with governments coming to be regarded as an essential agency of economic regulation by which the worst effects of slump could be avoided. In spite of areas of controversy about how far governments should intervene in specific fields of activity, there was general acceptance of the need for state intervention to an extent which in 1850 would have been deemed unthinkable. Overall, one could hardly say that the general effect of that intervention had been malevolent and in the 1930s it spelled hope and promise that a better life could be obtained. The problem as always was to find a compromise between the needs of the individual with his own desires and aspirations and the restraints upon some individuals which general community action entailed. In that sense the problem was perennial with each age redefining the relationship of the individual with society yet, in terms of achieving a general standard of living which ensured a measure of acceptable material comfort, it might be thought that the Anglo-Saxon democracies had performed none too badly.

REFERENCES

Chapter One

1 Lance E. Davis and others, *American Economic Growth: an Economist's History of the United States* (1972), p 33.
2 J. H. Clapham, 'Free Trade and Steel 1850–1886', in *Economic History of Modern Britain*, 2 (1932), p 14.
3 J. G. Williamson, *Late Nineteenth-Century American Development* (1974), Ch 1.

Chapter Two

1 Figures quoted in P. S. Bagwell and G. E. Mingay, *Britain and America, 1850–1939* (1970), pp 6, 10; Angus Maddison, *Economic Growth in the West* (1964), p 30.
2 Moses Abramovitz, *Resources and Output Trends* ... quoted in Lance E. Davis and others, *American Economic Growth: an Economist's History of the United States* (1972), p 206.
3 Donald N. McCloskey (ed), *Essays on a Mature Economy* ... (1971), pp 285–99.
4 Roderick Floud in Donald N. McCloskey (ed.) idem, p 313.

Chapter Three

1 R. A. Billington, *America's Frontier Heritage* (1966), p 160.
2 Harvey S. Perloff and others, *Regions, Resources and Economic Growth* (1960), p 124.
3 Idem, p 141.
4 Alan Conway, 'America, Half Brother of the World' in H. C. Allen and C. P. Hill (eds), *British Essays in American History* (1957), p 247.
5 Edith T. Penrose, *Theory of the Growth of the Firm* (1959), p 33.
6 E. H. Phelps Brown (with Margaret Browne), *A Century of Pay* (1968), pp 30–1.
7 Idem, pp 32–3.
8 Florence Peterson, *American Labor Unions: What They Are and How They Work*, 2nd edition (1963), p 1.
9 Henry M. Pelling, *America and the British Left* (1956), p 28.
10 J. G. Rayback, *History of American Labor* (1959), pp 144–7, 164–8.

Chapter Four

1 Allan G. Bogue, *From Prairie to Corn Belt* (1963), p 287.
2 F. M. L. Thompson, *English Landed Society in the Nineteenth Century* (1963), pp 310–18; E. L. Jones, *The Development of English Agriculture, 1815–1873* (1968), p 26.
3 Robert Higgs, *The Transformation of the American Economy, 1865–1914* (1971), pp 7–9.
4 P. L. Payne, 'Iron and Steel', in D. H. Aldcroft (ed), *The Development of British Industry and Foreign Competition, 1875–1914*, Ch 3 (1968), pp 71, 98–9.
5 R. E. Tyson, 'The Cotton Industry', in D. H. Aldcroft (ed), *The Development of British Industry and Foreign Competition, 1875–1914*, Ch 4 (1968), pp 100–27.
6 S. B. Saul (ed), *Technological Change: the United States and Britain in the Nineteenth Century* (1970).
7 Richard Duboff, 'The Introduction of Electric Power in American Manufacturing', *Economic History Review*, 2nd series, XX, 3 (1967).
8 Paul A. David, 'Transportation and Economic Growth: Professor Fogel on and off the Rails', *Economic History Review*, XXII, 3 (1969), p 525.
9 J. R. Kellett, *The Impact of Railways on Victorian Cities* (1969).
10 H. W. Parris, *Government and the Railways in Nineteenth Century Britain* (1965).

Chapter Five

1 S. B. Saul, 'The Export Economy', *Yorkshire Bulletin of Economic and Social Research*, 17, 1 (1965).
2 A. G. Kenwood and A. L. Lougheed, *The Growth of the International Economy, 1820–1960* (1971), p 43.
3 Cleona Lewis, *America's Stake in International Investments* (Washington, 1938), reprinted in H. U. Faulkner, *The Decline of Laissez-Faire, 1897–1917* (1951), p 87.

Chapter Six

1 H. S. Jevons, *The British Coal Trade* (1915).
2 George Soule, *Prosperity Decade, 1917–1929* (1947), p 175.
3 Idem, p 163.

Chapter Seven

1 H. W. Richardson, *Economic Recovery in Britain, 1932–39* (1967), p 300.
2 Lester V. Chandler, *America's Greatest Depression, 1929–41* (1970), p 1.

3 H. W. Richardson, op cit, p 44.
4 Idem, p 316.
5 Lester V. Chandler, op cit, p 177.
6 Idem, p 23.
7 Idem, p 229.
8 Idem, p 217, quoting *Historical Statistics of the United States*, p 283.

Chapter Eight

1 Charles P. Kindleberger, *The World in Depression, 1929–39* (1973), p 106.
2 Lester V. Chandler, *America's Greatest Depression, 1929–41* (1970), p 221.
3 Michael Tracy, *Agriculture in Western Europe* (1964), pp 168–9.
4 Quoted in G. C. Allen, *British Industries and their Organisation*, 4th edition (1959), p 46.
5 Quoted in George Soule, *Prosperity Decade, 1917–1929* (1947), pp 54, 108; and in Broadus Mitchell, *Depression Decade, 1929–1941* (1947), p 446.
6 Robert Sobel, *The Age of Giant Corporations* (1972), pp 31–2.
7 A. D. Chandler, *Strategy and Structure. Chapters in the History of the Industrial Enterprise* (1962).
8 John Child, *British Management Thought* (1969).
9 J. G. Rayback, *History of American Labor* (1959), p 290.

Chapter Nine

1 Import-export figures taken from D. H. Aldcroft, *The Inter-War Economy: Britain, 1919–1939* and from *Historical Statistics of the United States*.
2 R. M. Robertson, *History of the American Economy*, 2nd edition (1964), p 596.
3 M. Friedman and A. J. Schwartz, *A Monetary History of the United States, 1867–1960* (1963), p 355; see also pp 308–12, 351–9.

Chapter Ten

1 L. Robbins, *The Theory of Economic Policy in English Classical Political Economy* (1952), p 37.
2 Figures from B. R. Mitchell, *Abstract of British Historical Statistics* and from *Historical Statistics of the United States*.

BOOKS USED AND FURTHER READING

Chapter One

Ashworth, W. *An Economic History of England, 1870–1939* (1960), Chs I and II

Checkland, S. G. *The Rise of Industrial Society in England, 1815–1885* (1964)

Church, R. A. *The Great Victorian Boom* (1975)

Clapham, J. H. 'Free Trade and Steel, 1850–1886', in *An Economic History of Modern Britain*, II (Cambridge, 1932), Chs I and II

Clark, Victor S. *History of Manufactures in the United States*, II, 1860–93 (New York, 1929)

Cochran, Thomas C. 'Did the Civil War Retard Industrialization?' *Mississippi Valley Historical Review*, XLVIII (1961)

Conrad, Alfred H. and Meyer, John R. 'The Economics of Slavery in the Ante-Bellum South', *Journal of Political Economy*, 66 (April, 1958)

Court, W. H. B. *A Concise Economic History of Britain from 1750 to Recent Times* (Cambridge, 1954), Chs VIII and X

Engerman, Stanley L. 'The Economic Impact of the Civil War', *Explorations in Entrepreneurial History*, 3, 3 (Spring/Summer, 1966)

Fogel, R. W. and Engerman, S. L. *Time on the Cross* (Boston, Mass, 1974)

Franklin, John Hope. *Reconstruction after the Civil War* (Chicago, 1961)

Gallman, Robert E. 'Commodity Output, 1839–1899', National Bureau of Economic Research Conference on Research in Income and Wealth, *Trends in the American Economy in the Nineteenth Century* (Princeton, 1960)

Gilchrist, David T. and Lewis, W. David (eds). *Economic Change in the Civil War Era* (Greenville, Del, 1965)

Hacker, L. M. *The triumph of American Capitalism* (New York, 1940)

Hughes, J. R. T. *Fluctuations in Trade, Industry and Finance. A Study of British Economic Development, 1850–1860* (Oxford, 1960)

Imlah, A. H. *Economic Elements in the Pax Britannica* (Cambridge, Mass, 1958)

Jones, G. P. and Pool, A. G. *A Hundred Years of Economic Development in Britain* (1940), Chs II to VI

North, Douglass C. *Economic Growth in the United States, 1790–1860* (Englewood Cliffs, NJ, 1961)

——. *Growth and Welfare in the American Past* (Englewood Cliffs, NJ, 1966), Chs 6, 7 and 12

Potter, J. 'Atlantic Economy, 1815–60: the U.S.A. and the Industrial Revolution in Britain', in L. S. Pressnell (ed), *Studies in the Industrial Revolution* (1960)

Robertson, R. M. *History of the American Economy*, 3rd edition (New York, 1973)

Stover, J. F. *American Railroads* (Chicago, 1961), Ch III

Taylor, G. R. *The Transportation Revolution, 1815–1860* (New York, 1951)

——. 'The National Economy in 1860', Ch XVII of *The Transportation Revolution, 1815–1860* (New York, 1951)

Williamson, J. G. *Late Nineteenth Century American Development* (Cambridge, 1974), Ch I

Chapter Two

Abramovitz, Moses. *Resource and Output Trends in the United States since 1870* (New York, 1956)

Aldcroft, Derek H. 'McCloskey on Victorian Growth: a Comment', *Economic History Review*, 2nd series, XXVIII, 2 (1974)

Aldcroft, Derek H. and Richardson, Harry W. *The British Economy, 1870–1939* (1969)

Ashworth, W. *Economic History of England, 1870–1939* (1939)

——. 'The Late Victorian Economy', *Economica*, XXX (1966)

Beales, H. L. 'The Great Depression in Industry and Trade', *Economic History Review*, 1st series, V (1934)

Cochran, Thomas C. and Miller, William. *The Age of Enterprise. A Social History of Industrial America* (New York, 1942)

Conrad, A. H. 'Income Growth and Structural Change', in Seymour E. Harris (ed), *American Economic History* (New York, 1961)

Coppock, D. J. 'The Causes of the Great Depression, 1873–1896', *Manchester School*, XXIX (1961)

David, Paul A. 'The landscape and the machine: technical interrelatedness, land tenure and the mechanisation of the corn harvest', in Donald N. McCloskey, *Essays on a Mature Economy...*

Davis, Lance, E., Hughes, J. R. T. and McDougall, D. *American Economic History* (Homewood, Ill, 1969)

Davis, Lance E. and others. 'The Pace and Pattern of American Economic Growth', Ch 2 of *American Economic Growth: an Economist's History of the United States* (New York, 1972)

Deane, P. and Cole, W. A. *British Economic Growth, 1688–1959*, Cambridge. 2nd edition (Cambridge, 1967)

Faulkner, H. U. *The Decline of Laissez-Faire, 1897–1917* (New York, 1951)

Floud, Roderick. 'Changes in the productivity of labour in the British machine tool industry, 1856–1900', in Donald N. McCloskey, *Essays on a Mature Economy* . . .

Higgs, Robert. *The Transformation of the American Economy* (New York, 1971)

Kirkland, E. C. *Industry comes of Age. Business, Labor and Public Policy, 1860–1897* (New York, 1961)

——. *Dream and Thought in the Business Community* (1956)

McCloskey, Donald N. 'Did Victorian Britain fail?' *Economic History Review*, 2nd series, XXIII, 3 (1970)

——. 'Victorian Growth: a Rejoinder', *Economic History Review*, 2nd series, XXVII, 2 (1974)

——. (ed). *Essays on a Mature Economy: Britain after 1840* (1971), especially Ch 12: 'General discussion on the performance of the late Victorian Economy'.

Maddison, Angus. *Economic Growth in the West.* (1964)

Matthews, R. C. O. 'Some Aspects of Post-War Growth in the British Economy in Relation to Historical Experience', *Transactions of the Manchester Statistical Society* (1964)

Musson, A. E. 'British Industrial Growth during the Great Depression, 1873–1896', *Economic History Review*, 2nd series, XV, 3 (1963)

Pollard, S. *Development of the British Economy, 1914–1967*, 2nd edition (1969), Ch I. 'Great Britain at the end of the long peace'

Rostow, W. W. *The British Economy of the Nineteenth Century* (Oxford, 1948)

Sanderson, J. M. *The Universities and British Industry* (1972)

*Saul, S. B. *The Myth of the Great Depression, 1873–1896* (1969)

—— 'The Export Economy, 1870–1914', *Yorkshire Bulletin of Economic and Social research*, 17, 1 (1965)

*Temin, Peter. *Causal factors in American Economic Growth in the Nineteenth Century* (1973)

West, E. G. *Education and the Industrial Revolution* (1965)

Williamson, Jeffrey G. *Late Nineteenth Century American Development* (Cambridge, 1974)

*The works by Saul and Temin contain useful selective bibliographies.

Chapter Three

The Moving Frontier Thesis and Immigration

Billinton, R. A. *America's Frontier Heritage* (New York, 1966)

——. *Westward Expansion*, 3rd edition (New York, 1967)

Cochran, Thomas C. and Miller, William. *The Age of Enterprise. A Social History of Industrial America* (New York, 1962)

Conway, Alan. 'America, Half Brother of the World', in H. C. Allen and C. P. Hill (eds), *British Essays in American History* (1957)

Gilboy, Elizabeth W. and Hoover, Edgar M. 'Population and Immigration', in Seymour E. Harris, *American Economic History* (New York, 1961)

Habakkuk, H. J. *American and British Technology in the Nineteenth Century* (Cambridge, 1962)

Jones, M. A. *American Immigration* (Chicago, 1960)

Overton, Richard C. 'Westward Expansion since the Homestead Act', in H. F. Williamson (ed), *The Growth of the American Economy* (Englewood Cliffs, NJ, 1951)

Perloff, Harvey S. and others. *Regions, Resources and Economic Growth* (Baltimore, 1960)

Thomas, Brinley. *Migration and Economic Growth* (Cambridge, 1954)

Turner, F. J. *The Frontier in American History* (New York, 1920). Many other editions

Entrepreneurship

Aldcroft, D. H. 'The Entrepreneur and the British Economy, 1870–1914', *Economic History Review*, XVII, 1 (1964)

Aldcroft, D. H. (ed). *The Development of British Industry and Foreign Competition, 1875–1914* (1968)

Chandler, A. D. *Strategy and Structure: Chapters in the History of the Industrial Enterprise* (Cambridge, Mass, 1962). Contains material on General Motors and other firms before 1914

Cochran, Thomas C. *Railroad Leaders, 1845–1890* (Cambridge, Mass, 1953)

Emmet, Boris and Jeuck, John E. *A History of Sears Roebuck and Company* (Chicago, 1950)

Erickson, C. *British Industrialists: Steel and Hosiery, 1850–1950* (Cambridge, 1959)

Habakkuk, H. J. *American and British Technology in the Nineteenth Century* (Cambridge, 1962)

Hughes, J. R. T. *The Vital Few* (Boston, Mass, 1965; London, 1973)

Josephson, M. *Edison* (New York, 1959; London, 1961)

Kilby, Peter (ed). *Entrepreneurship and Economic Development* (New York, 1971)

McCloskey, Donald N. *Economic Maturity and Entrepreneurial Decline: British Iron and Steel, 1870–1913* (1974)

McCloskey, Donald N. and Sandberg, Lars. 'From Damnation to Redemption: Judgments on the late Victorian Entrepreneur', *Explorations in Economic History*, 9, 1 (Fall, 1971)

Miller, William (ed). *Men in Business* (Cambridge, Mass, 1952)

Nevins, Allan. *Rockefeller* (New York, 1940) 2 vols

Newcomer, Mabel. *The Big Business Executive: the factors that made him, 1900–1950* (New York, 1955)

Passer, Harold C. *The Electrical Manufacturers, 1875–1900* (Cambridge, Mass, 1953)

Payne, P. L. 'The Emergence of the Large-Scale Company in Britain, 1870–1914', *Economic History Review*, XX, 3 (1967)

——. *British Entrepreneurship in the Nineteenth Century* (1974)

Penrose, Edith T. *The Theory of the Growth of the Firm* (Oxford, 1959)

Saul, S. B. 'The Market and the Development of the Mechanical Engineering Industries in Britain, 1860–1914', *Economic History Review*, XX, 1 (1967)

—— (ed). *Technological Change: the United States and Britain in the Nineteenth Century* (1970)

Schumpeter, Joseph. *Business Cycles* (New York, 1939), 2 vols

Temin, Peter. 'The Relative Decline of the British Steel Industry, 1880–1913', in Henry Rosovsky (ed), *Industrialization in Two Systems* (New York, 1966)

Wilson, C. 'Economy and Society in late Victorian Britain', *Economic History Review*, XVIII, 1 (1965)

Trade Unions and the Labour Force

Allen, V. L. *The Sociology of Industrial Relations* (1971)

Clegg, H. A., Fox, Alan and Thompson, A. F. *A history of British Trade Unions since 1889*, I, 1889–1910 (1964)

Daugherty, Carroll R. 'The Changing Status of Labor', in H. F. Williamson (ed), *The Growth of the American Economy* (New York, 1951)

Fraser, W. Hamish. *Trade Unions and Society: The Struggle for Acceptance, 1850–1880* (1974)

Habakkuk, H. J. *American and British Technology in the Nineteenth Century* (Cambridge, 1962)

Hobsbawn, E. J. 'General Labour Unions in Britain, 1889–1914', *Economic History Review*, 2nd series, I, 2 and 3 (1949). Reprinted in E. J. Hobsbawm, *Labouring Men: Studies in the history of Labour* (1964)

Pelling, Henry M. *American Labor* (Chicago, 1960)

——. *America and the British Left* (1956)

——. *A history of British Trade Unionism* (1963)

Phelps Brown, E. H. (with Margaret Browne). *A Century of Pay* (1968)

Rayback, J. G. *A History of American Labor* (New York, 1959)

Renshaw, Patrick. *The Wobblies* (1967)

Taft, Philip. *The A.F. of L. in the time of Gompers* (New York, 1957)

——. *Organized Labor in American History* (New York, 1964)

Ulman, Lloyd. 'The Development of Trades and Labor Unions', in Seymour E. Harris, *American Economic History* (New York, 1961)

Chapter Four

Agriculture

Bogue, Allan G. *Money at Interest: The Farm Mortgage on the Middle Border* (Ithaca, NY, 1955)

——. *From Prairie to Corn Belt* (Chicago, 1963)

Bowman, John D. 'An Economic Analysis of Midwestern Farm Values and Farm Land Income, 1860 to 1900', *Yale Economic Essays*, V (Fall, 1965)

Chambers, J. D. and Mingay, G. E. *The Agricultural Revolution, 1750–1880* (1966), last two chapters

Faulkner, H. U. *The Decline of Laissez-Faire, 1897–1917* (New York, 1951), Chs XIII and XIV

Fletcher, T. W. 'The Great Depression of English Agriculture, 1873–1896', *Economic History Review*, XIII, 2 (1960). Reprinted in P. J. Perry (ed) below

Jones, E. L. *The Development of English Agriculture, 1815–1873* (1968)

Lewis, W. A. *The Theory of Economic Growth* (1955)

North, Douglass C. *Growth and Welfare in the American Past* (Englewood Cliffs, NJ, 1966), Ch 11

Orwin, C. S. and Whetham, E. H. *History of British Agriculture, 1846–1914* (1964)

Perry, P. J. (ed). *British Agriculture, 1875–1914* (1973)

Ross, Earle D. 'The Expansion of Agriculture', in H. F. Williamson (ed), *The Growth of the American Economy* (New York, 1951)

Rostow, W. W. *The Stages of Economic Growth* (Cambridge, 1960), 2nd edition, 1969

Scott, Roy V. *The Reluctant Farmers: The Rise of Agricultural Extension to 1914* (Urbana, 1970)

Shannon, F. A. *The Farmer's Last Frontier, 1860–1897* (New York, 1945)

Thompson, F. M. L. *English Landed Society in the Nineteenth Century* (1963)

The Development of Industry

Aldcroft, D. H. (ed). *The Development of British Industry and Foreign Competition, 1875–1914* (1968)

Ashworth, W. 'Changes in Industrial Structure', *Yorkshire Bulletin of Economic and Social Research*, 17, 1 (1965)

Chandler, Alfred D. jr. 'The Beginnings of "Big Business" in American History', *Business History Review*, XXXIII (Spring, 1959). Reprinted in James P. Baughman (ed), *The History of American Management* (Englewood Cliffs, NJ, 1969)

Clark, Victor S. *History of Manufactures in the United States*, II and III (New York, 1929)

Duboff, Richard. 'The Introduction of Electric Power in American Manufacturing', *Economic History Review*, XX, 3 (1967)

Faulkner, H. U. *American Economic History*, 8th edition (New York, 1960), Chs 20 and 21

Floud, R. C. 'The Adolescence of American Engineering Competition, 1860–1900', *Economic History Review*, 2nd series, XXVII, 2 (1974)

Kirkland, E. C. *Industry Comes of Age. Business, Labor and Public Policy, 1860–1897* (New York, 1961)

Levine, A. L. *Industrial Retardation in Britain, 1880–1914* (New York, 1967)

Nelson, R. L. *Merger Movements in American Industry, 1895–1956* (1959)

Payne, P. L. 'The Emergence of the Large-Scale Company in Britain, 1870–1914', *Economic History Review*, XX, 3 (1967)

Potter, J. 'Industrial America', in H. C. Allen and C. P. Hill (eds), *British Essays in American History* (1957)

Rosenberg, Nathan (ed). *The American System of Manufactures* (Edinburgh, 1969)

Sandberg, Lars. *Lancashire in Decline: a Study of Entrepreneurship, Technology and International Trade* (Columbus, Ohio, 1974)

Temin, Peter. *Iron and Steel in Nineteenth Century America* (Cambridge, Mass, 1964)

See also book list for *Entrepreneurship*, p 211.

Railways and the Economy

Allen, G. C. *British Industries and Their Organization*, 4th edition (1959), Ch I

Ashworth, W. 'The Late Victorian Economy', *Economica*, XXXIII (1966)

Bagwell, Philip S. *The Transport Revolution from 1770* (1974)

Barker, T. C. and Savage, C. I. *An Economic History of Transport in Britain*, 3rd edition (1975)

David, Paul A. 'Transport Innovation and Economic Growth: Professor Fogel on and off the Rails', *Economic History Review*, XXII, 3 (1969)

Dyos, H. J. and Aldcroft, D. H. *British Transport: An Economic Survey from the Seventeenth Century to the Twentieth* (Leicester, 1969)

Fishlow, Albert. *The Railroads and the Transformation of the Ante-bellum Economy* (Cambridge, Mass, 1965)

Fogel, R. W. *Railroads and American Economic Growth* (Baltimore, 1964)

Goodrich, Carter. *Government Promotion of Canals and Railroads, 1800–1890* (New York, 1959)

Hawke, G. R. *Railways and Economic Growth in England and Wales, 1840–1870* (Oxford, 1970)

McLelland, Peter D. 'Social Rates of Return on American Railroads in the Nineteenth Century', *Economic History Review*, 2nd series, XXV, 3 (1972)

Pollins, Harold. *Britain's Railways: An Industrial History* (Newton Abbot, 1971)

Reed, M. C. (ed). *Railways in the Victorian Economy: Studies in Finance and Economic Growth* (Newton Abbot, 1969)

Stover, J. F. *American Railroads* (Chicago, 1961)

Temin, Peter *Causal Factors in American Economic Growth in the Nineteenth Century* (1975), Section 5 on Railroads

Chapter Five

Overseas Trade and *Capital Export and Commercial Policy*

Ashworth, W. *Economic History of England, 1870–1939* (1960)

——. *The International Economy since 1850*, 2nd edition (1962)

Brown, A. J. 'Great Britain and the World Economy', *Yorkshire Bulletin of Economic and Social Research*, 17, 1 (1965)

Cairncross, A. K. *Home and Foreign Investment, 1870–1913* (Cambridge, 1953)

Cottrell, P. L. *British Overseas Investment in the Nineteenth Century* (1975)

Feinstein, C. H. *National income, Expenditure, and Output of the United Kingdom, 1855–1965* (1972)

Feis, Herbert. *Europe, the World's Banker* (New York, 1965)

Ford, A. G. 'Overseas Lending and Internal Fluctuations, 1870–1914', *Yorkshire Bulletin of Economic and Social Research*, 17, 1 (1965)

——. 'British Economic Fluctuations, 1870–1914', *Manchester School*, XXXVII (1969)

Hall, A. R. (ed). *The Export of Capital from Great Britain, 1870–1914* (1968)

Hawke, G. R. 'The United States Tariff and Industrial Protection in the late Nineteenth Century', *Economic History Review*, 2nd series, XXVII, 1 (1975)

Kenwood, A. G. and Lougheed, A. L. *The Growth of the International Economy, 1820–1960* (1971)

Kindleberger, C. P. 'The Rise of Free Trade in Western Europe, 1820–1875', *Journal of Economic History*, XXXV, 1 (1975)

Lewis, W. A. *Economic Survey, 1919–1939* (1964). Contains material on Britain in the nineteenth century

McCord, Norman. *Free Trade: Theory and Practice from Adam Smith to Keynes* (Newton Abbot, 1970)

Maizels, A. *Industrial Growth and World Trade* (Cambridge, 1963)

Richardson, H. W. 'British Emigration and Overseas Investment, 1870–1914', *Economic History Review*, XXV, 1 (1972)

Robertson, Ross M. *History of the American Economy*, 3rd edition (New York, 1973)

Saul, S. B. 'The Export Economy', *Yorkshire Bulletin of Economic And Social Research*, 17, 1 (1965)

——. *Studies in British Overseas Trade, 1870–1914* (Liverpool, 1960)

Taussig, F. W. *The Tariff History of the United States*, 8th edition (New York and London, 1931)

Thomas, Brinley. *Migration and Economic Growth* (Cambridge, 1954)

——. *Migration and Urban Development. A Reappraisal of British and American Long Cycles* (1972)

Wilkins, Mira. *The Emergence of Multinational Enterprise: American Business Abroad from the Colonial Era to 1914* (Cambridge, Mass, 1970)

Williamson, Jeffrey G. *American Growth and the Balance of Payments* (Chapel Hill, North Carolina, 1964)

The Banking Structure

Clapham, J. H. *Economic History of Modern Britain* (Cambridge, 1932) 3 vols

——. *The Bank of England* (Cambridge, 1944), 2 vols

Crick, W. F. and Wadsworth, A. P. *A Hundred Years of Joint-Stock Banking* (1936)

Friedman, M. and Schwartz, A. J. *Monetary History of the United States, 1867–1960* (Princeton, 1963)

Jones, A. G. and Pool, A. G. *A Hundred Years of Economic Development in Britain* (1940)

Myers, Margaret. 'The Investment Market after the Civil War' in H. F. Williamson (ed), *The Growth of the American Economy* (Englewood Cliffs, NJ, 1951)

Robertson, R. M. *History of the American Economy*, 3rd edition (New York, 1973)

Temin, Peter. *Causal Factors in American Economic Growth in the Nineteenth Century* (1975), Section 6, Banking

Chapters Six and Seven

Aldcroft, D. H. *The Inter-War Economy: Britain, 1919–1939* (1970)

Alford, B. W. E. *Depression and Recovery? British Economic Growth, 1918–1939* (1972)

Arndt, H. W. *Economic Lesson of the Nineteen-Thirties* (1944)

Chandler, Lester V. *America's Greatest Depression, 1929–1941* (New York, 1970)

Cochran, Thomas C. *Social Change in Industrial Society: Twentieth Century America* (1972)

Conkin, P. K. *The New Deal* (1968). Originally published as *F.D.R. and the origins of the Welfare State* (New York, 1967)

Dowie, J. A. 'Growth in the Inter-War Period; Some More Arithmetic,' *Economic History Review*, XXI, 1 (1968)

Galbraith, J. K. *The Great Crash, 1929* (New York, 1955; London, 1961)

Kindleberger, Charles P. *The World in Depression, 1929–1939* (London, 1973)

Leuchtenberg, W. E. *The Perils of Prosperity, 1914–1932* (Chicago, 1958)
——. *Franklin D. Roosevelt and the New Deal: 1932–1940* (1963)
Lewis, W. A. *Economic Survey, 1919–1939* (1949)
Mitchell, Broadus. *Depression Decade, 1929–1941* (New York, 1947)
Pollard, S. *Development of the British Economy, 1914–1967* (1969)
Potter, J. *The American Economy between the Two World Wars* (1974)
Richardson, H. W. *Economic Recovery in Britain, 1932–1939* (1967)
Romasco, H. U. *The Poverty of Abundance: Hoover, the Nation, the Depression* (1965)
Skidelsky, Robert. *Politicians and the Slump. The Labour Government of 1929–31* (1967)
Sobel, R. *The Great Bull Market; Wall Street in the 1920s* (New York, 1968)
Soule, George. *Prosperity Decade, 1917–1929* (New York, 1947)
Youngson, A. J. *Britain's Economic Progress, 1920–1966* (1966)

Chapter Eight

Agriculture
Chandler, Lester V. *America's Greatest Depression, 1929–1941* (New York, 1970)
Jones, G. P. and Pool, A. G. *A Hundred Years of Economic Development in Great Britain* (1940)
Mitchell, Broadus. *Depression Decade, 1929–1941* (New York, 1947)
Pollard, S. *Development of the British Economy, 1914–1967* (1969)
Soule, George. *Prosperity Decade, 1917–1929* (New York, 1947)
Tracy, M. *Agriculture in Western Europe* (1964)

Industry
Aldcroft, D. H. *The Inter-War Economy: Britain, 1919–1939* (1970)
Allen, G. C. *British Industries and their Organization*, 4th edition (1959)
Buxton, Neil. 'Entrepreneurial Efficiency in the British Coal Industry between the Wars', *Economic History Review*, XXIII, 3 (1970)
Chandler, Alfred D. jr. 'Management Decentralization: an Historical Analysis', *Business History Review*, XXX (June, 1956). Reprinted in James P. Baughman (ed), *The History of American Management* (Englewood Cliffs, NJ, 1969)
——. *Strategy and Structure: Chapters in the history of the Industrial Enterprise* (Cambridge, Mass, 1962)
Cochran, Thomas C. *American Business in the Twentieth Century* (Cambridge, Mass, 1972)
Coleman, D. C. *Courtaulds: an Economic and Social History*, 2 (Oxford, 1969),
Dunning, J. H. and Thomas, C. J. *British Industry* (1961)

Hannah, Leslie. 'Managerial Innovation and the rise of the large-scale company in Britain', *Economic History Review*, 2nd series, XXVII, 2 (1974)

Kirby, M. W. 'Entrepreneurial Efficiency in the British Coal Industry between the Wars: a Comment', *Economic History Review*, XXV, 4 (1972), and comments by other authors on the coal industry in the same issue

——. 'The Control of Competition in the British Coal Mining Industry in the Thirties', *Economic History Review*, 2nd series, XXVI, 2 (1973)

Reader, W. J. 'The Forerunners, 1870–1926', *Imperial Chemical Industries: a History*, I (1970)

Sobel, Robert. *The Age of Giant Corporations. A Microeconomic History of American Business, 1914–1970* (Westport, Conn, 1972)

Wilson, Charles. *The History of Unilever* I and II (1954),

The Industrial Labour Force
Farman, Christopher. *The General Strike* (1972)
Pelling, Henry M. *American Labor* (Chicago, 1960)
——. *A history of British Trade Unionism* (1963)
——. *A short history of the Labour Party*, 2nd edition (1965)
Rayback, J. G. *History of American Labor* (New York, 1959)
Renshaw, Patrick. *The General Strike* (1975)
Soule, George. *Prosperity Decade, 1917–1929* (New York, 1947)
Symons, Julian. *The General Strike* (1959)
Taft, Philip. *Organized Labor in American History* (New York, 1964)

Chapter Nine

Aldcroft, D. H. *The Inter-War Economy: Britain, 1919–1939* (1970)
Arndt, H. W. *Economic Problems of the Nineteen-Thirties* (1944)
Chandler, Lester V. *America's Greatest Depression, 1929–1941* (New York, 1970)
——. *Benjamin Strong: Central Banker* (Washington, 1958)
Drummond, I. M. *British Economic Policy and the Empire, 1919–1939* (London, 1972)
Falkus, M. E. 'United States Economic Policy and the "Dollar Gap" of the 1920s', *Economic History Review*, 2nd series, XXIV, 4 (1971)
Glynn, S. and Lougheed, A. L. 'A Comment on United States Economic Policy and the "Dollar Gap" of the 1920s', *Economic History Review*, 2nd series, XXVI, 4 (1973)
Howson, Susan. 'The Origins of Dear Money, 1919–1920', *Economic History Review*, 2nd series, XXVII, 1 (1974)
Kindleberger, Charles P. *The World in Depression, 1929–1939* (1973)
Lewis, W. A. *Economic Survey, 1919–1939* (1949)
Moggridge, D. E. *The Return to Gold, 1925* (Cambridge, 1969)

Moggridge, D. E. *British Monetary Policy, 1924–1931. The Norman Conquest of $4.86* (Cambridge, 1972)

Muchmore, Lynn. 'The Banking Crisis of 1933: Some Iowa Evidence', *Journal of Economic History*, XXX (1970)

Nevin, E. *The Mechanism of Cheap Money. A Study of British Monetary Policy* (1955)

Pollard, S. (ed). *The Gold Standard and Employment Policies between the Wars* (1970). Contains articles by R. S. Sayers and J. R. Hume

Robertson, R. M. *History of the American Economy*, 3rd edition (New York, 1973)

Wicker, Elmus R. *Federal Reserve Monetary Policy, 1917–1933* (New York, 1966)

Youngson, A. J. *Britain's Economic Growth, 1920–1966* (London, 1967)

Chapter Ten

Alderman, Geoffrey. *The Railway Interest* (Leicester, 1973)

Ashworth, W. *Economic History of England, 1870–1939* (1960)

Bruce, Maurice. *The Coming of the Welfare State* (1961)

Cain, P. J. 'Railway Combination and Government, 1900–1914', *Economic History Review*, 2nd series, XXV, 4 (1972)

Coll, Blanche D. *Perspectives in Public Welfare. A History* (Washington, 1969)

Fabricant, Solomon. *The Trend of Government Activity in the United States since 1900* (New York, 1952)

Fainsod, M., Gordon, Lincoln and Palamountain, Joseph C. *Government and the American Economy* (New York, 1960)

Fearon, Peter. 'The British Airframe Industry and the State, 1918–1935', *Economic History Review*, 2nd series, XXVII, 2 (1974)

Fraser, Derek. *The Evolution of the British Welfare State* (1973)

Gilbert, Bentley B. *British Social Policy, 1914–1939* (1970)

——. *The Evolution of Natial Insurance in Britain. The Origins of the Welfare State* (1966)

Goodrich, Carter. *Government Promotion of Canals and Railroads, 1800–1890* (New York, 1960)

—— (ed). *The Government and the Economy* (New York, 1967)

Harris, Jose. *Unemployment and Politics: A Study in English Social Policy* (Oxford, 1972)

Hay, J. R. *The Origins of the Liberal Welfare Reforms, 1906–1914* (1975)

Kolko, Gabriel. *Railroads and Regulation, 1877–1916* (Princeton, 1965)

Parris, H. W. *Government and the Railways in Nineteenth Century Britain* (1965)

Peacock, Alan T. and Wiseman, Jack. *The Growth of Public Expenditure in the United Kingdom*, 2nd edition (1967)

Robbins, L. *The Theory of Economic Policy in English Classical Political Economy* (1952)

Rose, Michael E. *The English Poor Law, 1780–1930* (Newton Abbot, 1971)
——. *The Relief of Poverty, 1834–1914* (1972)
Taylor, A. J. *Laissez-faire and State Intervention in Nineteenth Century Britain* (1972)
Winch, Donald. *Economics and Policy* (1969)
Woodroofe, Kathleen. *From Charity to Social Work in England and the United States* (1962)
Youngson, A. J. 'Economic Thought and Policy between the Wars', Ch VIII in *Britain's Economic Growth, 1920–1966* (1967)

INDEX

Names of authors quoted or referred to in the text are in italics.

Abnormal Importations (Customs Duties) Act (1932), 128
Abramovitz, Moses, 30, 206, 209
Addison Act (1919), 201
Agricultural Adjustment Act (1933), 143, 152; (1938), 153
Agricultural colleges, 71
Agricultural credit, 151
Agricultural implements, 75
Agricultural machinery, 12–13, 17, 27, 29–30, 49–50, 72, 75, 78, 146
Agricultural Marketing Act (1929), 151; (1931), 154; (1933), 154
Agricultural workers' *see* Workers, agricultural
Agriculture, American, 9, 17, 26, 39, 41–2, 44, 64–71, 108, 117, 136, 143–4, 146–53, 187; Board of, 71, 108, 147; British, 9, 28, 64–71, 136, 143–4, 146–51, 153–4; Department of, 70, 71; Productivity of, 17, 27, 30, 64, 143, 150; Share of labour force in, 9, 26, 28; Share of in National Income or Output, 70, 117, 148, 149; State intervention in, 146–8, 150–4
Aircraft production, 110, 112, 156, 158, 193
Aldcroft, D. H., 49, 50, 207, 211, 213, 214, 216, 217, 218
Alford, B. W. E., 157, 216
Allen, G. C., 84, 207, 214, 217
Allen, V. L., 58, 212
Amalgamated Association of Miners, 59
Amalgamated Engineering Union, 170
Amalgamated Society of Engineers, 57
American Federation of Labor (AFL), 56, 61, 62, 168
Anti-trust legislation, 195
Arndt, H. W., 138, 216, 218
Ashworth, W., 35, 84, 91, 112, 192, 198, 208, 209, 213, 214, 215, 219
Australia, 13, 92, 96
Austria, 125, 126, 127
Automobiles, *see* Motor vehicles

Bagehot, Walter, 19
Bagwell, P. S., 205, 214
Balance of payments, American, 12, 89–90, 94; British, 11, 37, 91, 118, 175
Balance of trade, American, 12, 89, 116, 174; British, 11, 90, 107, 118, 137
Balfour, A. J., 100
Bank Charter Act (1844), 103
Bank of England, 19, 101–4, 163, 179–80, 181, 183, 186
Bank for International Settlements, 126
Bank of the United States, 130, 187–8
Banking, American, 22, 23, 39, 101–5, 119–20, 124, 126, 130, 140, 184, 185–90, 194; British, 101, 105, 129, 185–6
Barclay & Co Ltd, 105
Barley, 67, 71
Barnes, George, 167
Beales, H. L., 34, 209
Beard, C. A., and *Beard, M. R.*, 20, 208
Belgium, 95, 182
Bessemer process, 18, 73, 74
Biddle, Nicholas, 102
Billington, R. A., 40, 41, 205, 210
Birmingham, 134, 138

Bogue, Allan G., 69, 206, 212
Booth, Charles, 199–200
Boots and shoes, 10, 76
Bowman, J. D., 69, 213
British Dyestuffs Corporation, 164, 193
British Iron and Steel Federation, 158, 163, 202
British Shipping (Assistance) Act (1935), 162
British Sugar Corporation, 193
Building Construction, 47, 96, 115, 129, 131, 141, 159, 201
Burn, D. L., 74, 163

Cairncross, A. K., 93, 97, 215
California, 13, 70
Canada, 94, 96, 107
Capital, American export of, 32, 46, 94–5, 107, 116–17; American import of, 32, 93–4; British export of, 32, 46, 93, 95–7
Capital formation and investment, 22, 32, 42, 92–7, 128, 132, 134, 159
Capital/labour ratio, 27, 30
Chandler, A. D., 109, 160–1, 207, 211, 213, 217
Chandler, L. V., 133, 207, 216, 217
Cheap money, 129, 183–4
Chemicals, 10, 49, 73, 110, 115, 120, 134, 159
Chicago, 10, 16, 17, 42, 75, 142
Child, John, 161, 207
Cincinnati, 10, 17, 42, 142
Civil War, American, 13, 16, 19, 20–4, 58, 65, 102–3, 192
Clapham, J. H., 91, 205, 208, 216
Clark, V. S., 23, 74, 208, 213
Cigarettes, consumption of, 149
Coal, 10, 18, 27–8, 72, 84, 91, 110
Coal industry, American, 28, 77–8, 82, 114, 142, 158–9, 163, 169; British, 27–8, 33, 36, 37, 49, 68, 72, 76–7, 110–11, 113–14, 139, 158–9, 162, 169, 202
Coal Mines (Reorganization) Act (1930), 162
Cobden, Richard, 12
Cochran, T. C., 23–4, 43, 48, 54, 208, 209, 210, 211, 216, 217
Cole, W. A., 25, 209
Colonial Conference (1902), 99
Committee (Congress) for Industrial Organization, 171
Commodity prices, 122, 136, 152
Company Unions, 171
Conrad, A. H., 21, 208, 209
Conservative party, 99, 167, 169, 198
Consumption, 44, 48, 110, 119, 121, 124, 129, 134, 156, 160
Conway, Alan, 44, 205, 210
Cooke, Jay, 34
Copper, 10, 17, 26, 72–3, 141
Coppock, D. J., 37, 209
Corn Laws, Act to Repeal (1846), 64
Corn Production Act (1917), 148; (1920), 148
Corn Production (Repeal) Act (1921), 148
Cotton, 10, 11, 15–16, 17, 21, 65, 70, 90–1, 147, 149, 164, 176
Cotton Industry, American, 50, 78, 141, 158; British, 10, 18, 33, 37, 118, 162, 202
County War Agricultural Committees, 146
Court, W. H. B., 65, 208
Courtaulds, 38, 49

Credit Anstalt, 126, 182, 183
Cunliffe Committee, 111, 179–80
Currency, American, 22–3

Dairy farming, 65–6, 67, 70, 108
David, P. A., 29, 82–3, 206, 209, 214
Davis, Lance E., 9, 205, 209
Deane, P. 25, 209
Defence expenditure, 191–4
Democratic party, 21, 98
Departmental Committee on Railways (1909), 86
Department of Scientific and Industrial Research, 194
Dickens, Charles, 28
Dillingham Commission, 45–7
Dingley tariff, 99
Disraeli, Benjamin, 58
Dollar, devaluation of (1934), 178
Douglas, Paul, 165
Dowie, J. A., 118, 157, 216
Dowlais Iron Company, 73
Drainage, agricultural, 30
Duboff, Richard, 79, 206, 213
Du Pont, 109, 161
Durant, William C., 38, 53
Dyestuffs, 174

Early start thesis, British, 33
Economic growth, 26–34, 35, 38, 54, 63, 113, 118, 158
Edison, Thomas, A., 43, 51
Education, expenditure and investment in, 17, 18, 31, 196–8, 201
Education, Federal Bureau of, 71
Education system, American, 31, 43
Eight Hours Act (1909), 62
Electric arc furnace, 110
Electrical engineering, 132, 134
Electrical equipment, 156
Electrical Industry, American, 80, 109, 158; British, 37, 135
Electrical supply (light and power), 37, 51, 159, 160, 198
Electrical Trades Union, 170
Electricity Act (1926), 120, 135, 198
Empire Marketing Board (1926), 151
Engerman, S. L., 21, 23, 24, 208
Engineering, 10, 18, 49–50, 80, 91, 110, 158
Entrepreneurs, 30, 32, 33, 48–54, 140, 141
Exchange Equalisation Account, 129, 184
Exports, American, 11, 12, 15, 17, 27, 37, 42, 65, 70, 75, 76, 89–92, 108, 126, 128, 137–8, 143, 148, 152, 174–8; British, 10, 11, 15–16, 32, 37, 50, 72, 77, 88–92, 110, 113, 116, 118, 123, 126, 137, 139, 174–6, 178–9; Invisible, 11, 37, 19–91, 118, 137, 174, 176

Fabricant, Solomon, 199, 219
Farm Incomes, 67–9, 108, 143, 149, 150, 152–3
Farm Mortgages, 69, 148, 150
Farmers Cooperatives, 151
Federal Deposit Insurance Corporation, 189
Federal Farm Board, 151–2
Federal Intermediate Credit Act (1923), 151
Federal Reserve Act (1913), 104, 186
Federal Reserve Bank of New York, 180, 184, 186, 187
Federal Reserve Board, 104–5, 185–6, 189
Federal Reserve monetary policy, 119–20, 125–6
Federal Reserve system, 104, 119, 130, 140, 184, 188
Feinstein, C. H., 93
Fiduciary issue, 103
Firth, Sir William, 163
Fishlow, A., 82–4, 214
Fletcher, T. W., 67, 213
Floud, R. C., 30, 205, 209, 213
Flour milling, 10, 42, 76
Flour processing and production, 17, 74
Fogel, R. W., 21, 81–4, 208, 214
Ford, A. G., 95, 215
Ford, Henry, 38, 62, 163, 168, 203

Fordney-McCumber tariff, 107, 116, 173
France, 55, 91, 95, 97, 123, 126, 173, 181, 182, 183
Free Trade, 28, 71, 98–100, 153, 178, 194
Friedman, Milton, 129–30, 187, 207, 216
Frontier thesis, American, 26, 40–4
Fruit growing, 65, 67, 70, 149

Galbraith, J. K., 119, 121, 124, 216
Gallmann, Robert E., 20, 208
Gas Industry, British, 37, 51, 73, 198
General Motors, 38, 161
General and Municipal Workers Union, 170
General Strike (1926), 164, 167, 169
Germany, 55, 91, 95, 97, 100, 122, 123, 126, 127, 147, 173, 180–4
Glass, 17, 159
Gold, discoveries of, 13, 26; production of, 14, 35
Gold Standard, 46, 97, 117, 119, 122, 174, 179–84
Gompers, Samuel, 61, 168
Goodrich, Carter, 195, 214, 219
Government economic intervention, 112, 146–8, 139–41, 150–5, 158, 161–4, 191–204
Grangers, 67
Great Exhibition (1851), 9, 13
Great Plains, 41, 66
Greenbacks, 22
Green, William, 168
Gross National Product, 34; American, 25, 81, 124–5; British, 25, 125; *see also* National Income

Habakkuk, H. J., 30, 43, 48, 58, 211, 212
Hacker, L. M., 20, 208
Harrod-Domar model, 32
Hawke, G. R., 83, 214, 215
Hawley-Smoot tariff, 125, 178
Haymarket episode, 60
Hettinger, Alfred, jr., 130–1
Higgs, Robert, 73, 206, 210
Hobsbawn, E. J., 60–1, 212
Homestead Act (1862), 65, 68
Hoover, Herbert, 125
House building, 115, 134, 135
Housing, 201

Illinois, 17, 20, 66, 69, 75
Imlah, J. H., 11, 208
Immigration, American, 12, 16, 31, 39, 44–7
Imperial Airways, 164
Imperial Chemical Industries, 120, 161, 164, 169, 193
Imperial preference, 153, 178
Imperial Tobacco Company, 52, 78
Import Duties Act (1932), 128, 153
Import Duties Advisory Committee, 128, 154, 178
Imports, American, 10, 11, 15, 23, 99, 116, 122, 174, 177; British, 10, 11, 16, 28–9, 64–5, 76, 118, 149, 154, 174, 176–8; Invisible, 89
India, 14, 15, 26, 92
Industrial Workers of the World (Wobblies), 56, 61, 63, 168
Industry, American, 10, 17, 23–4, 30, 71–80, 109, 119, 141–3, 156, 157–61, 168–9, 172; British 10–11, 18–19, 71–4, 76–80, 109–11, 118–19, 132, 134–6, 156–63, 169–70; *see also* under separate industries
Industry, productivity in, 30–1, 51
Inflation, in American Civil War, 22, 23
International Harvester Company, 75, 78
International monetary situation, 14, 34, 106, 117–18, 121–3, 126–8, 173, 175, 179–85
International trade, *see* World trade, general trends in
Inter-State Commerce Act (1887), 85, 196
Invisible exports, *see* Exports, Invisible
Iowa, 66, 69, 70
Iron industry, American, 18, 24, 73, 78, 82, 114, 141; British, 10–11, 18–19, 33, 37, 49, 73–4, 76, 99, 113, 178
Iron ore, 26, 72, 74

Jackson, Andrew, 102
Japan, 26, 109
Jevons, H. S., 110, 206
Jones, M. A., 45, 211

Kansas, 21, 42, 69, 75
Kellett, J. R., 85, 206
Kenwood, A. G., 93, 206, 215
Keynes, J. M., 179, 180, 182, 203
Kindleberger, C. P., 148–9, 207, 216, 218
Kirkland, E. C., 34, 210, 214
Knights of Labor, 56, 59–60, 61
Knights of St Crispin, 59

Labour force, 9, 28; composition of in America, 45–7
Labour party, 56, 61–2, 162, 166, 167, 169
Labour Representation Committee, 61–2
Laissez-faire, 191, 201
Lancashire, 10, 16, 18, 78
Land, as a factor in economic growth, 26–8
Land area, 26, 29–30
Land Grant Acts, 16
Landownership, 19, 29, 49, 67–9, 149
Land rents, 67–8, 150
Land values, 29, 68, 150
Lead, 10, 26, 72
Leather, 17, 76
Lewis, Cleona, 94, 206
Lewis, John L., 168, 171
Lewis, W. A., 64, 91, 213, 215, 216, 218
Lib-Labs, 58
Liberal party, 58, 200
Limited liability, 194–5
Livestock farming, 65, 70, 108, 149
Lloyd George, 166, 201
London, 28, 97, 134, 138, 139, 181, 182, 183
London Clearing House, 104
London Trades Council, 57
Lougheed, A. L., 93, 206, 215, 218
Lumber, 10–11, 72, 76, 141

Macdonald, Ramsay, 131
Machine tools, 49, 50
Macmillan Committee, 127
Maddison, Angus, 25, 206
Management, changing practice in, 156, 160–1
Man-made fibres, 118–19, 160
Mann-Elkins Act, 85
Market gardening, 65, 69, 149
Markets, changes in, 13, 27, 35, 53, 65, 71, 115, 134, 155, 175
Matthews, R. C. O., 38, 210
May Committee, 127, 182
McCloskey, D. N., 30, 51, 205, 210, 211
McCormick agricultural machinery, 13, 17, 75
McKinley tariff, 53, 74, 99
Meat packing, 10, 42–3, 74–5, 90
Meat production, 66, 70
Mergers, 79
Meyer, J. R., 21, 208
Miller, W., 43, 48, 209, 210, 211
Miners Federation of Great Britain, 170
Miners National Union, 59
Mingay, G. E., 205, 213
Ministry of Munitions, 111
Missouri Compromise, 21
Mitchell, Broadus, 133, 207, 216, 217
Mitchell, B. R., 193, 207
Moggridge, D. E., 180, 218
Mond, Sir Alfred, 169
Money supply, general, 14, 100; American, 34, 126, 129–30, 138, 140–1, 188, 189
Montgomery Ward, 115
Morgan, Pierpont, 51
Morrill tariff, 15, 19, 73, 98
Motor cycles, 49
Motor vehicles, 49, 80, 97, 109, 114–16, 119, 132, 134, 135, 141, 158–60, 169, 174–5, 176
Multi-divisional corporations, 160–1
Munitions of War Act (1915), 166
Musson, A. E., 37, 210

National Banking Acts (1863–4), 23, 103
National Bank Act (1887), 104
National Debt, American, 22; British, 106–7, 118
National Income, 25, 34, 38, 82–3, 88, 113, 124, 131, 132, 156, 166; Ratio of foreign trade to, 88–9
National Industrial Recovery Act (1933), 142, 170
National Labor Relations Act (1935), 171
National Labor Relations Board, 171
National Labor Union, 59
National Monetary Commission Report (1912), 104
National Recovery Administration, 161, 163–4
National Typographic Union, 58
Nebraska, 13, 21, 69
Nelson, R. L., 79, 214
Net National Product, 9, 25; *see also* National Income
Netherlands, 95, 125
Nevins, A. D., 51, 211
Newcomer, Mabel, 53–4, 211
New Deal, 134, 139, 142–4, 189, 199, 202–3
New England, 13, 41, 69, 75, 199
New Model Union, 57
New Unionism, 60
New York, 42, 75, 180, 184, 186, 187
Norman, Montagu, 181
Norris–La Guardia Act, 170
North, D. C., 20, 208, 209, 213
Northrop loom, 78
Notes, circulation of, 102–4

Oil, 26, 73, 109, 111, 134
Oil Industry, American, 24, 159, 163
Old age pensions, 200
Orwell, George, 139
Osborne judgement, 62
Ottawa Conference, 128, 154, 178
Overseas investment, 11, 15, 32, 92–7, 107, 116–17, 122
Overseas trade, *see* Exports and World trade

Paper, 75–6, 115
Parris, H. W., 86, 206, 219
Payne, P. L., 52–3, 73, 206, 212, 214
Peel, Robert, 86
Pelling, H. M., 56, 166, 169, 205, 212, 218
Pennsylvania, 58, 142
Penrose, Edith T., 48, 205, 212
Perloff, H. S., 41, 205, 211
Peterson, Florence, 55–6, 205
Petroleum products, 115, 141, 159, 176
Phelps Brown, E. H., 55, 80, 165–6, 205, 212
Picketing, 58
Pollard, S., 38, 137, 210, 216, 217, 218
Population, American, 31–2, 41, 46–7; Rural American, 70; Urban American, 70
Populists, 67
Pork, 17, 75
Potter, J. M., 16, 209, 214, 216
Powderly, Terence V., 60
Prairies, 65–6, 70
Prest, A. R., 113
Printing, 17
Public Works Administration, 142
Publishing, 17

Radio production, 110, 135, 138, 156, 159, 160
Railway Act (1921), 86, 196
Railway Department, Board of Trade, 86, 196
Railway and Canal Traffic Acts (1888 and 1894), 86, 195
Railways, American, 14–16, 20–2, 32–3, 36, 42, 81–5, 158, 195–6; British, 14, 32, 81, 83–7, 195–6
Railway locomotives, 49, 50
Railway mileage, 14, 16, 19
Rayback, J. G., 60, 206, 207, 212, 218
Rayon, 115; *see also* Man-made fibres
Rearmament, before World War II, 193
Republican party, 21

Reconstruction Finance Corporation, 188–9
Regulation of Railways Act (1871), 86
Rice, 11
Richardson, H. W., 124, 128, 132, 136, 137, 139, 176, 206, 207, 215, 216
Ring spinning, 78
Robbins, L., 191, 207, 219
Rockefeller, John D., 51
Roepke, H. G., 74
Romasco, H. U., 125, 216
Roosevelt, Franklin D., 133, 140, 142, 152, 164, 171, 184, 189
Rostow, W. W., 64, 210, 213
Rowntree, B. Seebohm, 49, 200
Royal Commission, On the Depression in Trade and Industry (1885), 34; On the Poor Law (1909), 200; On Trade Unions (1867), 57; On Unemployment Insurance (1931), 127
Royal Dockyards, 192
Rubber, 115, 122, 159

Safeguarding of Industries Act (1921), 173
Sailing ships, 18
St Louis, 42, 75
Samuel Commission (1925), 167
Sandberg, L., 51, 214
Sanderson, Michael, 32
Sankey Commission (1919), 167
Saul, S. B., 34–5, 37, 49–50, 78, 90, 97, 206, 210, 212
Savings, 22
Schlote, W., 91
Schumpeter, J. A., 48, 135, 164, 212
Scientific management, 62
Scoby-Smith Committee, 162, 202
Sears, R. W., 38, 53
Sears Roebuck, 38, 53, 115, 130, 161
Second Bank of the United States, 102
Sewing machines, 13, 50
Sheffield Outrages, 57
Sherman Anti-Trust Act (1890), 195
Shipbuilding, 156–7; British, 18, 33, 37, 39, 72, 78, 97, 109, 113, 157, 162, 202
Shipping earnings and services, 11, 35–6, 111, 114, 116
Siemens open-hearth process, 73
Silk, 76
Silver, discovery of, 13, 26
Singer's sewing machine, 13
Size of firm, 52–3, 61, 155, 194
Slavery, 17, 20–1, 23
Smiles, Samuel, 191
Smith, Adam, 191
Social mobility, 31, 40, 43, 52–4
Sobel, Robert, 159, 207, 217, 218
Social mobility, 31, 40, 43, 52–4; in America, 40–1, 43; in Britain, 48–9
Social saving, from railways, 83
Social services and welfare, 112, 199, 201–2
Soda, 10
Soule, G., 119, 206, 207, 217, 218
South Wales, 16, 18, 28, 37, 53, 72, 73–4, 114, 163, 166, 201
Spencer, Herbert, 191
Standard Oil, 161
Steam engines, 49
Steamships, 18, 35, 157
Steel industry, 156–7; American, 18, 24, 36, 47, 51, 73–4, 78, 109, 114, 141, 158; British, 18, 33, 37, 49, 73–4, 76, 99, 109, 113, 139, 158, 162, 178, 202
Steinbeck, John, 139
Stock market speculation, 121, 123–4, 187
Strong, Benjamin, 130, 180, 186
Sturmey, S. G., 149
Subsidies, for American shipbuilding, 157–8; for British agriculture, 154; for British housing, 201; for British sugar beet, 151, 154
Sugar, 74, 122, 151
Sugar beet, 150–1, 164, 193
Sugar refining, 74, 76
Supreme Court, 153, 163, 171
Sweden, 26, 55, 125

Taff Vale judgement, 62
Tariffs, American, 13, 15–16, 39, 53, 74, 98–100, 107, 116, 118, 125, 143, 173, 177, 194; British, 128, 136, 153–4, 163, 178; European, 28, 77, 100, 117, 154, 173, 183
Taussig, F. W., 99, 215
Tawney, R. H., 201
Taylor, Frederick Winslow, 62
Technical education, 197
Technology, changes in, 12–13, 18–19, 24, 29–30, 43, 112, 133, 155–6, 158, 175, 191, 193
Temin, P., 51, 210, 212, 214, 215
Tennessee Valley Authority, 164, 203
Textile machinery, 49–50
Textiles and textile industry, 37, 72, 76–8, 91, 107, 109, 118, 139, 169
Thomas, Brinley, 46, 211, 215
Thomas, D. A., 36, 110
Thomas-Gilchrist process, 74
Thompson, F. M. L., 68, 206, 213
Timber, 25
Tin, 10, 122
Tinplate, 10, 16, 18, 49, 53, 74, 99
Tobacco, 11, 65, 70, 76, 147, 149, 176
Tory landowners, 64
Tracy, Michael, 153, 207, 217
Trade Agreements Act (1934), 177
Trade Disputes Act (1927), 169
Trade Unions, American, 31, 56–63, 165, 168–72; British, 39, 56–63, 112, 166–70
Trades Union Congress, 56, 167, 169
Transport and General Workers Union, 170
Turner, Ben, 169
Turner, Frederick Jackson, 40, 211
Tyson, R. E., 76–7, 206

Unemployment, 113, 120, 127, 133–4, 138, 142, 157, 159, 161, 166, 169, 170, 201–4
Unemployment Insurance, 127, 200–1
Unilever, 161
United Mine Workers, 168, 170
United States Steel Company, 52, 158
United States War Department, 192
United Textile Workers, 170

Vegetable production, 66, 67, 115, 149
Votes for women, 112

Wage boards, 200
Wage rates, 31, 47, 55, 56, 59, 63, 129, 165–7, 202
Wages, Agricultural, 150
Wages (Regulation) Act (1924), 150
Wall Street, 121, 124
War Debt, Repayment of, 117
War Loan, 183
Waterways, 81–4
Watney, Combe and Reid, 52, 78
Webb, Sidney and Beatrice, 57
West, E. G., 32
Wheat, 10, 11, 28, 64–5, 66, 70, 71, 81, 108, 122, 136, 147, 149, 154
Wheatley Act (1923), 201
Whisky, 17
Wilkins, Mira, 94, 215
Williamson, J. G., 22, 33, 90, 205, 209, 210, 216
Wilson, C., 50, 212, 218
Wisconsin, 70, 75
Wobblies, *see* Industrial Workers of the World
Wool, 10, 67, 70
Woollen Industry, American, 10, 12, 76, 141; British, 10, 18, 37, 118
Workers, agricultural, 9, 28, 44–5, 70, 150
Workers, skilled, 44, 47, 57, 61–2, 166; Unskilled, 44, 47, 59, 60–1, 166
World trade, American share of, 90, 179; British share of, 88, 90–1, 175, 179; General trends in, 13–14, 35, 65, 90–1, 106–7, 113, 116, 122, 125, 137–8, 155, 174–6, 178–9, 185, 200
World War I, 38–9, 91, 95, 101, 105, 106–12, 136, 138, 146–8, 156, 161, 164, 201
World War II, 172, 204

Yellow-dog contracts, 63, 170
Youngson, A. J., 183, 217, 219